Edexcel GCE History

The Experience of Warfare in Britain 1854–1929

Rosemary Rees • Geoff Stewart

Series editors: Martin Collier   Rosemary Rees

Unit 2 Student Book

CP038500

CORNWALL COLLEGE

A PEARSON COMPANY

Heinemann is an imprint of Pearson Education Limited, a company incorporated in England and Wales, having its registered office at Edinburgh Gate, Harlow, Essex, CM20 2JE. Registered company number: 872828

www.heinemann.co.uk

Heinemann is a registered trademark of Pearson Education Limited

Text © Rosemary Rees and Geoffrey Stewart 2008

First published 2008

12 11 10 09

10 9 8 7 6 5 4 3

British Library Cataloguing in Publication Data is available from the British Library on request.

ISBN 978 0 435308 26 1

Edited by Florence Production Ltd, Stoodleigh, Devon
Designed by Florence Production Ltd, Stoodleigh, Devon
Typeset by Florence Production Ltd, Stoodleigh, Devon
Produced by Florence Production Ltd, Stoodleigh, Devon
Original illustrations © Pearson Education Ltd 2008
Cover design by Siu Hang Wong
Picture research by Zooid Pictures
Printed in China (CTPS/03)

Acknowledgements

The author and publisher would like to thank the following individuals and organisations for permission to reproduce photographs:

© akg-images p. 6; © Alamy/Classic Images p. 44; © Alamy/Mary Evans Picture Library pp. 12, 148; © Alamy/Photo Art Collection (PAC) p. 38; © Art Archive pp. 74, 111; © Art Archive/Imperial War Museum p. 136; © Art Archive/Musée des 2 Guerres Mondiales, Paris p. 137; © Bridgeman Art Library p. 157; © Bridgeman Art Library/National Army Museum, London p. 2; © Corbis/Hulton-Deutsch Collection pp. iv, 71, 164, 182, 189; © Getty Images/Hulton Archive p. 7; © Getty Images/Popperfoto p. 123; © Imperial War Museum pp. 126, 148, 151, 185; © Library of Congress p. 167; © Mary Evans Picture Library cover, p. 43; © Punch pp. 66, 190; © St. Helens Local History and Archives Library p. 139; © Topfoto p. 18; © Topfoto/David Wimsett/UPPA.co.uk p. 38; © Topfoto/Fotomas p. 23; © Topfoto/World History Archive p. 55; © University of Kent British Cartoon Archive/Mirror Pix. W.K. Haselden p. 183

Every effort has been made to contact copyright holders of material reproduced in this book. Any omissions will be rectified in subsequent printings if notice is given to the publishers.

Websites

The websites used in this book were correct and up-to-date at the time of publication. It is essential for tutors to preview each website before using it in class so as to ensure that the URL is still accurate, relevant and appropriate. We suggest that tutors bookmark useful websites and consider enabling students to access them through the school/college intranet.

Contents

George Cruikshank (1792–1878)
'The British Beehive', 1867

Introduction: What was Britain like in the 1850s?

In 1854 Britons of whatever class could claim to belong not only to the most liberal state in Europe, but also to the richest and most powerful on the Earth. Great Britain was possessed of the world's greatest empire, the most formidable navy and the world's most advanced economy. London was the world's financial capital and the pound sterling the nearest thing there was to a world currency. Britain seemed to offer the world a vision of change and improvement. To many, both within the British Isles and outside, it seemed the growing point of humanity.

On page iv at the start of this introduction, there is a drawing by the famous cartoonist George Cruikshank. His career was notable for the fact that he illustrated the work of one of the most famous novelists of the day, Charles Dickens. Cruikshank was also the foremost political satirist of his time. However, there is little cynicism in this cartoon.

Facts and change

'Now what I want is, Facts. Teach these boys and girls nothing but Facts. Facts alone are wanted in life.'

So spoke Mr Gradgrind in the opening of Charles Dickens' novel of 1854, *Hard Times*. The book was appropriately named as for many who lived in Britain in the mid-nineteenth century, times were indeed hard. But the facts of life in Britain in 1854, looked at from the perspective of the early twenty-first century, might appear as an alien world. Much that we take for granted did not exist. Much that is condemned or even forbidden today was completely legal. Electrical power had not transformed home and place of work. Horses were still vital for moving men and goods; their plentiful droppings in the streets of cities rendered a crossing sweeper a desirable accessory for pedestrians. Opium (heroin) was a key component in popular sleeping draughts for children and drugs in general were completely unregulated. A gentleman pedestrian might carry a sword stick in the larger cities, not trusting to the relatively newly created police to keep him safe. The rapidly growing, grimy cities apart, it might appear a slow moving and essentially rural world. The majority of people in Britain lived in small communities, and the most common job was that of agricultural labourer. But whether city or country dweller, the majority of those living in both town and country would seem poverty-stricken and deprived compared to their twenty-first-century descendants.

SKILLS BUILDER

What impression does the image on the opposite page give of mid-Victorian Britain?

v

Definition

Census

This is a survey of the population undertaken once every ten years. The first census was in 1801.

Definition

Meritocratic

is when position and power are based on talent and merit, not birth

This was not a static, unchanging Britain but one that seemed to throb with the excitement of a new world being born. The Parliamentary Report on the 1861 **census**, which was published two years later, recorded the momentous news that Britain had become a preponderantly urban nation with more living for the first time in towns and cities than in villages and country parishes. Indeed, urban Britain expanded rapidly. Villages became towns and towns became cities. Fields and woods were increasingly covered with factories and houses and the new urban communities were linked by the new iron roads, along which ran the steam powered railway engines. Here was a revolution affecting time and place. In the 1820s it had taken the fastest coach twenty-four hours to travel the two hundred miles between York and London. By the 1850s it could be done in less than five.

Political élite

If a slow moving rural world was being replaced by a faster moving urban one, the political system and social relationships still reflected the old rural world. Two earls, a viscount and the son of a duke were prime ministers in the 1850s; in 1854 the prime minister was Lord Aberdeen. All were thus aristocrats, whose families owned extensive landed estates. Parliament was still dominated by landed gentlemen and the upper reaches of the civil service and the army were filled with the relatives of aristocratic and gentry families. This situation was not, however, unchallenged and there was a growing demand for a more **meritocratic** and efficient approach to government. This was the world of the Crimean War, a conflict that was to lead to the challenging of perceptions and change.

1 The Crimean War 1854–56: 'Theirs not to reason why'

What is this unit about?

This unit focuses on the conduct of the Crimean War, and in particular on the reportage by **William Russell** of *The Times*, who emerged as the first recognisable war reporter, and on the photography of **Roger Fenton**, who became the first war photographer. Through these and other eyewitness accounts, a picture of wasteful military muddles will emerge, as well as images of outstanding heroism. The impact of these accounts on the British at home will be addressed.

Key questions

* How was the Crimean War reported?
* What impact did the reportage have on Britain?

Timeline

1853

30 November	Turkish fleet destroyed by the Russians at the Battle of Sinope

1854

May	British field army of about 28,000 men (with French forces of the same size) landed at Varna
28 June	British forces ordered to invade the Crimea
5 September	Allies leave Varna for Crimea
20 September	Battle of Alma: allied forces defeat Russian troops blocking the road to Sebastopol at the River Alma
24 September	Allies begin siege of Sebastopol
17 October	First allied bombardment of Sebastopol
24 October	Battle of Balaclava: 93rd Highlanders hold 'thin red line'
25 October	Battle of Balaclava: charge of the Light Brigade
5 November	Battle of Inkerman: an unsuccessful attempt by the Russians to destroy the British Army as it lays seige to Sebastopol

1855

Jan–March	Terrible Russian winter
8 March	Roger Fenton arrives at Balaclava
9 September	Russians evacuate Sebastopol

1856

29 February	Armistice in the Crimea
30 March	Treaty of Paris signed

Historical health warning!

This unit, and the one that follows, cover roughly the same time period, but in different ways. This unit focuses on the different ways in which the war was reported and, specifically, on the twin enemies facing the British troops: the Russians and the Russian winter. The next unit addresses the administrative muddle and confusion that the reportage brought to the attention of the British public. They have been separated out for reasons of clarity, but you will need to cross-reference between the two units in order to gain the fullest understanding of the dynamics of the period.

Definition

Stoic

Brave and uncomplaining.

SKILLS BUILDER

Look carefully at this painting (and even more carefully if you want to spot Queen Victoria!). Discuss the following question in your group and remember to back up what you think with evidence from the painting.

What impression does this painting give you about attitudes to the outbreak of war in 1854?

How is the Crimean War remembered?

The Crimean War was the only European war fought by Britain between 1815 and 1914. But it was remarkable for far more than that. It was a war renowned for military incompetence and administrative muddle; it was a war in which the **stoic** suffering of the ordinary British soldiers stood out in stark contrast to the dash, bravado and sheer stupidity of their commanders; it was a war in which wives were allowed to accompany their husbands for the last time; it was a war in which the heroism and recklessness of the charge of the Light Brigade at Balaclava created a myriad of controversies that still puzzle and enrage today. The Crimean War, too, made and broke reputations. It made the reputation of Florence Nightingale and, latterly, of Mary Seacole. It broke the commander-in-chief, **Lord Raglan** (see page 28), and ruined the reputations of Lords Lucan and **Cardigan** (see page 28). It had a long-term impact on British society that was to change institutions and create a profession.

The Crimean War was one of the first major wars from which a large number of eye-witness accounts have survived, and it was the first major war from which photographs and newspaper reportage hit the breakfast tables and parlours of the Victorian middle class and well-to-do. Because of this, it was a war that raised doubts about the competence of a small, aristocratic élite to run the British Army, about the ability of the British government and about the efficiency of the British administration.

Source A

1.1 *The Farewell to the Scots Fusilier Guards at Buckingham Palace, 28 February 1854,* painted in 1854 by George Housman Thomas and bought by Queen Victoria

Action Crimea! What was the Crimean War about?

The Crimean War, like most wars, was about power and control and it was about fear. In the first fifty years of the nineteenth century, the Russian Empire had doubled its size in Europe and the Russian army was steadily advancing through central Asia until its regiments were closer to Delhi than they were to the Russian capital of St Petersburg. This presented a double threat to Britain. British politicians believed that British interests in India were being directly threatened by the Russian army's advance through Afghanistan. They also believed that their short overland route to India was being threatened by the prospect of Russian control of the eastern Mediterranean, in particular, the area around the Black Sea.

Source B

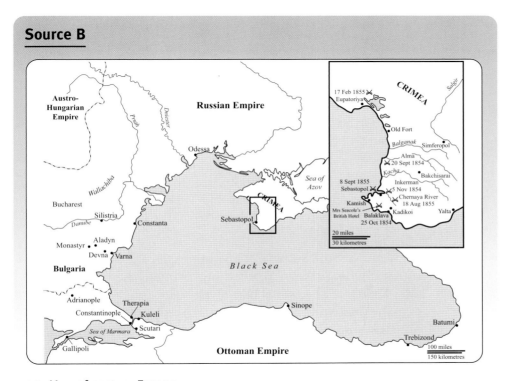

1.2 Map of eastern Europe

The Tsar of Russia, Nicholas I, was anxious to move in and carve up the Turkish Empire. On 9 January 1853 he told Sir George Hamilton Seymour, the British ambassador in St Petersburg, 'We have on our hands a sick man – a very sick man; it will be a great misfortune if one of these days he should slip away from us. Especially before all necessary arrangements have been made.' In other words, the Tsar regarded the Turkish Empire as weak and likely to collapse – and he wanted Russia to have part, or all, of it. The problem, for Russia (look at Source B above), was that Turkey controlled the exit from the Black Sea to the Mediterranean. Russia wanted ice-free ports for its fleet and access to the Mediterranean – and then the world. The collapse of the Turkish Empire could provide just what Russia wanted. Britain, on the other hand, was determined to prevent this from happening. Britain needed the area around the

Black Sea to be in friendly hands as it was the key to maintaining their existing route to India.

Matters came to a head when Russia claimed, not for the first time, their need to protect the interests of Greek Orthodox Christians in the Turkish Empire. The Turkish Empire was, of course, predominantly Muslim. At the same time, Franco-Russian relationships reached an all-time low over a dispute concerning the privileges of Catholic and Orthodox monks, and in particular over who held the keys to the **Church of the Holy Sepulchre** in Jerusalem, which was within the Turkish Empire. The French supported the Catholics, and the Russians supported the Orthodox monks. In 1852 the Turkish Sultan decided in favour of the Catholic monks. These quarrels tended to align France and Britain against Russia, largely because they both feared Russian expansionist ambitions. But worse was to come:

- Early in 1853 the Tsar sent Prince Menshikov (who had a reputation as a bully when it came to negotiations) to Constantinople, along with the Russian admiral commanding the Black Sea Fleet and the Chief of Russian forces on the Danube. Their mission was to maintain the privileges of the Orthodox Christians and to insist on Russia's right to protect the Sultan's Christian subjects.

- When Menshikov arrived in Constantinople, the Turks were busy suppressing a revolt in Christian Montenegro. Menshikov simply added this to his list of demands, insisting that the Turkish troops withdraw from Montenegro. However, when Menshikov left Constantinople in May 1853, he knew these demands had been rejected.

- In order to 'encourage' the Sultan's cooperation, the Russian government announced that unless Turkey did what they wanted, Russian troops would occupy Moldavia and Wallachia. These were provinces bordering the River Danube and were not part of the Turkish Empire, although Turkey had loose control, but into which Russia was allowed to go to maintain law and order.

- However, behind the scenes the British ambassador, Lord Stratford de Redcliffe, had been encouraging the Sultan to reject Russia's demands. Learning of Russia's threats, Britain and France decided to intervene. On 15 June 1853, a combined French and British fleet was sent to the Dardanelles to show solidarity with Turkey. All over Europe, diplomats scurried to try to prevent a war.

- A draft compromise, drawn up by Austria, was rejected by the Sultan.

- In July, the Tsar ordered Russian troops into Moldavia and Wallachia.

- In August, the British parliamentary session was closed for the summer recess. Queen Victoria, making the closing speech that reflected the views of her government, earnestly hoped that war would not come.

- On 5 October 1853, buoyed up by the expectation that Britain and France would help him rather than see the Turkish Empire collapse, the Sultan formally declared war on Russia.

Embarkation, setting up camps – and war!

On 5 April 1854, the first contingent of British troops arrived at the Dardanelles and disembarked at Gallipoli, where the French soldiers were already billeted. As more and more British troops arrived, they were moved first to Constantinople and then to Scutari. Military historian Denis Judd describes both places as distinctly unimpressive.

Source C

Though Constantinople seemed, from the sea, a city of delicate minarets, cypress groves and exotic vegetation, its blue skies swept with plovers and storks, the reality was different. Soldiers soon discovered that the streets were filthy, and often so badly paved as to be downright dangerous. Men stumbled to avoid dead rats and dogs, and the pushing, jostling crowds, but there was no avoiding the stench that assailed their nostrils. Of course, there were compensations. In the narrow, dirty back streets the troops were able to find cheap wine and cheap whores. It was soon reckoned that you could get drunk for sixpence and syphilis for a shilling.

Scutari was no paradise, either. Lord Raglan [the British commander-in-chief] described his headquarters as a 'furiously hot' wooden building, 'low on the beach where all the filth of Constantinople is driven either by the wind or the current and so great is the abominable smell thereof that for the last ten days I have been driven from the room I used to sit in and have been forced to receive and transact business in my bedroom.' The British troops at Scutari were encamped either behind Lord Raglan's house, or in and around the great Turkish army barracks which were soon to become the notorious hospital for the reception of the British sick and wounded. Among the British forces passed Jewish money-changers, and assorted Turks, Greeks and Armenians peddling wares ranging from sherbet to horses, and from lemonade to young girls.

From Denis Judd *The Crimean War* published in 1975

SKILLS BUILDER

How useful is the description given in Source C in helping you to understand the problems faced by the British soldiers?

In considering this question you need to take into account the following:

- the content of the source;
- the context in which it is written;
- the situation of the author;
- his purpose in writing Source C;
- the nature of the evidence.

In the middle of May, as the weather grew hotter, Lord Raglan and the French and Turkish commanders, agreed that the Anglo-French force should sail to the Black Sea port of Varna. From there, the allied force could easily move to relieve the Russian siege of Silistria, a strategically important town on the River Danube. On 28 May British and French troops moved to Varna. By mid-June the Russian forces were in retreat; by mid-July they were safely back over the River Pruth.

Everything could have stopped at this point: Russia was no longer a threat to the Turkish Empire. The world could get back to normal. But it didn't. It didn't stop because the allied governments had convinced themselves that the Russian naval base of Sebastopol had to be taken, and the Russian fleet destroyed. British crowds demonstrated in favour of the war being continued, and Queen Victoria told her uncle, King Leopold of the Belgians, that the war was 'popular beyond belief'. Glumly, the Chancellor of the Exchequer, William Gladstone, raised income tax from 7d to 1s 2d in the pound to pay for it. On 23 June, the British government ordered Lord Raglan to invade the Crimea.

How was the Crimean War reported?

Enter Roger Fenton and William Russell

Source D

1.3 Roger Fenton

1.4 William Russell

SKILLS BUILDER

Quickly – what are your first impressions of these two men, looking just at their photographs? Jot them down or discuss them in your group.

They don't look particularly revolutionary, do they? Yet what they were to do in the Crimea was to revolutionise the way people thought about war. It was to begin, too, a whole genre of war reportage that brought the battlefields of the world to people's breakfast tables.

Biography

Roger Fenton 1819–69

Born in Lancashire, Roger Fenton was part of a manufacturing and business family. He studied in London and Paris, where he became fascinated by photography. Returning to London in 1844 to start a career as a solicitor, he kept up his interest in photography and founded the Royal Photographic Society in 1853. Queen Victoria was one of his patrons and he photographed her and her family several times.

Thomas Agnew & Sons of Manchester wanted to produce an album of photographs of the Crimean War that would be suitable for sale, and Fenton jumped at the opportunity. He was instructed not to record the horrors of war – and the technology of the time, in any case, did not allow him to photograph moving scenes such as battles. Fenton arrived at Balaclava in March 1855 with two alcoholic assistants and a specially converted horse-drawn wagon in which they lived, slept and worked. They stayed until June of that year, sharing the wagon with 5 cameras, 700 glass plates and a great deal of equipment. Overall, Fenton took some 400 usable photographs while he was in the Crimea, and in October 1855 nearly all of them were exhibited in London and were then taken on tour throughout Britain. Enthusiastic and highly skilled, Fenton was a regular contributor to many of the photographic exhibitions in the 1850s.

SKILLS BUILDER

Read the biography of Roger Fenton in the biography box. How far would you be able to regard his photographs as an accurate record of the Crimean War?

Source E

1.5 A photograph of some officers and men of the 4th Dragoon Guards relaxing in their camp in the Crimea. It was taken by Roger Fenton either at the end of 1854 or the beginning of 1855.

SKILLS BUILDER

How useful is this photograph to historians investigating the Crimean War?

(Hint: you will need to incorporate some of the answer you gave to the last 'Skills Builder' task.)

Biography

William Howard Russell 1820–1907

Born in Dublin and educated at Trinity College, Russell read for the Bar, taught mathematics and worked as a correspondent for *The Times* newspaper from 1841. *The Times* sent Russell to the Crimea, and in doing so made him the first professional journalist to cover a war. Russell went without the permission of the army or the government and, indeed, both institutions would have preferred him to have stayed at home. His reports exposed appalling conditions and administrative incompetence and did much to prepare the ground that resulted in Florence Nightingale being allowed to take nurses to the Crimea. The frankness of his reports shocked Victorian England and did much to swing public opinion against the war and in favour of reform.

However, Russell's reports have to be treated with some caution. He was violently anti-Turk and anti-French. Furthermore, Russell cannot have witnessed all the events he describes and, as the identity of his informants is unknown, the reliability of their accounts cannot be verified. He was absent from the Crimea during most of the appalling winter of 1854–55, spending most of December in comparative luxury in Constantinople before returning to the Crimea at the end of the month. Russell left the Crimea for good early in December 1855. He was knighted in 1895.

Source F

On 19 September 1854, early in the morning, the British soldiers began their march from the landing beach to the Russian naval base at Sebastopol.

> The day was warm, and our advance was delayed by the wretched transport provided to carry the baggage, an evil which will, I fear, be more severely felt in any long drawn out operations. Everything not absolutely indispensable was sent by ship.
>
> The country beyond the salt lake, near which we were encamped, is perfectly destitute of tree or shrub, and consists of wide plains, marked at intervals of two or three miles with hillocks and long irregular ridges of hills running down towards the sea. It is but little cultivated, except in the patches of land around the infrequent villages built in the higher recesses of the valleys.
>
> At last, the smoke of burning villages and farmhouses announced that the enemy in front was aware of our march. It was a sad sight to see the white walls of the houses blackened with smoke – the flames ascending through the roofs of peaceful homesteads – and the ruined outlines of deserted hamlets. Many sick men fell out and were carried to the rear. It was a painful sight – a sad contrast to the magnificent appearance of the army in the front of the column – to see litter after litter carried past to the carts, with the poor sufferers who had dropped from illness and fatigue.

William Russell writing in *The Times*, September 1854

SKILLS BUILDER

1 What hints does Russell give of problems to come?

2 What impression of the war would this report probably have given to people reading it back in Britain?

3 To what extent can we rely on the reportage of the Crimean War as delivered by Roger Fenton and William Russell?

Fenton and Russell were not the only voices commenting on the Crimean War. Doctors and surgeons, soldiers – and their wives – kept journals and diaries as well as writing copious letters home. While *The Times* newspaper shocked and horrified its readers, and its proprietors saw the circulation figures soar from 42,500 to 58,500 in the first year of the war, letters and journals that were not necessarily intended for publication played an important part, too, in shaping public opinion.

What happened at the Battle of Alma, 22 September 1854?

The Russian commander Menshikov decided not to attack the British and French during the first day of their march south on 19 September (see Source F). Instead, he and his troops took up positions three miles south of the Alma River. The Russian position was on high ground and, Menshikov believed, easy to defend. The French and British commanders halted their troops close to water, ready for the inevitable battle the following day. It was here that cholera began to take its toll.

Notwithstanding the threat of an epidemic, St Arnaud, the French commander, rode over to discuss strategy and tactics with Lord Raglan. Outlining his plan of action in a mixture of French and English, St Arnaud was assured by Raglan of British cooperation. But Raglan said very little beyond this. He told his divisional commanders nothing of the French plans and had none of his own. No proper reconnaissance had been carried out and so Raglan had no idea of the strength of the Russian forces that would oppose him the following morning. The crucial nature of the battle had escaped him. If the allies were defeated in their first encounter with the Russians, that would be the end of the Crimean adventure. On the other hand, if the allies won, the way would be open for an advance on Sebastopol, which was the whole object of the campaign.

Source G

The front of the Russian line above us had burst into a volcano of flame and white smoke – the roar of the artillery became terrible – we could hear the heavy rush of the shot, those terrible dumps into the ground, and the crash of trees, through which it tore with resistless fury and force, splinters and masses of stone flew out of the walls. The shot came flinging close to me, one, indeed, killing one of the two bandsmen who were carrying a **litter** close to my side. It knocked away the side of his face and he fell dead – a horrible sight. Before me all was smoke. The rush of shot was appalling and I recollect that I was particularly annoyed by the birds, which were flying about distractedly in the smoke and I thought they were fragments of shell.

William Russell wrote an account of the Allies' attack that was published in *The Times* newspaper in September 1854

Definition

Litter

A stretcher for carrying the sick or wounded.

The Russians were so confident of winning the battle that picnic parties of men, women and children came out from Sebastopol to watch the great allied defeat. The French began the attack, following their commander's battle plan but were soon pinned down. Then the British, devoid of any particular battle plan of their own, went for a full frontal assault, uphill, on the Russian position. And they won. The Russians were forced to flee with some 1,755 men dead and around 6,000 casualties. The British lost 363 men with 1,600 wounded. The way to Sebastopol was opened – but at what cost?

Source H

No notice was given to me that sick or wounded would be sent here; consequently no preparation was made for their reception. But early next morning a small steamer came alongside with 86 soldiers. Six of these had been wounded in the cavalry skirmish the night before the battle, and had suffered amputation. No document, nor order about them, was sent, and I considered no others were coming, and proceeded to arrange them on the main deck. About noon, boat after boat came alongside with the sick and the wounded. About 6pm, finding that there were nearly 500 on board, and that others were alongside, I requested the first lieutenant, in the absence of the commander, to prevent others from coming on board. The sick and the wounded were placed indiscriminately on the decks, to the great risk of the wounded, for with diseases such as cholera and dysentery extensively prevailing, the atmosphere becomes quickly tainted. Great distress was experienced by the lack of urinals and bedpans, one only of each being on board; and from the lack of these, many blankets were thrown overboard by my order when they became foul.

In conclusion, I would say that, although I do not feel called upon to blame any one, there can be no doubt that, as from the time the army landed in the Crimea, a battle was impending and sickness was very rife, some arrangements should have been made, and certain vessels fitted for the purpose.

An eyewitness account from James Peters, the naval surgeon on board *HMS Vulcan* writing about the events of 1854

Source I

When I was looking at the wounded men going off today, I could not see an English ambulance. Our men were sent to the sea, three miles distant, on jolting **arabas** or tedious litters. The French – I am tired of this disgraceful comparison – had well-appointed covered hospital vans.

From William Russell's dispatch to *The Times* newspaper in September 1854

SKILLS BUILDER

1 To what extent does William Russell's dispatch support the account given by James Peters?

2 Look back to Source F and to the answer you gave to the question 'What hints does William Russell give of problems to come?' How far do Sources H and I help to confirm that the answer you gave was correct?

Source J

Verse 1

You loyal Britons pray draw near
Unto the news I've brought you
    here,
With joy each British heart doth
    cheer
For the victory gained at Alma.
It was in September, the 18th day,
In spite of the salt sea's dashing
    spray,
We landed safe in the Crimea,
Upon our route for Alma

Chorus
Britain's sons may long remember,
The glorious 20th of September
We made the **Russian bears**
    surrender
Upon the heights of Alma

Verse 3

And when the Alma came in view
The stoutest heart it would subdue
To see the Russians motley crew
Upon the heights of Alma
They were so strongly fortified
With batteries on the mountain
    side
Our generals viewed their force
    and cried
'We'll get hot work at Alma!'

Verse 7

To Sebastopol the Russians fled
And left their wounded and their
    dead;
The river that day, I am sure, ran
    red
With the blood that was spilt at
    Alma.
And though the battle we have got
And gallantly our heroes fought,
Yet dearly was that victory bought
For thousands fell at Alma

From a **broadside** (see page 10), published in 1854, called 'The Battle of Alma'. It would have been recited or sung on the streets, particularly in Scotland, because the Highland Brigade played a large part in the final stages of the battle. The broadside itself consists of ten verses and a chorus.

SKILLS BUILDER

- What is the tone of this broadside?
- What reaction would you expect it to generate among those who listened to it on the streets in Britain?

Definition

Russian bears

Russia is often depicted as a bear, just a Britain is shown as a lion.

What happened at the Battle of Balaclava, 25 October 1854?

The Russians, commanded by Menshikov and desperate to break the Allies' siege of Sebastopol, began to advance with 25,000 men on the British supply base at the port of Balaclava.

(i) The Thin Red Line

On 25 October, the morning of the fateful charge of the Light Brigade, the Russian cavalry advance on Balaclava was halted by the 93rd Highland regiment. Facing a formidable cavalry charge, their tough commander, Sir Colin Campbell, admonished them, 'There is no retreat from here, men. You must die where you stand.' 'Aye, Sir Colin,' they are supposed to have replied, 'And needs be, we'll do that.' Traditionally, when infantry faced a cavalry charge, they formed up into a square. Sir Colin would have none of this and formed his men into a long line, two deep. William Russell, watching from the hills above, wrote that only a 'thin red streak tipped with a line of steel' stood between the Russian cavalry and the defenceless British base of Balaclava. As he watched, the 93rd halted the Russian advance, leaving them to be routed by Lucan's Heavy Brigade. Twenty-seven years later, Robert Gibb painted the 93rd defying the Russian cavalry.

Source K

1.6 'The Thin Red Line' painted by Robert Gibb in 1881

SKILLS BUILDER

Read these two statements:

Statement A: 'The picture is of little use. It was painted seventeen years after the event and so can tell us nothing reliable or useful.'

Statement B: 'The fact that the picture was painted so many years afterwards means that the event had long-term importance.'

Which view do you agree with, and why?

(ii) The charge of the Light Brigade

We are going to be focusing here on one cavalry charge, the charge of the Light Brigade, on the way in which it was reported and reaction to it back in Britain. During the Battle of Balaclava, Lord Raglan ordered Lord Lucan, his cavalry commander, to stop the Russians from removing captured cannon from the Causeway Heights that overlooked two valleys close to

Balaclava. Confusion among the commanders, centring on the gestures of the bearer of the written order, Captain Nolan, and the verbal explanation he gave, led to Lucan sending the Light Brigade up the wrong valley against the wrong guns. What happened next has become a by-word for military ineptitude and matchless courage. The French General Bosquet was moved to say 'C'est magnifique, mais ce n'est pas la guerre' ('It is magnificent, but it is not war').

Definition

Redoubt

A stronghold or fortification.

Source L

I shall proceed to describe, to the best of my powers, what occurred under my own eyes, and to state the facts which I have heard from men whose veracity is unimpeachable.

It appears that the Quartermaster-General, Brigadier Airey gave an order in writing to Captain Nolan to take to Lord Lucan, directing his Lordship 'to advance' his cavalry.

A braver soldier than Captain Nolan the army did not possess. He rode off with his orders to Lord Lucan. He is now dead and gone. God forbid that I should cast a shade on the brightness of his honour, but I am bound to state what I am told occurred when he reached his Lordship. I should explain that the Russian cavalry retired, leaving men in three **redoubts** they had taken. They had also placed some guns on the heights over their position, and about 30 guns were drawn up along their line. Our cavalry had moved up to the ridge across the valley. When Lord Lucan received the order from Captain Nolan and had read it, he asked, we are told, 'Where are we to advance to?' Captain Nolan pointed with his finger to the line of the Russians and said, 'There are the enemy, and there are the guns, sir, before them; it is your duty to take them,' or words to that effect, according to the statements made since his death.

Lord Lucan, with reluctance, gave the order to Lord Cardigan to advance upon the guns. The noble Earl, though he did not shrink, also saw the fearful odds against him. As they passed towards the front, the Russians opened on them from the guns in the redoubt on the right, with volleys of musketry and rifles. They swept proudly past, glittering in the morning sun in all the pride and splendour of war. We could scarcely believe the evidence of our senses. Surely that handful of men are not going to charge an army in position? Alas! It was but too true – their desperate valour knew no bounds, and far indeed was it removed from its so-called better part – discretion.

They advanced in two lines, quickening their pace as they closed towards the enemy. A more fearful spectacle was never witnessed by those who, without the power to aid, beheld their heroic countrymen rushing to the arms of death. At the distance of 1,200 yards the whole line of the enemy belched forth, from 30 iron mouths, a flood of smoke and flame, through which hissed the deadly balls. Their flight was marked by instant gaps in the ranks, by dead men and horses, by steeds flying wounded or riderless across the plain. The first line is broken, it is joined by the second, they never halt or check their speed an instant, with diminished ranks, thinned by those 30 guns, which the Russians had laid with the most deadly accuracy, with a halo of flashing steel above their heads, and with a cheer which was many a noble fellow's death-cry, they flew into the smoke of the batteries, but ere they were lost from view the plain was strewed with their bodies and with the carcasses of horses. Through the clouds of smoke we could see their sabres flashing as they rode up to the guns and dashed between them, cutting down the gunners as they stood.

At 11.35 not a British soldier, except the dead and the dying, was left in front of the bloody Muscovite guns. Our loss, as far as it could be ascertained, in killed, wounded and missing at 2 o'clock today, was as follows: 4th Light Dragoons 79 lost; 8th Hussars 66 lost; 11th Hussars 85 lost; 13th Light Dragoons 69 lost; 17th Lancers 110 lost; Total lost 409.

This was a melancholy day, in which our Light Brigade was annihilated by their own rashness, and by the brutality of a ferocious enemy.

An extract from William Russell's report on the charge of the Light Brigade that was published in *The Times* on 14 November 1854. He watched the charge from a hill overlooking the valley.

SKILLS BUILDER

1 William Russell watched the charge of the Light Brigade from a hill overlooking the valley down which the charge was made. How likely is it that the account, as published in *The Times,* was accurate?

2 What was Russell's attitude to the charge? How do you know?

3 Why do you think *The Times* published Russell's dispatch?

Source M

My Dear Parents

I take the pleasure (having stolen a few moments) to write these few lines to inform you that I am, God be thanked for it, enjoying good health, after having been engaged in a hard fought battle with the Russians on 25th October. I am, however, sorry to say that a great many of my poor comrades met with their death wounds, but in an heroic manner. The Light Dragoon regiments got a dreadful cutting up. My regiment came from England 300 strong, and now we have not more than 100 left from deaths from sickness, and killed in battle.

I shall never forget 25th October – shells, bullets, cannon-balls and swords, kept flying around us. I escaped them all, except a slight scar on my nose from the bursting of a shell and a slight touch on the shoulder from a cannon-ball, after it had killed one of our horses.

The Russians fight hard and well, but we will make them yield yet. Dear mother, every time I think of my poor comrades, my blood runs cold to think how we had to gallop over the poor wounded fellows lying on the field of battle, with anxious looks for assistance – what a sickening scene! In one part of the battle I lost my horse, owing to the one in front of me being shot dead, and my poor horse fell over it, and I was unhorsed; in getting up my horse took fright and got from me, but fortunate for me, I saw another that some poor fellow of the 8th Hussars had been killed from, I mounted it in a moment and was in the rank again. On our return from the charge, I got my own horse again, he had galloped to the camp, and dear parents, I was as glad when I saw him there as if I had got half the world given to me.

I have not time to say more as things look rather queer, and as if we will soon be engaged again with the enemy. I hope to hear from you soon, and when I return to Old England, if God spare me, I will tell you all.

Part of a letter written by William Pearson, of the 4th Light Dragoons, to his parents. He took part in the charge of the Light Brigade.

SKILLS BUILDER

1 How far does William Pearson's account of the charge of the Light Brigade support what William Russell reported about the charge?

2 Would you consider Source K or Source L to be the more reliable account?

3 William Pearson and his parents lived in Penrith, Cumbria. They sent his letter to their local paper, the *Kendal Mercury* and it was published on 18 November 1854. Why would Mr and Mrs Pearson have done this, do you think?

In England, Alfred, Lord Tennyson, was so moved by Russell's description of the charge of the Light Brigade that, in the same year, he wrote the following poem.

Source N

Half a league, half a league,
Half a league onward,
All in the valley of Death
Rode the six hundred.
'Forward, the Light Brigade!'
'Charge for the guns!' he said:
Into the valley of Death
Rode the six hundred.

'Forward, the Light Brigade!'
Was there a man dismay'd?
Not tho' the soldier knew
Someone had blunder'd:
Theirs not to make reply,
Theirs not to reason why,
Theirs but to do and die:
Into the valley of Death
Rode the six hundred.

Cannon to right of them,
Cannon to left of them,
Cannon in front of them
Volley'd and thunder'd;
Storm'd at with shot and shell,
Boldly they rode and well,
Into the jaws of Death,
Into the mouth of Hell
Rode the six hundred.

Flash'd all their sabres bare,
Flash'd as they turn'd in air,

Sabring the gunners there,
Charging an army, while
All the world wonder'd:
Plunged in the battery-smoke
Right thro' the line they broke;
Cossack and Russian
Reel'd from the sabre stroke
Shatter'd and sunder'd.
Then they rode back, but not
Not the six hundred.

Cannon to right of them,
Cannon to left of them,
Cannon behind them
Volley'd and thunder'd;
Storm'd at with shot and shell,
While horse and hero fell,
They that had fought so well
Came thro' the jaws of Death
Back from the mouth of Hell,
All that was left of them,
Left of six hundred.

When can their glory fade?
O the wild charge they made!
All the world wondered.
Honour the charge they made,
Honour the Light Brigade,
Noble six hundred.

From 'The Charge of the Light Brigade' written in 1854 by Alfred, Lord Tennyson

SKILLS BUILDER

1 What message do you think Tennyson was trying to get across to his readers? How far does this message differ from that embedded in the broadside, 'The Battle of Alma' (Source J)?

2 Can you suggest any reasons why there should be a difference?

What was the impact of the Russian winter, January 1855?

The French and British troops did not only have to face the Russian troops, they had to contend with the horrors of a Russian winter, which reached its height in January 1855. It was at this point that it became clear that the British Army was no longer functioning as a military force.

Source O

The British Army was no longer capable of undertaking any operations. Indeed, it could hardly survive. Its logistical support had collapsed through lack of foresight and gross incompetence. There was just enough food to keep the soldiers alive, but they lacked suitable clothing and decent accommodation. They were falling ill and dying at an increasing rate. Without reinforcements the British Army was diminishing in size and unable to do more than stay in its positions. Luckily, the Russians were unable to mount an attack. If they had, it is doubtful whether the British Army would have been able to put up any effective resistance.

From Clive Ponting *The Crimean War* published in 2004

Source P

There are now five or six inches of snow on the ground and a cutting wind from the north-east. Last night was the most severe we have had yet; our tents frozen stiff as boards, so that this morning the door flaps could hardly be undone. Everything was frozen, my boots and trousers quite stiff, and my waterproof bedcover. My cold pork for breakfast was quite hard and ink frozen up. Even now it freezes in my pen. Our poor men suffer much, their blankets were frozen on them last night. I cannot see how we can hold the trenches in this weather, and shall not be surprised if the siege [of Sebastopol] is ended.

From the journal of Temple Godman, an officer in the Heavy Brigade, 6 January 1855

Source Q

Many of these men were all but dead. With closed eyes, open eyes and ghastly attenuated faces, they were borne along, two and two, only a thin stream of breath visible in the frosty air showing that they were alive. One figure was a horror – a corpse, stone dead, strapped upright in its seat, its legs hanging stiffly down, the eyes staring wide open, the teeth set on the protruding tongue, the head and body nodding with frightful mockery of life at each stride of the mule over the broken road. Another man I saw with the raw flesh and skin hanging from his fingers, the naked bones of which protruded into the cold air, undressed and uncovered.

Part of one of William Russell's dispatches to *The Times* in January 1855. Here he is describing the sick and dying being sent to Balaclava.

SKILLS BUILDER

How far do Sources P and Q support what Clive Ponting is saying about the effects of the Russian winter in Source O?

What was the impact of the reportage of William Russell and Roger Fenton?

William Russell

William Russell's frank revelations about the conduct of the Crimean War, its military mismanagement and administrative incompetence (more of which you will read about in the next unit) shocked middle-class Victorian England. Russell's graphic descriptions of the army in the field were a sober contrast to the romantic, jingoistic heroism that had hitherto dominated the reporting of conflict. Indeed, it was Russell's sober, matter-of-fact, objective reporting that did much to undermine the government and destroy the reputation of Lord Raglan, the army commander-in-chief. However, it wasn't simply a matter, for *The Times,* of publishing Russell's dispatches without comment. By the end of November the plight of the army stirred the newspaper itself to mount a campaign to bring the mismanagement of the war to the public's attention. The newspaper's editor, John Delane, decided to sanction a journalistic attack on Lord Raglan and his staff which was spearheaded by a dispatch from Russell.

Source R

It is now pouring with rain – the skies are black as ink – the wind is howling over the staggering tents – the trenches are turned into dykes – in the tents the water is sometimes a foot deep – our men have not either warm or waterproof clothing – they are out for twelve hours at a time in the trenches – they are plunged into the inevitable miseries of a winter campaign – and not a soul seems to care for their comfort or even for their lives.

Part of a dispatch from William Russell, printed in *The Times* on 25 November 1854

Source S

There are people who think it an unhappy outcome of affairs that the Commander-in-Chief and his staff should be decorated, ennobled, duly named in dispatches and ready to return home to enjoy pensions and honours amid the bones of fifty thousand British soldiers, than that the stability of office and the good-humour of society should be disturbed by a single recall or a new appointment over the heads now in command.

From a leader printed in *The Times* in December 1854. A leader is an article written by an editor.

Military historian Denis Judd considers the impact of Russell's war reportage and the attitude taken by *The Times* below.

Source T

The horrors brought so vividly to light by *The Times* shattered the patriotic complacency of opinion at home. The British public was searching furiously for a scapegoat during the winter of 1854–5. Who was to blame? That 'old traitor, Aberdeen' (the Prime Minister)? Lord Raglan? His staff? The Secretary of State for War (the Duke of Newcastle)?

The huge volume of criticism and complaint had its effect. In February 1855 the Aberdeen government fell; the bellicose [warlike] Lord Palmerston became Prime Minister and Lord Panmure went to the War Office. The new administration was apparently determined to make drastic improvements in the running of the war.

From Denis Judd *The Crimean War* published in 1975

SKILLS BUILDER

Look back over the reportage of William Russell (Sources F, G, I, L, Q and R) and re-read his biography box. Would you consider him to be a biased reporter?

Discuss your thoughts with others in a discussion group.

Roger Fenton

Remember that Roger Fenton was sent to the Crimea by the commercial firm of Thomas Agnews & Co, who were relying on his images to make the company a profit. The market they were aiming at consisted primarily of soldiers and their families, but they thought there might be other 'interested parties' as well. How right they were.

Fenton had two main problems with which to contend. He was in the Crimea to record a war. But Victorian sensibilities decreed that no dead bodies should be shown. Secondly, photographic technology had not advanced sufficiently to enable him to take photographs where the subjects were moving. This was just a bit limiting for a war photographer!

Bored with taking photographs of officers, men and ships in Balaclava, he asked a friend to take him to a 'good view'. The friend immediately took him to a narrow ravine running between the British camps in the plains and the Russian fortifications. Fenton was amazed at what he saw 'Round shot and shell lay like a stream at the bottom of the hollow all the way down; you could not walk without treading upon them.' The soldiers called the place 'The Valley of the Shadow of Death' after a phrase in the 23rd Psalm. To them, and to the hordes that travelled to the Crimea to watch the battles, this was a well-known place. Fenton was to make it familiar the length and breadth of Britain.

Source U

1.7 The photograph *Valley of the Shadow of Death* taken by Roger Fenton in 1855

Fenton managed to take about 360 photographs showing different aspects of the Crimean War, and on 26 June 1855 he returned to England. Simon Grant, editor of *TATE etc*, Europe's largest Art magazine, explains what happened next.

Source V

The photographs went on show at the Water Colour Society in Pall Mall in September, the first of three London venues. Versions of the exhibition then toured the country for eight months, taking in Manchester, Leeds, Liverpool, Birmingham and Yeovil. They were a huge success. While audiences were more accustomed to smoke-filled battle scenes, often done by studio painters creating a propaganda picture based on a second hand account from a returning soldier, Fenton's minimal approach coincided with a new feeling of empathy towards the military. Fuelled by William Howard Russell's reports in *The Times* of the terrible conditions that the troops faced, Fenton had touched on an appetite for documentary – for telling it how it was.

From Simon Grant *A Terrible Beauty*, 2008

And finally . . .

In this unit you have studied many different ways of reporting the war to the people back home. Which, in your judgement, was the most effective?

What have you learned in this unit?

You have learned that the Crimean War was fought because British politicians believed that Russian expansion was threatening Britain's ability to hold India and also to control the Mediterranean Sea. You have addressed the importance of the Battle of Alma in opening the way to Sebastopol, and your study of two incidents within the Battle of Balaclava will have alerted you to shortcomings in the command structure of the British Army. Finally, your study of the effect the Russian winter had on the British troops will have prepared you for the administrative ineptitude which you will study next.

What skills have you used in this unit?

You have worked with source material to begin to explore the terrain over which the troops would be fighting. You have looked at the different ways in which the war was reported and have cross-referenced between them in order to assess which method was the most effective. You have analysed in depth the work of William Russell and Roger Fenton and you have considered the impact war reportage had on the British public.

SKILLS BUILDER

At the time of the Crimean War, photography was not sufficiently advanced to allow photographers to take pictures of any form of movement.

How far would you agree with the view that, because of this, there was no point in having photographers at a war?

Use Sources E and U in your answer.

SKILLS BUILDER

1 What should be the role of war correspondents?

   Set up a debate on the motion 'This house believes that war correspondents should report factually and without emotion.' Remember to get someone to propose the motion and someone to oppose it. After that, everyone can join in the debate.

2 Identify a twentieth-century and a twenty-first-century war correspondent.

   Use the Internet to find at least one report from each of them.

   To what extent do they differ from those sent to *The Times* by William Russell?

3 How much notice should the British public take of reports from war zones?

Exam style question

This is the sort of question you will find appearing on the examination papers as an (a) question.

Study Sources W, X and Y.

How far do Sources X and Y challenge Source W about the effective supplying of the army?

Source W

Mr Commissary-General Filder deserves the greatest raise for his exertions in supplying our men with food. The stories which have been circulating respecting the insufficiency and irregularity of the supply of meat, biscuits and spirits are base lies. No army was ever fed with more punctuality, and no army, I believe, was ever so well fed under such very exceptional circumstances. No man in this army has ever been without his pound of good biscuit, his pound and a half or pound of good beef or mutton, his quota of coffee, tea, rice and sugar or his gill of excellent rum, for any one day, except it has been through his own neglect.

From a dispatch from William Russell, published in *The Times* newspaper on 8 November 1854

Source X

You cannot imagine anything more uncomfortable than wet and cold weather in camp. The ground here when it rains is in some places almost as bad as a marsh and the wet tent does not form a cheerful place to go into, particularly as there are no chairs, or any fire, in fact, nothing more than the canvas walls. All cooking is done in the open air, and the wind either almost scatters the fire or the rain puts it out. Latterly, during the last two weeks, owing to the bad weather and the state of the roads, the Commissariat have been unable to get up their full supplies and the tea and sugar have not been issued.

From a letter written home by George Lawson, a doctor at the Crimea

Source Y

The winter is setting in and we have just had two days' rain. The horses are up to their fetlocks in mud and slush, through which one must paddle to get to them; the saddles soaked, the tents so crowded that the men have no room in them for their arms, which must therefore lie in the rain. In our tents everything is wet, except what one can wrap up in a waterproof; mud outside and mud within. The men, of course, are worse off, most having no change of clothes. Their clothes get wet in the daytime, and their cloaks, and these they must sleep in as also their boots. We had twenty-two cases of sickness this morning. Dysentery is on the increase. If we are left like this the horses must die and the men will suffer even more. Unless they make us and our horses huts soon, we shall be quite useless by the spring, even if we get through the winter.

From the journal of Temple Godman, an officer in the Heavy Brigade,
12 November 1854

Exam tips

- **Don't** bring in a lot of your own knowledge. All (a) questions focus on the analysis, cross-referencing and evaluation of source material. Your own knowledge won't be credited by the examiner, and you will waste valuable time writing it out.
- **Do** remember that the only own knowledge you should introduce will be to put the sources into context. This means, for example, that you might explain that Russell was absent from the Crimea for most of the appalling winter of 1854–55.
- **Don't** describe (or even re-write) the sources: the examiner will have a copy of the exam paper!
- **Do** draw inferences from the sources concerning what they show about the effectiveness of supplying the army, and cross-reference the inferences for similarity and difference.
- **Do** reach a supported judgement about 'how far' Sources X and Y challenge Source W by carefully weighing the similarities and differences.

RESEARCH TOPIC

Local history

Look carefully at your local built area.

What indications can you find of the impact of the Crimean War?

(Hint: look out for Alma Terrace, Balaclava cottages, Raglan Road and other such names.)

What does this tell you about:

(a) the date of the development;

(b) the importance, locally, of the Crimean War?

2 The Crimean War 1854–56: 'Someone had blundered'

What is this unit about?

This unit focuses on the administrative chaos that was revealed by the reportage of the Crimean War and on the reactions to that chaos back in Britain. The role of Florence Nightingale in the Crimea is considered through a case study; the nature of her work and the role she played in the Crimea is addressed, along with a consideration of whether the myth of the 'lady with the lamp' was borne out by reality. The unit ends with a consideration of the work of Mary Seacole, the other major player in nursing in the Crimea.

Key questions

- How serious was the supposed chaos in the administration of the Crimean War?
- What was the impact of the work of Florence Nightingale and Mary Seacole?

Timeline

1854

July	The Ottoman Barracks at Scutari cleaned out and made ready as a hospital
Autumn	Mary Seacole's request to become one of Florence Nightingale's nurses at Scutari rejected
September	The General Hospital established in the Crimea
12 October	*The Times* Fund set up
13 October	*Patriotic* fund set up
23 October	Florence Nightingale and 38 nurses leave England
5 November	Florence Nightingale and nurses arrive at Scutari
8 November	Lord Raglan informs the Commissariat that the troops will be wintering in camps around Balaclava
14 November	Crimea hit by the 'Great Storm'
25 November	*The Times* begins its campaign to bring the state of affairs in the Crimea to the attention of the British public

1855

6 March	Sanitary Commission arrives at Scutari
Spring	Mary Seacole's 'British hotel' established outside Balaclava
April	The Castle Hospital established in the Crimea
28 June	Death of Lord Raglan
9 September	Fall of Sebastopol

Source A

2.1 A contemporary cartoon called *Mis(s)management*, printed in Denis Judd *The Crimean War* published in 1975

How well supplied were the troops?

You read in the last unit about the terrible suffering of men and horses as a result of the dreadful Russian winter of 1854–55. You might reasonably have drawn the conclusion that there wasn't much that could be done in the face of such appalling weather conditions. Read the following sources and see whether or not they help change your mind or, at least, develop your ideas as to whether matters could have been managed better.

The weather or human error?

Source B

I am full of apprehension as to our power of keeping this Army supplied during the coming winter. In this crowded little harbour [Balaclava] only a proportion of our vessels can be admitted at a time. With all the siege and other stores which are being disembarked, we can do little more than land sufficient supplies to keep pace with the daily consumption of the troops; and to add to our difficulties, the road from the harbour to the camp, not being a made one, is impassable after heavy rains. Our obstacles in these respects will be increased as the winter comes. We shall have many more stores to convey than we have hitherto had – fuel, for instance. In short, I am full of anxiety and dread on the subject.

Part of a letter written by Sir James Filder, the head of the commissariat, to the British Treasury on 14 November 1854. Confident that the army would have taken Sebastopol and would have been wintering there in the shelter of a well-resourced town, Lord Raglan had not entertained the idea of failure. Consequently he didn't tell Filder until 8 November that the army would be wintering in the Crimea and Filder had no time to make adequate preparations.

However, the government in London had more foresight than its military commanders. From August they had been requisitioning supplies sufficient to equip their army through a winter in the open and in October ships containing the necessary supplies set out. Meanwhile, back in the Crimea, the situation worsened.

Source C

By the end of the first week of November, as the weather worsened, the situation of the cavalry was becoming difficult. The horses had no shelter and there was no transport to take fodder up to the camp. By 12 November the horses were surviving on a handful of barley a day. Lord Cardigan, who was spending four to five days at a time on his yacht, refused to allow the Light Brigade to move to Balaclava where the horses could be fed. He also ordered that no horse was to be killed unless it had a broken leg or an incurable disease. The result was that the horses died slowly of starvation over several days, usually lying in the mud.

From Clive Ponting *The Crimean War* published in 2004

Just when it must have seemed that the situation couldn't get any worse, it did. The Crimea was hit by a tremendous storm. The Russians, safe inside Sebastopol, were reasonably well protected. The British Army, encamped in tents outside, suffered dreadfully. Tents disappeared, hospital marquees were flattened and barrack roofs ripped off in the gale force winds. Balaclava harbour was awash with ships' cargoes: planks and spars, blankets, guns, gunpowder and cartridges, socks, chamber pots and greatcoats. Outside the harbour, twenty-two ships were forced to ride out the storm, half of which were sailing ships. There was room in Balaclava harbour, but the port authorities refused to let the ships in, though some desperate captains forced their way over the harbour bar. Historian Clive Ponting takes up the story again in Source D.

Source D

Of the ships outside Balaclava harbour, *Resolute*, carrying ammunition, sank, but the crucial loss was that of the steamship *Prince*. This was carrying nearly all the supplies that had been ordered by the War Office in August. In total, the clothing losses were 25,000 fur caps, 8,000 sealskin coats, 15,000 pairs of leather boots, 40,000 fur coats, 40,000 pairs of leggings and 10,000 gloves. These stocks would have been enough to equip the small British Army for the winter. The stores could be replaced, but it would take several months for the items to be made and shipped out to the Crimea. Equally important was the loss of more than twenty days' supply of hay for the horses. Without this fodder the horses would die and there would be no way of moving supplies (particularly food) to the troops several miles away on the heights before Sebastopol. When the horses died, the troops would have to do this work themselves. The harbour master at Balaclava, Captain Christie, who had refused to let ships into the harbour, took most of the blame for the disaster. He was told he would be court-martialled, but died and was posthumously awarded a CB.

From Clive Ponting *The Crimean War* published in 2004

SKILLS BUILDER

Look back over Sources B–D. Clearly, British troops in the Crimea were not being appropriately supplied to enable them to survive the winter. Who was to blame? There are several candidates:

Lord Raglan   Lord Cardigan   Sir James Filder
Captain Christie   The weather

Working in small groups, decide what contribution each made to the disaster.

Now weigh the responsibility each bore and reach a balanced, supported judgement as to where the blame lay.

Compare your findings with those of other groups. Have you arrived at the same conclusion? Have you weighted the evidence differently? If so, explain why.

An historian, Denis Judd, came up with his answer. He believed that there was one over-riding factor, and that was the lack of coordination between the different departments that were supposed to be responsible for different aspects of the army's supply, welfare and equipment. He identified:

- The Secretary of State for War and the Colonies
  Responsible for military policy;
- The Secretary-at-War
  Responsible for army finance and business;
- The Commander-in-Chief
  Unable to initiate any measure involving finance without the agreement of the Secretary-at-War;
- The Adjutant-General
  Responsible for recruiting, discipline, pay, arms and clothing;
- The Quartermaster-General
  Responsible for movement, quartering, barracks, camps and transport;
- The Board of General Officers
  Advised the Adjutant-General on clothing and equipment;
- The Master-General of the Ordnance
  Responsible for the artillery and engineers;
- The commanding officers of the various regiments
  Dealt with various contractors for fuel and rations;
- The Commissariat officers
  Responsible for providing rations and fuel, managing butcheries and bakeries while the army was abroad and was responsible to the Treasury;
- The Medical Staff Corps (doctors and quarter-masters to the hospitals)
  Responsible for various elements to the Secretary-at-War, the Commander-in-Chief and the Ordnance Office;
- The Paymaster-General
  responsible for making payments and answerable to the army treasury.

SKILLS BUILDER

Does Denis Judd's answer make you change your mind about yours?

What was the reaction in Britain?

Source E

I see in a leading article of *The Times* of the 23rd of last month* (which is an excellent one) that you at home are beginning to find out the true state of things here. It would make the people of England's blood boil to see one half of the miseries the finest Army she ever sent out, have been made, and still are being made, to suffer. Added to this is the horrible waste, mismanagement and culpable neglect of the public and private stores sent out for us so generously by the public. The Army are most thankful for them, that is for the intention, but as to the things themselves, they never get them. They are either left on board the transports to rot, or carried into some of the deserted houses at Balaclava, which that most infernal commissariat have converted into what they call stores, there they are piled in heaps, in an undesirable state of confusion, and when anything is applied for, you find Mr Commissary Jones, Smith or Robinson smoking a cigar (which most likely has been sent out for the army but which he has bagged) who tells you that really he is very sorry, he believes that the article you want is somewhere in the stores, but just where he has not the slightest idea, and at present he has no time to look for it. The consequence is, the poor devil has to go to the nearest shop and pay 200% for an article which, if the affairs were carried on as they ought to be, would have been received from the government for nothing or, at worst, for what they cost in England. If he does not do this, he must starve from hunger or cold, as the case may be. Now this is – I give you my honour – the true state of things.

An extract from a letter from Captain W.P. Richards to his sister Caroline, written on 12 January 1855 from outside Sebastopol

SKILLS BUILDER

What can you learn from Source E about the relationship between the Army in the Crimea and the British public?

*Remember, that in November 1854 *The Times* newspaper began a concerted campaign to bring the state of affairs in the Crimea to the attention of the British public (see page 17).

The horrors of the Crimean War were brought to light by the reportage of William Russell in *The Times* and challenged the patriotic complacency of the British public. In direct response to the Crimean dispatches printed in *The Times,* Sir Robert Peel, son of the former Prime Minister, sent the newspaper a cheque for £200 for supplying comforts to the sick and wounded. This formed the basis of *The Times* 'Crimea Fund', which rapidly amassed over £7,000. But Sir Robert Peel wasn't the only high-ranking person to express concern about the goings-on in the Crimea.

Source F

The sad privations of the Army, the bad weather and the constant sickness are causes of the deepest concern and anxiety to the Queen and the Prince. The braver her noble Troops are and the more patiently they bear all their trials and sufferings the more miserable we feel at their long continuance.

The Queen trusts that Lord Raglan will be very strict in seeing that no unnecessary privations are incurred by any negligence of those whose duty it is to watch over their wants. The Queen heard that their coffee was given them green instead of being roasted and several other things of the kind. It has distressed the Queen, as she feels so conscious that they should be made as comfortable as circumstances can admit of. The Queen earnestly trusts that the larger amount of warm clothing has not only reached Balaclava but has been distributed and that Lord Raglan has been successful in procuring the means of hutting for the men. Lord Raglan cannot think how much we suffer for the Army and how painfully anxious we are to know that their privations are decreasing.

Part of a letter, written on 1 January 1855, by Queen Victoria to Commander-in-Chief Lord Raglan

SKILLS BUILDER

Are you surprised that the Queen should write to her Commander-in-Chief in this way?

Does this mean that she had been influenced by the dispatches in *The Times*?

What was Lord Raglan's reply?

Source G

With truth Lord Raglan can assure your Majesty that his whole time and all his thoughts are occupied in endeavouring to provide for the various wants of your Majesty's troops. It has not been in his power to lighten the burden of their duties. Much having been said, as Lord Raglan has been given to understand, in private letters, of the inefficiency of his staff, he considers it to be due to your Majesty, as a simple act of justice to those individuals, to assure your Majesty that he has every reason to be satisfied with their exertions.

Part of Lord Raglan's reply to the letter from Queen Victoria, dated 2 January 1855

SKILLS BUILDER

How far do Sources B and E challenge what Lord Raglan (Source G) says in reply to Queen Victoria's letter?

As spring approached, the situation began to improve. R.L.V. ffrench Blake, himself a regular officer in the 17th/21st Lancers from 1933–49, and who researched the Crimean War, describes what happened.

Source H

As spring approached, the administrative chaos was gradually cleared. A system for the supply of provisions to central depots on the plateau was established; Turkish labour was recruited for construction work; a railway from Balaclava to the area of the Telegraph on the Woronzov Road was completed; transport was borrowed from the French; Spanish mules arrived from Barcelona.

Mr Filder, the Commissary-General, began to restore order in Balaclava with the help of Admiral Boxer who had been appointed to organise the port. Greatcoats and boots began to arrive; the crowd of dishonest **sutlers** and contractors who had been operating unchecked in Balaclava, was brought under control. Huts became available, but as it took two artillery wagons with ten horses, or 180 men, to move a single hut up to the Heights, progress was slow. Fresh meat and oranges arrived from Malta; by February the army was on the mend. By March, race-meetings were being organised, football and cricket were being played in the camps. It was time to turn against the enemy once more.

From R.L.V. ffrench Blake *The Crimean War* published in 1971

Definition

Sutler

A person who followed an army and sold its provisions.

Fitzroy James Henry Somerset, 1st Baron Raglan (1788–1855)

Born at Badminton he was commissioned into the 4th Light Dragoons in 1804, transferred to 43rd Foot in 1808 and took part in the Peninsular Campaign as aide-de-camp to General Sir Arthur Wellesley, the future Duke of Wellington whose niece he married in 1814. He was badly wounded at the Battle of Waterloo (1815) that finally ended Napoleon's European ambitions, and had to have his right arm amputated. He was promoted to the rank of Major-General, became military secretary at the Horse Guards, Colonel and then Lieutenant-General of 53rd Foot. In 1852 he was appointed Privy Counsellor and given the title Baron Raglan. Two years later at the outbreak of the Crimean War, and despite never having led troops in war, he was given command of the British forces. Although promoted to Field Marshal, it quickly became apparent that he was not suited for high command and he was widely criticised, specifically in William Russell's dispatches to *The Times* and in particular for his orders resulting in the charge of the Light Brigade. He died in the Crimea, probably from dysentery, in June 1855.

James Thomas Brudenell, 7th Earl of Cardigan (1797–1868)

Born at Hambleden, Buckinghamshire. Handsome and full of dash and gallantry, it was said that he didn't know what fear was, but contemporaries also said that he was extraordinarily stupid. He was commissioned in the 8th Hussars in 1824, bought command (a common thing to do for the sons of the wealthy) of the 15th Hussars in 1832 and was removed for misconduct in 1834. Two years later he bought the command of the 11th Hussars and in 1837 succeeded to the family title. He and Lucan were brothers-in-law and hated each other. During the Crimean War, Lucan lived alongside his men while Cardigan dined and slept on his luxurious yacht. During the Battle of Balaclava, Cardigan led the charge of the Light Brigade, shouting 'Here goes the last of the Brudenells', but he survived. He was the first into the 'Valley of Death' and the first out, unscathed, leaving immediately for his yacht and champagne. After Crimea he returned to England where he was regarded as a hero and showered with honours. He worked as Inspector-General of Cavalry from 1855–60 and died from injuries sustained as a result of a fall from his horse in 1868.

What medical services were available in the Crimea?

The medical services that were available in the Crimea were a reflection of the state of medical knowledge at the time and the ability of those in control to ensure that that medical knowledge was used appropriately for the benefit of sick and wounded soldiers.

How were the medical services organised?

In February 1853, the Army Medical Department and the Ordnance Medical Department were amalgamated into one department under Dr Andrew Smith, who had a small staff of six. It was impossible to do this any earlier because the Duke of Wellington (whose opinions on military matters were rarely challenged after his victory over Napoleon at Waterloo in 1815) was adamantly opposed to any reform of the army medical services. Andrew Smith and his small department thus had to create a war-ready department virtually from scratch. When Crimean engagements intensified and invasion was imminent, Dr Smith was told, wrongly, that the British force would number some 10,000 men. At that point he had no wagons in which to transport the wounded to camp and base hospitals; no stretcher-bearers and no doctors. Colonel Tulloch, heading up the Hospital Conveyance Corps 'solved' the problem of stretcher-bearers. His staff was made up of army pensioners, and they were swung into action on the battlefields as stretcher-bearers for the wounded and dying, removers of the dead, and general servants of the officers. This was a disastrous move.

A major problem was that Lord Raglan, believing that space on board ships was best given over to troops, ordered that only a small number of medical assistants (roughly four per hundred men) would be necessary and should embark for the Crimea. As for doctors, they were to be recruited on a volunteer basis. The two designated hospital ships at Varna in August 1854 were taken over as troop transporters, and it wasn't until early in 1855 that four hospital ships were in operation. The same confusion that reigned regarding general supplies found its way into the distribution of medical supplies. For example, in order to make way for troops, the captain of one of the two originally designated hospital ships off-loaded all the medical supplies stacked on board. They weren't found until four months later, by which time a large proportion were unusable.

The effectiveness of the British approach to the organisation and administration of medical services is summed up by Lieutenant Colonel Anthony Sterling. He fought in the Crimean War and later made many criticisms about the ways in which the war was run.

Source J

The mistake that has been made has been a very common one in our country. Certain military establishments have not been kept up in peacetime because people took it into their heads that war would never come. In France there is a permanent wagon-train always organised, a permanent commissariat and also a permanent ambulance. The English people destroyed these above named departments that existed during the Spanish war. The British government, on deciding upon war, should have instantly begun to organise them again.

From Lieutenant Colonel Anthony Sterling *The Story of the Highland Brigade* published in 1895

Source I

Whether it was a scheme for saving money by utilising the poor old men or shortening the duration of their lives and pensions, it is difficult to say. But they have been found in practice rather to require nursing themselves than to be able to nurse others. At Gallipoli and in Bulgaria they died in numbers, while the whole of them were so weak as to be unable to perform the most ordinary duties. The man who conceived the idea that the hard work of a military hospital could be performed by worn-out and aged cripples must have a slight knowledge of warfare or profited little by experience.

From a report sent to *The Times* by Thomas Chenery, their Constantinople correspondent, and published in September 1854

Where were hospitals established?

The major base hospital established in Scutari, where the old Ottoman barracks were converted by the British into the Barrack Hospital, could accommodate around 6,000 men. Across the Black Sea, in the Crimea itself, four hospitals were set up.

- The General Hospital opened in September 1854 as soon as British troops arrived in the area.

- The Castle Hospital opened in April 1855 with some 2,500 beds.
- The Land Transport Corps had its own hospital at Karani.
- A convalescent hospital was set up at the St George Monastery.

What treatment was available?

The treatments that were available mirrored, but in cruder ways because of circumstances, that which was available in hospitals in Britain. Out in the Crimea, the main form of 'treatment' was the amputation of shattered limbs, and this carried with it a 25 per cent likelihood of death from shock or infection. Anaesthesia, in the form of ether or chloroform, was used in the Crimea but its impact was limited. Sufficient supplies rarely got to the hospitals and, even when they did, there was a deep-rooted belief among some medical staff that the use of anaesthetics during an operation weakened the patient. Shot was gouged out of bleeding flesh and gaping wounds were stitched, but there was always the ever-present risk of infection.

Clean water and sanitation: the greatest problem of all?

By far the biggest problem for the medical services in any battlefield situation was the provision of clean water and sanitation. Hundreds of men, camped in the open with barely a change of clothing and facing the appalling weather and supply conditions you read about earlier, were bound to become prey to disease. It was the same in the hospitals. Lack of washing facilities led to lice infestation and to the risk of typhus and typhoid. Lack of sanitation led to dysentery and cholera.

British forces suffered 18,058 casualties in the war, but of these only 1,761 were killed by enemy action. The remaining 16,297 died from their wounds or from disease and by far the largest number succumbed to disease. Indeed, in the winter of 1854–55, more than one-third of the British Army died from disease and most of these deaths occurred in hospitals.

It must be remembered, however, that lack of clean water and poor sanitation were killers on mainland UK too. It was in 1854, the year of the major Crimea battles and the arrival of Florence Nightingale in the Crimea, that John Snow removed the handle from the Broad Street pump thus proving (but not to everyone's satisfaction) the link between water and cholera. Louis Pasteur's germ theory of disease was a decade away and so was Joseph Lister's work on antisepsis.

Enter Florence Nightingale

Into this maelstrom of mess and muddle came **Florence Nightingale** (see page 31). She was invited to head the nursing staff at the Scutari Barrack Hospital through the influence of two powerful friends, Sidney Herbert (Secretary at War at the beginning of the Crimean conflict) and

SKILLS BUILDER

Read Sources I and J and use the information in this unit.

Who, or what, was to blame for the standard of medical services offered to British troops in the Crimea?

his wife Elizabeth. No other candidates were considered. Florence was to be accompanied to the Crimea by a team of 38 nurses, selected by a committee that included Elizabeth Herbert. The committee was careful to keep a religious balance among the volunteer nurses. Fourteen came from various Anglican orders, ten from Catholic nursing orders and the remaining fourteen from various unaffiliated English hospitals. Florence Nightingale's brief was clear. She was to be in charge only of the nurses at the Scutari base hospital, and she was at all times to be under the authority of the medical officer, Dr Menzies.

Case study: Florence Nightingale

Angel of mercy?

Florence Nightingale became a legend in her own lifetime. Praised and honoured by the British public for what they believed to be her success in improving nursing conditions for the sick and wounded Crimean soldiers at Scutari, they created the myth of the 'Lady with the Lamp'. The British public saw Florence Nightingale as an angel of mercy, moving gently among the sick and dying, administering comfort and care, bringing hope out of despair. How correct was this image? How much basis does it have in hard fact? The purpose of this case study is to investigate the significance of the role played by Florence Nightingale in the Crimean War and to consider the impact this had on the British public.

Biography

Florence Nightingale 1820–1910

Named after the city of her birth, Florence was the second child and second daughter of William and Frances Nightingale, a wealthy couple who were touring Europe for two years on their honeymoon. Back in England, the family divided its time between their homes in Derbyshire and Hampshire. Educated at home by her father, Florence was an academic child who was expected to make a good marriage. She would have none of this, and finally persuaded her parents to allow her to undertake three months' nursing training in 1851 at Kaiserwerth, near Dusseldorf. Unusually for the time and her background, Florence's father settled £500 a year on her for life, which enabled her to live independently. She took up, for three months, a post as Superintendent of the Establishment for Gentlewomen during Illness at 1, Harley Street, London, in 1853.

Outcry in *The Times* led to Sidney Herbert, the Minister at War, appointing her to oversee the introduction of nurses into military hospitals in Turkey and she arrived at the Barrack Hospital, Scutari, in November 1854. Returning home at the end of the war in 1856 she disappeared from public view for some time and it is now thought that she was coming to terms with the reasons for the high death rates at Scutari. Her greatest achievement was to raise nursing to the level of being a respectable profession for women. In 1860, with public subscriptions to the Nightingale Fund, the Nightingale Training School for nurses was established at St Thomas's Hospital, London. In the same year she published *Notes for Nursing* which has been translated into eleven languages and is still in print today.

Dirt, disease and death rates

Source 2A

On Thursday last we had 1715 sick and wounded in this hospital (among whom 120 cholera patients) and 650 severely wounded in the other building, called the General Hospital, of which we also have charge – when a message came to me to prepare for 570 wounded on our side of the hospital who were arriving from the dreadful affair [see page x] of 5 November at Balaclava, where some 1763 wounded and 442 killed, besides 96 Officers wounded and 38 killed. We had but half an hour's notice before they began landing the wounded. Between one and nine o'clock, we had the mattresses stuffed, sewn up, and laid down, alas! only upon matting on the floors, the men washed and put to bed and all their wounds dressed.

Not a sponge nor a rag of linen, not anything have I left. Everything is gone to make slings and stump pillows and shirts. These poor fellows have not had a clean shirt nor been washed for two months before they came here, and the state in which they arrive from the transport is literally crawling. I hope in a few days we shall establish a little cleanliness. But we have not a basin nor a towel nor a bit of soap nor a broom – I have ordered 300 scrubbing brushes. But one half of the Barrack is so sadly out of repair that it is impossible to use a drop of water on the stone floors, which are all laid upon rotten wood, and would give our men fever in no time.

Part of a letter from Florence Nightingale to Dr William Bowman, written on 14 November 1854. William Bowman was an ophthalmologist on the staff of King's College Hospital, London. In 1844, he had helped found the St John's House Institution for training nurses and four of Florence Nightingale's nurses were trained there.

Source 2B

(1) It appears that, in these Hospitals, the Purveyor considers washing both of linen and of the men a minor 'detail', and during the three weeks we have been here, though our remonstrances have been treated with perfect civility, yet no washing whatever has been performed either of body-linen or of bed-linen except by ourselves and a few wives of the wounded. The dirty shirts were collected yesterday for the first time and on Monday it is said they are to be washed. We are organising a little Washing Establishment of our own for the bandages etc. When we came here, there was neither basin, towel nor soap in the wards, nor any means of personal cleanliness for the wounded except for the following. Thirty were bathed every night by Dr MacGrigor's orders in slipper-baths, but this means a washing once in eighty days for 2,300 men.

The consequences of all this are fever, cholera, gangrene, lice, bugs, fleas and maybe erisypelas – from the using of one sponge among many wounds.

(2) The fault here is not with the Medical Officers but in the separation of the department which affords every necessary supply, except medicines, to them – and in the insufficient supply of minor officers in the Purveying Department under Mr Wreford, the Purveyor General – as well as the inevitable delay in obtaining supplies, occasioned by the existence of one single Interpreter only.

(3) The Officers here link the apparent meanness in the system to you. They fix their attention on the correctness of their book-keeping as the primary object of life.

(4) The requirements are unity of action and personal responsibility.

(5) Another cause is the imperfection of distinct orders in England as to packing. The ship 'Prince' had on board a quantity of medical comforts for us which were so packed under shot and shell that it was found impossible to off-load them here and so it went on to Balaclava where the ship sank in the great storm.

All the above is written in obedience to your private instructions. Do not let me appear as a government spy here, which would destroy all my usefulness.

Part of a letter written by Florence Nightingale on 25 November 1854 to Sidney Herbert. This was the first of many such letters.

SKILLS BUILDER

What are the differences, and what are the similarities, between these two letters, both written by Florence Nightingale within less than a fortnight?

How would you explain these differences?

Now read Source 2C.

How far is Source 2C supported by Sources 2A and 2B?

Source 2C

It was at Scutari that Florence Nightingale battled as valiantly as any soldier in the field to improve conditions. The men were piled up in corridors, lying on unscrubbed, rotting floors crawling with vermin. In her early days in the hospital at Scutari there were more than a thousand patients suffering from acute diarrhoea and only twenty chamber pots to go round! The privies were blocked up and an inch of liquid filth floated over the floor. The men's food often lay in this revolting mess. The vile stench from the hospital penetrated the walls and could be smelled from some distance away.

Florence Nightingale had a fund of £30,000 to manage, and out of this she purchased some of the necessities so badly needed at the Barrack Hospital. She also worked with incredible energy and devotion, often going without sleep, superintending the multiple tasks that confronted her – cleansing the wards, ensuring that fresh bed linen was available, tending the dying, and arranging for the preparation of special nutritious diets.

From Denis Judd *The Crimean War* published in 1975

Source 2D

Nightingale did not arrive at Scutari until 4 November 1854. By then the hospital was running well. At the end of September, Thomas Chenery reported to 'The Times' that 'the preparations for the reception of the sick and wounded have been as complete as those for the active business of the war'. The old Ottoman barracks had been 'cleaned and whitewashed' and were 'sufficiently comfortable'. He added that 'the health of the men is wonderfully improved by the air of the Bosphorous'. Sidney Herbert sent out – at the suggestion of Dr Andrew Smith, the Head of the Medical Department, a commission to investigate the state of the hospitals. Nightingale travelled out with them in October and immediately after their arrival Dr Spence (who was to die a week later on the 'Prince' outside Balaclava harbour) reported to London: 'Just returned from Scutari, perfectly delighted to find things so well managed.' A friend of Sidney Herbert, Mr Bracebridge, reported at the same time that the hospital was 'clean and airy' and that there were 'few bad smells'. Although Florence Nightingale tried to portray the situation at Scutari as appalling before she arrived, this was not the case.

From Clive Ponting *The Crimean War* published in 2004

SKILLS BUILDER

1 To what extent does Source 2D challenge Source 2C about the conditions in the Scutari Barrack Hospital in 1854?

2 How would you explain the difference between these accounts?

3 Which account would you trust? Why?

Source 2E

It is clear that, quite independently of the medical treatment of the sick and wounded, there is an urgent necessity for improved sanitary arrangements in our hospitals at Scutari and elsewhere. Proper ventilation has been neglected, and various other sanitary arrangements have been either not thought of, or not carried into effect. There are two very able and active men who have been connected with the Board of Health and whom I have much employed about sanitary matters – Dr Sutherland and Dr Grainger. I wish very much that you would send them out at once to Constantinople, to Scutari and Balaclava and the Camp, not to interfere at all with the medical treatment of the sick and wounded, but with full powers to carry into immediate effect such sanitary improvements and arrangements in regard to the hospital buildings and to the Camp as their experience may suggest. I am convinced that this will save a great many lives.

Part of a letter written by Prime Minister Lord Palmerston to his Minister of War, Lord Panmure, in February 1855

Source 2G

They put in hand a programme of basic sanitary improvements that, as elsewhere, produced a significant fall in the death rate. The hospital in Scutari was positioned above a huge cesspool. This was dug out and drained, floors were renewed, walls painted with disinfectant, double rows of mattresses changed to single ones and the wards and corridors were cleared of rubbish every day. Their programme was an indictment of the previous management (including that of Florence Nightingale) and the death rate was subsequently reduced from 42 per 1,000 in March 1855 to 2 per thousand by June of that year.

Historian Clive Ponting, in his book *The Crimean War* published in 2004, comments on the work of the Sanitary Commission

Source 2F

The physically deteriorating effect of the Scutari air has been much discussed, but it may be doubted. The men sent down to Scutari in the winter died because they were not sent down until they were half dead – the men sent down now live and recover because they are sent in time.

Part of a letter from Florence Nightingale to the Minister of War, Lord Panmure, in August 1855

Source 2H

Her work with *Farr in analysing the differences between the mortality in different areas, and specifically between the front line hospitals in the Crimea and the base hospitals at Scutari, had shown that the epidemic that had killed 18,000 men out of an army intended to number 25,000 had not been caused by inadequate food, overwork or lack of shelter as everyone believed. It had been primarily caused by bad hygiene. The worst affected places had been those where overcrowding had aggravated the effect of bad sanitation. And by far the worst of these, where 5,000 men had been killed by bad hygiene in the winter of 1854/5, was Florence Nightingale's own base hospital at Scutari. In the five months before the Sanitary Commission arrived, between November 1854 and March 1855, Nightingale had not been running a hospital. She had been running a death camp.

From Hugh Small *Avenging Angel* published in 1998

*William Farr (1807–83) was a medical statistician. He was appointed Compiler of Abstracts at the General Register Office (now known as the Office for National Statistics).

SKILLS BUILDER

Read Sources 2E, 2F and 2G.

Would you agree with the view that says 'Lord Palmerston clearly knew more about the care of soldiers than Florence Nightingale'?

In Source 2H, historian Hugh Small believes that Florence Nightingale had been running a death camp. Look back over the sources you have worked with so far in this case study. Which would you use to support this view? Which would you use to challenge this view?

Disagreements and disputes

Source 2I

5th December 1854

Dear Miss Gipps

I have no time but to make the shortest communication, as you may suppose when I tell you that I have not yet written to my own people.

I have now had one month's experience of the St John's Sisters.

Mrs Drake is invaluable, kind, careful, modest.

Mrs Lawfield, though not skilful (she does not know a fracture when she sees it) is one of the most valuable nurses I have from her great propriety of conduct and kindness.

With regard to the other four, I fear that nothing can be made of them here, tho I have no doubt that, as private nurses in England, they may be very good. Their manners are so flibberty-gibbet that they do not command the respect imperatively necessary where forty women are turned loose among three thousand men. They do not keep the rules which I have made to ensure female decorum, but run scampering over the wards by themselves at night, feeding the men without medical orders. Their dressings of wounds are careless and slovenly [sloppy], and they will not take a hint, except from me. I have consequently employed them less in nursing, and more in making stump pillows etc for the men that otherwise I should have done, with the view of protecting them. And they said, which is very true, that they did not come out for needlework. I fear they must be recalled, which I should very much prefer to happen because you want them, rather than because I don't.

> Not all the nurses who accompanied Florence Nightingale to Scutari were happy there. Some wrote home complaining of her harsh discipline and inability to compromise. On her part, Florence Nightingale felt the need to complain to their superiors back in the UK about their lack of commitment. This is her letter to Miss Gipps.

Source 2J

I cannot pass over your letter without expressing regret that, in a matter of such grave import to the nurses as a complaint about their conduct to the authorities of the Institution to which they belong, expressions should have been used which seem to betoken a lack of consideration towards women who volunteered to aid in carrying out, under your control and guidance a good, though difficult and arduous work in an hitherto untried field of labour.

I am at a loss to know what amount of significance you wish me to attach to the term 'flibberty gibbet'. I think you will recollect that your most express instruction to these nurses, and which you asked me to impress upon them, was that they were to obey no one but you nor to take orders from anyone else.

The complaint of lack of skill to pronounce decidedly upon a fracture etc etc., I can but reply that the Council of this institution have only contemplated training women who should observe, & carefully carry out, as nurses, the directions of a physician or surgeon, and have not trained the women to possess any skills of actual surgeons.

You will not imagine, dear Miss Nightingale, from anything in this letter, any lack of appreciation on my part of your own arduous labours, or of the difficulties you have to encounter in arranging that those under you and working with you shall orderly and effectually carry out your wishes & intentions, for I am quite sure you will readily understand my feeling that whilst it is my duty, as the appointed head of these nurses, to suffer no fault or wrong behaviour to pass unrebuked. I am equally bound to care for their well being during the performance of any duty to which they may be sent.

Miss Jones, the Lady Superintendent of St John's House, replied to the letter sent by Florence Nightingale to Miss Gipps. The nurses, about whom Florence Nightingale complained, came from St John's House.

SKILLS BUILDER

Do you think Miss Jones has effectively defended her nurses against the complaints made about them by Florence Nightingale?

Source 2K

(i) 10 December 1854

I have found from this last month's experience that had we come out with twenty [women] instead of forty, we should not only have been less hampered with difficulties, but the work itself would have been actually better and more efficiently done. About ten of us have done the whole work. The others have only run between our feet and hindered us, and the difficulty of assigning to them something to do without superintendence has been enormous.

(ii) 15 December 1854

When I came out here it was with the distinct understanding (expressed both in your own handwriting and in the printed announcement which you put in the *Morning Chronicle* which is here in everyone's hands) that nurses were to be sent out at my requisition only, which was to be made only with the approval of the medical officers here.

I have toiled my way into the confidence of the medical men. I have, by excessive vigilance day & night, introduced something like a system into the disorderly operations of these women [the nurses who went out with her to Scutari]. But the Medical Officers (under whose orders my written instructions and my own judgement equally

Source 2K continued . . .

agree in placing me) while expressing themselves satisfied with things as they are, have repeatedly given their opinion that more women cannot usefully be employed nor properly governed. And in this opinion I entirely agree.

At this point of affairs arrives, at no one's requisition, a fresh batch of women, raising our number to eighty-four. You have sacrificed the cause, so near to my heart. You have sacrificed me, a matter of small importance now. You have sacrificed your own written word to a popular cry.

The government decided that more nurses should be sent out to Scutari and to the newer hospitals in the Crimea. A number of Catholic nuns, under the control of their Mother Superior, travelled out. They were followed by Mary Stanley, a close friend of Elizabeth Herbert, and twenty-three Protestant nurses. Florence Nightingale was furious. These are extracts from two of the letters she wrote to Sidney Herbert, Elizabeth's husband, on the subject.

Source 2L

When Mary Stanley arrived at Scutari, she reported 'It is a horrid place – no one trusts another – no one speaks well of another. I am so shocked at the falseness of people. They abuse you behind your back and flatter you to your face.' Many of Stanley's nurses went to Balaclava to assist the surgeons in the Crimean hospitals, undertaking much more difficult work than was being done in the base hospital at Scutari. Florence Nightingale, having rejected Mary Stanley and refused to go to the Crimea herself, now found Stanley's conduct 'inexplicable', and accused her of plotting 'to set up an opposition'. As the number of nurses increased, Florence Nightingale's position became much less important. By the spring and early summer of 1855, about 230 nurses were with the British Army in the east. Nightingale was in charge of thirty-nine of them and this was not the largest group – that belonged to her rival, Mary Stanley, with a group of forty-seven.

From Clive Ponting *The Crimean War* published in 2004

SKILLS BUILDER

How far does Clive Ponting (Source 2L) explain why Florence Nightingale was so angry that more nurses were being sent out to Scutari and the Crimean hospitals?

Reputation and Reality

Source 2M

She is a 'ministering angel'. As her slender form glides quietly along each corridor, every poor fellow's face softens in gratitude at the sight of her. When all medical officers have retired for the night, she may be observed alone, with a little lamp in her hands, making her solitary rounds.

From *The Times* newspaper, May 1855

Source 2N

The wounded from the battle plain,
In dreary hospitals of pain,
The cheerless corridors,
The cold and stony floors.

Lo! In that house of misery
A lady with a lamp I see
Pass through the glimmering gloom,
And flit from room to room.

And slow, as in a dream of bliss,
The speechless sufferer turns to kiss
Her shadow, as it falls
Upon the darkening walls

A lady with a Lamp shall stand
In the great history of the land,
A noble type of good,
Heroic womanhood.

The American poet Henry Wadsworth Longfellow
wrote a poem called *Santa Filomena* in 1858.
These are four verses from the poem.

Source 2O

2.2 This image of Florence Nightingale, called *The Lady with the Lamp* was published in the *Illustrated London News* at Christmas 1891.

SKILLS BUILDER

Study Sources 2M, 2N and 2O.

How far are these sources projecting similar images of Florence Nightingale?

How close do these images come to reality?

2.3 Mary Seacole

Mary Seacole: the real angel of mercy?

This oil painting on a piece of board was found in a car boot sale in 2005. It was cleaned up and now hangs in the National Portrait Gallery, London. Who is it of, and what had she to do with the Crimean War?

The portrait, painted in 1869 by Albert Charles Challen, is of **Mary Seacole** (see page 39), whom many people at the time regarded as being the real angel of mercy during the Crimean conflict.

Official rejection: colour prejudice at work?

Units from Jamaica were fighting in the Crimean War and, inevitably, news of the terrible medical conditions there filtered back. This provided the trigger for Mary Seacole's decision to travel to London, carrying letters of recommendation from Jamaican doctors, to offer her services as a nurse in the conflict.

Biography

Mary Seacole née Grant 1805–81

Born in Kingston, Jamaica, as Mary Grant, the daughter of a white Scottish officer in the British Army and a free Jamaican Creole woman, Mary learned her nursing skills from her mother who, as a 'doctress' ran a boarding house for invalid soldiers and sailors. Mary married Edwin Horatio Hamilton Seacole, a Jamaican merchant and godson of Lord Nelson, in 1836 and travelled with him around the Caribbean, Central America and England. After her husband's death in 1844, Mary set up a hotel in Cruces, Panama, with her brother Edward where she successfully treated cholera victims. In 1853 the Jamaican medical authorities asked her to return, which she did, to care for victims of a yellow fever epidemic.

Mary offered her nursing services to the British authorities, and when this offer was rejected, paid for her own passage out to the Crimea. With a relative she formed the company 'Seacole and Day' to purchase stores and provisions for the Crimean troops. Spurning the safety of Scutari, she set up the 'British Hotel' close to the front line outside Balaclava, where she provided food and provisions for the troops. She also ministered to the wounded and dying on the battlefield. She returned to England, bankrupt, at the end of the war, where funds were raised by the public, soldiers and ex-soldiers to support her. She wrote a book *Wonderful Adventures of Mary Seacole in Many Lands* which sold well, the royalties from which kept her in her old age.

Source K

Mary Seacole applied in turn to the War Office, the army medical department, the quartermaster-general's department, and the secretary for war. She produced fine testimonials and pointed out that she already knew many of the officers and soldiers in the regiments concerned, having nursed them when they were stationed in Jamaica.

But authority closed ranks against this plump, middle-aged West Indian lady in her flamboyant red or yellow dress and blue straw bonnet from which flowed a length of scarlet ribbon. She was turned away by everybody.

From Peter Fryer *Staying Power: The History of Black People in Britain*
published in 1984

SKILLS BUILDER

Mary Seacole clearly suspects that she wasn't invited to join Florence Nightingale's group of nurses because of colour prejudice. Clearly we can never know the truth of the matter. However, look back to page 31, and at the ways in which nurses were selected. On balance, do you think it likely that colour had anything to do with Mary Seacole's rejection?

Mary Seacole herself describes what happened and provides an explanation in her autobiography.

Source L

In my country, where people know our value, it would have been different. But here [England] it was natural enough that they should laugh, good-naturedly enough, at my offer. Once again I tried and had an interview with one of Miss Nightingale's *companions. She gave me the same reply, and I read in her face the fact that, had there been a vacancy, I should not have been chosen to fill it. Was it possible that American prejudices against colour had some root here? Did these ladies shrink from accepting my aid because my blood flowed beneath a somewhat duskier skin than theirs?

From Mary Seacole *Wonderful Adventures of Mary Seacole in Many Lands* published in 1857

* This 'companion' was Elizabeth Herbert, friend of Florence Nightingale and wife to Sidney Herbert who, at the time, was Secretary at War.

When Mary Seacole did get to the Crimea, one of her first actions was to seek out Florence Nightingale at the Barracks Hospital in Scutari. Ron Ramdin, who has written many books on Black and Asian history, describes, in his words and those of Mary Seacole, what happened.

SKILLS BUILDER

When you have read Source M, will you need to change in any way the answer you gave to the last 'Skills builder' question? Why? Or why not?

Source M

Face to face, it was a meeting of historic significance, for here were two women of their times, both motivated by a common cause – to serve Britain. They were 19th century women from opposite ends of the socio-economic spectrum, one white from the heart of the Empire, the other black (or non-white) from a colonial backwater, one a pioneering paid administrator at the beginning of a new profession of nursing, the other a sutler who paid her own way and roughed it towards the war zone, one white and young, the other dark and much older. How did they perceive each other?

According to Mary Seacole, Miss Nightingale read Dr F's letter [a reference Mary Seacole had brought with her from Jamaica] which lay on the table beside her and in her 'gentle but eminently practical and business-like way she asked "What do you want, Mrs Seacole? Is there anything we can do for you? If it lies in my power, I shall be very happy."' Although these words were well-received, as it was there was nothing that Miss Nightingale could do for Mrs Seacole. The fact remained that no offer of employment was made to her. Mary's next request was of greater immediacy – a bed for the night. But even this request did not have the best of outcomes. Eventually a bed was found in the washerwoman's quarters.

From Ron Ramdin *Mary Seacole* published in 2005

The firm of Seacole and Day

So how did Mary Seacole 'rough it towards the war zone' (Source M)? Determined to get to the Crimea, Mary Seacole teamed up with a distant relative, Thomas Day. He had business in Balaclava. Together they hatched a plan and set up a company: Seacole and Day. The idea was that this company would buy medicines and home comforts (like tea and blankets) and set up a store and 'hotel' close to the front line at Balaclava. And it worked. Mary Seacole lived on the ammunition ship *Medora* until her store, which quickly became known as the 'British Hotel' was fully set up and functioning, at Spring Hill near Kadikoi, about two miles inland from Balaclava by the side of the road leading to the main British camp. The store opened in the spring of 1855, and allowed men to buy food and sit and talk in the warm and the dry. No gambling was allowed and the store closed at 8.00 p.m. She organised her own supply chain from Constantinople, and majored in supplying freshly baked Turkish bread to the troops. All this was done under the protection of the local Turkish commander, who befriended Seacole.

But that wasn't all that Mary Seacole did. She was there at the front line of all the major battles (except that she was too late for the Alma) and tended the wounded and the dying.

How effective was Mary Seacole?

It is best to let Mary Seacole, those who were treated by her, or who observed her at work, tell their stories.

Source N

So strong was the old impulse within me, that I waited for no permission, but seeing a poor infantryman stretched upon a pallet, groaning heavily, I ran up to him at once, and eased the stiff dressings. Lightly my practised fingers ran over the familiar work, and well was I rewarded when the poor fellow's groans subsided into a restless uneasy mutter. He had been hit in the forehead, and I think his sight was gone. I stooped down, raised some tea to his baked lips. Then his hand touched mine, as though the discovery had arrested his wandering senses. 'Ha! This surely is a woman's hand.' He continued to hold my hand in his feeble grasp, and whisper 'God bless you, woman, whoever you are, God bless you!' Over and over again.

From Mary Seacole *Wonderful Adventures of Mary Seacole in Many Lands* published in 1857. Here she recounts what happened when she first arrived at Balaclava.

Source O

She was a wonderful woman. All the men swore by her, and in case of any malady would seek her advice and use her herbal medicines in preference to reporting themselves to their own doctors. That she did effect some cures is beyond doubt, and her never failing presence among the wounded after a battle and assisting them made her beloved by the rank and file of the whole army.

From Frederick Harris D. Vieth *Recollections of the Crimean Campaign and the Expedition to Kinburn in 1855* published in 1907. Frederick Harris D. Vieth had fought in the Crimean War as a lieutenant in the 63rd West Suffolk Regiment.

Source P

Here I met a celebrated person. A coloured woman, Mrs Seacole. Out of the goodness of her heart and at her own expense, she supplied hot tea to the poor sufferers while they waited to be lifted into the boats.

She did not spare herself if she could do any good to the suffering soldiers. In rain and snow, day after day, she was at her post. With her stove and kettle, in any shelter she could find, she brewed tea for all who wanted it – and there were many.

Part of a letter home, written by Dr Reid, a surgeon in the British Army, in 1855

Source Q

She [Mary Seacole] not only, from the knowledge she had acquired in the West Indies, was enabled to administer appropriate remedies for their ailments, but, what was of as much importance, she charitably furnished them with proper nourishment, which they had no means of obtaining except in hospital and most of that class had an objection to go into hospital.

Part of a letter home written by Sir John Hall, Inspector-General of Hospitals, on 30 June 1856

Source R

(i) 27 September 1855

In the hour of their illness, these men have found a kind and successful physician, a Mrs Seacole. She is from Kingston, Jamaica, and she doctors and cures all manner of men with extraordinary success. She is always in attendance near the battlefield to aid the wounded and has earned many a poor fellow's blessing.

(ii) 11 April 1857

I have seen her go down under fire with her little store of creature comforts for our wounded men, and a more tender or skilful hand about a wound or broken limb could not be found among our best surgeons. I saw her at the assaults on the Redan, at the battle of the Tchernaya, at the fall of Sebastopol, laden with wine, bandages and food for the wounded or the prisoners. Her hands, too, performed the last offices for some of the noblest of our slain. Her hut was surrounded every morning by the rough navvies and Land Transport men, who had a faith in her proficiency in the healing art, at which she justified by many cures and by removing obstinate cases of diarrhoea, dysentery, and similar camp maladies.

William Russell was an enthusiastic supporter of Mary Seacole. These are two extracts from his dispatches.

Source S

I was generally up and busy by daybreak, sometimes earlier, for in the summer my bed had no attractions strong enough to bind me to it after 4 o'clock. There was plenty to do before the work of the day began. There was the poultry to pluck and prepare for cooking, which had been killed on the previous night; the joints to be cut up and got ready for the same purpose; the medicines to be mixed; the store to be swept and cleaned.

By 7 o'clock the morning coffee would be ready. From that time until 9 o'clock officers on duty in the neighbourhood or passing by would look in for breakfast. About half past nine my sick patients began to show themselves. In the following hour they came thickly and sometimes it was past twelve before I had got through this duty. They came with every variety of suffering and disease; the cases I most disliked were the frostbitten fingers and feet in winter.

From Mary Seacole Wonderful Adventures of Mary Seacole in Many Lands published in 1857. Here she describes her daily routine.

SKILLS BUILDER

There are six sources here, N–S, all describing aspects of Mary Seacole's work in the Crimea.

1 What can you learn from them about what she did?

2 How reliable are the sources as evidence of her work in the Crimea?

On 9 September 1855, the Russians evacuated Sebastopol. Mary Seacole, as she had always promised, was the first woman to go inside.

And finally . . .

Source T

2.4 A contemporary picture called 'Lady tourists to the Crimea on board HMS *Hecla*'

Question

Now answer the question with which this final section began: How effective was Mary Seacole in the Crimea?

Question

If conditions during the Crimean war were so bad, why did tourists visit the battlefields?

What have you learned in this unit?

You have learned that the administrative chaos that characterised the management of the Crimean War was exacerbated by the 'Great Storm' of November 1854, and you have considered whether or not the multiplicity of administrative departments contributed to the chaos. You have understood that the reportage of William Russell created concern in Britain, from ordinary people to Queen Victoria, about the ways in which the troops were being cared for, and that this concern led to the creation of various contributory funds that were intended to provide comforts for the troops. You have learned about the medical services that were available during the Crimean conflict and how they reflected, more or less, the state of medical knowledge in Britain. The case study on Florence Nightingale has focused on whether or not she did any good at Scutari, her relationships with her nurses and those in authority and the myth that grew up round her. Finally, you have learned that the maverick nurse, Mary Seacole, was working in the Crimea and that she was providing a very different kind of service from that offered by Florence Nightingale.

What skills have you used in this unit?

You started by analysing a cartoon for 'message' and utility. You then worked with sources, cross-referencing and drawing inferences, in order to draw conclusions about who or what was to blame for the disastrous way in which supplies to the Crimean War were handled. Faced with some further information, you re-evaluated the previous conclusion you had drawn. You used your empathetic skills to consider the relationship of Queen Victoria with her commander-in-chief when it came to the welfare of the troops. You embarked on a case study of Florence Nightingale, using your skills of inference making, cross-referencing, evaluation of utility and reliability and empathy in order to evaluate the role she played in the Crimean conflict and the ways in which this role translated into a myth. You used similar skills to evaluate the role played by Mary Seacole.

SKILLS BUILDER

1 How might the ladies drawn in Source T explain what their motives were in travelling out to watch a war?

2 Would you agree that unofficial workers in a conflict zone (like Mary Seacole) can do more harm than good?

3 Now for a difficult question but one which you might be able to answer in discussion with others in your class: Why does war create myths?

Exam style question

This is the sort of question you may find on the examination paper as a (b) question.

Use Sources U and V and your own knowledge.

Do you agree with the view that Mary Seacole, and not Florence Nightingale, was the real 'angel of mercy' during the Crimean War?

Source U

2.5 A lithograph of one of the wards in the Barrack Hospital, Scutari, published in 1856

Source V

Florence Nightingale's admirable hospital was several hundred miles from the Crimean peninsula. Mary Seacole did not pretend to Nightingale's formidable gifts of organisation, but she was in the very front line. Her 'British Hotel' in Balaclava was an important refuge. The 'ranks' who had a fear of hospitals felt more at ease with 'Mother Seacole' than in the Turkish field hospitals. She treated patients suffering from cholera and dysentery. She was attentive to their practical needs. Officers and men had permanent colds throughout the Crimean winters. There were no pocket handkerchiefs until Mary Seacole established her stores. Miss Nightingale's hospital was where you were taken if you were wounded or fell sick. Mary Seacole was on hand for the troops in the long months when nothing much appeared to be happening and, unlike some officers, she showed courage under fire.

From A.N. Wilson *The Victorians* published in 2002

Exam tips

- **Do** be clear about the question focus – what is being claimed? In this case, what is being claimed is that the real 'angel of mercy' during the Crimean War was Mary Seacole and not Florence Nightingale.
- Be **clear** that you know what is meant by 'angel of mercy' and define it.
- **Analyse** the sources to establish points that support and points that challenge the view given in the question.
- **Develop** each point by reference to your own wider knowledge, using it to reinforce and/or challenge the points derived from the sources.
- **Combine** the points into arguments for and against the stated view.
- **Evaluate** the conflicting arguments.
- Present a **judgement** as to the validity of the stated view.

And above all, **plan** your answer.

Start now by using the exam tips to draw up a plan that would deliver an answer to this question. You might find that using a spider diagram would be the best way to do this.

RESEARCH TOPIC

Florence Nightingale and Mary Seacole were not the only women involved in the Crimean War. Four wives, for example, were chosen to accompany every regiment. Fanny Duberly was one such woman. Find out what contribution she made to the war effort.

3 The Crimean War 1854–56: what were the outcomes?

What is this unit about?

This unit focuses on the main outcomes of the Crimean War. The importance of the Peace of Paris in solving the disputes with which the war began is considered. The significance of the McNeill-Tulloch Report in beginning the process by which control of the army was moved from the Crown and the generals to parliament is addressed and a link is made with Cardwell's Army Reforms and competitive entry to the civil service in the 1870s. The role of Florence Nightingale in setting up the Nightingale School for Nurses is analysed and the differences in the treatment by British society of her and Mary Seacole are considered.

Key questions

- What were the most significant outcomes of the Crimean War?
- To what extent were Florence Nightingale and Mary Seacole treated differently by British society on their return to Britain?

Timeline

1855

29 November	National appeal launches the Nightingale Fund
Autumn	Publication of the McNeill-Tulloch Report

1856

30 March	Peace of Paris signed
April	Army Board of Enquiry into the McNeill-Tulloch report
July	Mary Seacole and Thomas Day arrive back in England

1857

2 July	Publication of Mary Seacole's autobiography *Wonderful Adventures of Mary Seacole in Many Lands* that sold for 1s 6d a copy
27 July	Concert held in Kennington, London, to raise money to support Mary Seacole

1860	Nightingale Training School for Nurses established at St Thomas's Hospital, London
1870	Entry to the civil service to be by competitive examination
1870–71	Cardwell's Army Reforms

It was over. After all the mud and mismanagement, the death and disease, Russia had been defeated and the Allies had triumphed.

Source A

BOROUGH OF STAFFORD

PEACE REJOICINGS.

ON THURSDAY, THE 29TH OF MAY INSTANT,
IT IS REQUESTED THAT ALL

BUSINESS MAY BE SUSPENDED
AND THE DAY KEPT

AS A GENERAL HOLIDAY,
IN ORDER TO CELEBRATE

THE RATIFICATIONS OF PEACE.

The Aged Poor, both Men and Women, will be
regaled in the Covered Market Hall with Roast
Beef, Plum Pudding, and Ale, at ONE O'CLOCK
at noon. All Poor persons, of FIFTY-FIVE Years
of age and upwards, who wish to participate in this
Feast must apply for Tickets on TUESDAY NEXT,
the 20th instant, at the Guildhall, Stafford, at Four
o'clock in the Afternoon.

JOHN GIFFIN, Mayor.
GUILDHALL, 15th May, 1856

3.1 A poster put up by the Borough of Stafford in 1856 as part of the peace celebrations after the Crimean War

SKILLS BUILDER

What does this poster tell you about attitudes to the peace?

The Peace of Paris that ended the Crimean War was greeted, as the end of all wars are, with general rejoicing. Regiments of returning soldiers were reviewed, cannons were fired in public parks, parties were held and half a million people flocked to London to celebrate along with the two million Londoners already indulging in festivities. Music was composed (for example Albert Lindahl wrote *Alma, a Battlepiece for the Pianoforte*), a species of crocus was named 'Crimean crocus' and men and boys wore balaclava helmets. But was it all worth it? 18,058 British soldiers and sailors died in the Crimean War. Of these, only 1,761 were killed by enemy action. The rest died from their wounds or (more commonly) from disease. Maybe even these sacrifices would have been justified if the causes of the war had been put to rest.

Did the Peace of Paris end the disputes which started the war?

On 30 March 1856 the final peace treaty was signed in Paris. By its terms:

- Russia retained Sebastopol, Balaclava and all areas occupied by the Allies.

- The Black Sea was to be neutralised: no naval bases or arsenals were to be maintained on its shores, and no ship of war could enter the Black Sea through the Bosphorus.

- The River Danube was to be an international waterway open to all shipping.

- Turkish sovereignty over the Danubian principalities was guaranteed by the Great Powers, and the principalities were to be grouped into a new state called Romania.

- The Sultan declared he was prepared to improve the conditions of all Christians within the Ottoman Empire.

Question

Look back to pages 3–4 and the causes of the Crimean War.

In your judgement, had the Peace of Paris solved the disputes that caused the Crimean war?

Throughout the peace negotiations, Prime Minister Lord Palmerston had urged the Foreign Secretary Lord Clarendon to hold out for tougher terms. Although Palmerston presented the Treaty to his Cabinet in a positive way, it was denounced in the House of Commons as being too lenient and the heralds who proclaimed it in the City of London were hissed as they did so despite the fact that Russia had been beaten and bankrupted. It did not attack Turkey again for twenty years.

To what extent did the Crimean War experience impact on the development of nursing as a profession?

The Nightingale Fund

Sidney Herbert decided to exploit the wave of national enthusiasm that flooded the country as a result of what they believed Florence Nightingale had achieved at Scutari. On 29 November 1855, in a public meeting in Willis's Rooms, London, he launched a national appeal for subscriptions to the 'Nightingale Fund'. His aim was to raise enough money to support her, and his, scheme to improve the standard of female nursing. It was an emotional meeting. Herbert read out a letter from a soldier who had been a patient of Nightingale's at Scutari: 'What a comfort it was to see her pass. She would speak to one and nod and smile to many more, but she could not do it to all, you know. We lay there by hundreds; but we would kiss her shadow as it fell, and lay our heads on the pillow again, content.' Many of Florence Nightingale's influential friends were there. A committee was set up, with Sidney Herbert as its honorary secretary, and a resolution was passed that stated that the 'Nightingale Fund' was to 'enable Miss Nightingale to establish an institute for the training, sustenance and protection of nurses, paid and unpaid'. Money flooded in: more than several million pounds by today's standards. Queen Victoria sent Nightingale an inscribed diamond brooch and an invitation to visit when she returned to Britain. So there it was: enough money to set up a permanent institution for the training of nurses to fit them for employment in hospitals. But nothing is ever that simple. Sidney Herbert wrote to Florence Nightingale, telling her what had happened. She gave him two replies, one official and one private.

Source B

Exposed as I am to be misinterpreted and misunderstood, in a field of action in which the work is new, complicated and distant from many who sit in judgement upon it, – it is indeed an abiding support to have such sympathy and such appreciation brought home to me in the midst of labour and difficulties all but overpowering. I must add, however, that my present work is such that I would not desert for any other, so long as I see room to believe that what I may do here is unfinished. May I then, beg you to express to the Committee that I accept their proposal, provided I may do so on their understanding of this great uncertainty as to when it will be possible for me to carry it out?

Part of Florence Nightingale's official reply to the Nightingale Fund Committee.
She was still at Scutari when she wrote this on 6 January 1856.

Source C

My dear Mr Herbert

I have written a letter as you desired, in order to relieve you from Trouble & responsibility which are a bad reward for all your kindness and confidence in this matter.

The confidence which you and the Subscribers to this Fund have shewn me has been so generous and extraordinary that it is perhaps hardly necessary for me to allude to a very natural letter which I am told has appeared in *The Times*, to the effect that I must furnish a prospectus of what I am going to do before I can expect to have money subscribed to do it. I think this perfectly reasonable, if I had originally asked for the money which, of course, I did not. I would not furnish a cut and dried prospectus of my plans because everything which succeeds is not the production of a Scheme, of Rules and Regulations made beforehand, but of a mind observing and adapting itself to wants and events.

Part of Florence Nightingale's private reply to Sidney Herbert, written on 6 January 1856

Whether she wanted to or not, a Nightingale Training School was set up. The web-site of the Florence Nightingale Museum, attached to St Thomas's Hospital, London, describes its importance.

Source D

Florence Nightingale's greatest achievement was to raise nursing to the level of a respectable profession for women. In 1860, with the public subscriptions of the Nightingale Fund, she established the Nightingale Training School for nurses at St Thomas' Hospital. Mrs Sarah Wardroper, Matron of St Thomas', became the head of the new school. The probationer nurses received a year's training which included some lectures but was mainly practical ward work under the supervision of the ward sister. 'Miss Nightingale', as she was always called by the nurses, scrutinised the probationers' ward diaries and reports

From 1872, Florence Nightingale devoted closer attention to the organisation of the School, and almost annually for the next thirty years she wrote an open letter to the nurses and probationers giving advice and encouragement. On completion of training, Florence Nightingale gave the nurses books and invited them to tea. Once trained, the nurses were sent to staff hospitals in Britain and abroad and to established nursing training schools on the Nightingale model. In 1860, her best known work, *Notes on Nursing*, was published. It laid down the principles of nursing: careful observation and sensitivity to the patient's needs. *Notes on Nursing* has been translated into eleven languages.

From the Florence Nightingale Museum web-site

SKILLS BUILDER

1 What is the difference between the two letters in Sources B and C?

2 Why do you think Sidney Herbert asked Florence Nightingale to write a public and a private letter?

3 In your judgement, and using the evidence of these two letters, do you think Florence Nightingale really wanted to set up a nursing school?

Historian Hugh Small, however, views the situation somewhat differently.

Source E

Apart from her service at Scutari, Florence Nightingale's name is best known for the nurse training school that was eventually established at St Thomas's with the Nightingale Fund's money. Most modern historians agree that Nightingale's early biographers created a myth by exaggerating the importance of this school, the independence of its nurses, and Nightingale's personal involvement in it. They have been unable to explain why she took so little interest in a project that had been so close to her heart before and during the war. During the war, Nightingale had accepted responsibility for the Fund which was to bear her name, and had agreed to a board of trustees and a trust deed aimed at establishing an institute for training hospital nurses. When she returned from the war she postponed a decision on how to use the money and after she had recovered from her collapse she suddenly appeared to want nothing more to do with it.

Press, public and politicians bombarded her with demands that she dedicate the rest of her life to carrying out the original nursing objectives of the Fund, in a teaching hospital and under the supervision of the medical profession. It must have seemed to her as if she was being condemned to repeat her errors at Scutari for the rest of her life.

Sidney Herbert and his wife still wanted to improve the standard of the hospital nursing profession, and Herbert continually pestered Nightingale to use the Fund because he felt responsible for persuading the public to give money to it and he was being criticised for not putting it to good use. Not surprisingly, she tried to resign from her position with the Fund, but Herbert would not allow it. By 1859 Nightingale was claiming that her health prevented her from supervising the use of the Fund. Eventually, Herbert began to organise a scheme to use the money to establish a nurse training school in Kings College Hospital and it seems to have been this that stirred Nightingale into action at St Thomas's.

A new [St Thomas's] hospital was built on the banks of the Thames opposite the Houses of Parliament. Nightingale did succeed in designing the new buildings, using her favourite scheme of many separate 'pavilions' to improve ventilation. The Nightingale Fund set up its nurse training school there but Nightingale ignored its activities, claiming to be incapacitated by illness.

From Hugh Small *Florence Nightingale: Avenging Angel* published in 1998

SKILLS BUILDER

1 How far does Hugh Small in Source E challenge what is said about Florence Nightingale's involvement in nurse training in Source D?

2 How best can the differences between Sources D and E be explained?

What was the impact of the Crimean War on the British Army?

Two main problems had gradually become clear to the politicians and, but to a lesser extent, to the public. The first, and most glaringly obvious, was the mismanagement of supplies; the second, and possibly the more difficult to criticise because it was steeped in custom and practice, was the sharp division between officers and men. This was partly because of the ways in which recruitment worked, but was thrown into sharp relief during the Crimean conflict where some officers were receiving hampers from Fortnum & Masons, an exclusive London food hall, while their men suffered terribly from scurvy while cases of lime juice lay undisturbed in army warehouses.

The McNeill-Tulloch Report

In February 1855, the government, alarmed at reports of the mismanagement of supplies, instructed Sir John McNeill and Colonel Alexander Tulloch to go out to the Crimea to investigate. Lord Panmure, the Minister of War, wrote them two sets of instructions. The first set instructed the two men to enquire into the civilian side of matters: how the supplies were obtained and sent out. The second set of instructions ordered the men to 'further make enquiry into the alleged delay in unshipping and distributing the clothing and other stores supplied for the use of the troops.' These instructions required McNeill and Tulloch to investigate the role of the army in the debacle. The first set of instructions was made public; the second was not.

The Report, when it was published, caused a furore. Civilian mismanagement was exposed, but, more importantly for the politicians, so was military negligence. The Report, despite a whitewashing by an army Board of Enquiry that sat in April 1856, served the politicians' purpose. It was the politicians who wanted to bring the army more under the control of parliament and less under the control of the monarch and the generals, but a lot of careful and delicate manoeuvrings had to take place before this was possible.

The Cardwell Army Reforms 1870–71

By the time of Prime Minister Gladstone's first administration that began in December 1868, the government felt able to institute specific army reforms proposed by the Secretary for War, Edward Cardwell. In a series of Acts, Parliament agreed the following measures:

- Various military departments were combined under one roof: the War Office.
- The country was divided into local regimental districts, with single battalion regiments being merged into two-battalion regiments, the idea being that one battalion would serve overseas while one would be garrisoned at home for training. Local militia formed the third battalion of a particular regiment.
- The length of overseas service was cut from twelve years to six.

- Traditionally, the sons of the wealthy had been able to buy a commission in a specific regiment of their (or their father's) choice. They didn't have to show any military ability or ability at managing men. The purchase of commissions was abolished and replaced by a system of promotion through merit.
- The Commander-in-Chief was to be answerable to the Secretary for War and, through him, to Parliament.
- Flogging of ordinary soldiers in peacetime was forbidden.
- Soldiers could choose to spend time in the reserves rather than regular service. They were paid 4 pence a day for doing so, provided they undertook a short period of training each year and guaranteed to return to their regiment when required to do so in times of national emergency.

The government regarded these reforms as a necessary attack on government inefficiency and privilege. Inevitably, they angered the aristocracy.

Cardwell had certainly addressed many problems but not all. Resistance from entrenched interests was often too strong. No General Staff was appointed to forward plan on the Prussian model. Although the breech-loading Martini Henry rifle was adopted for the infantry, breech-loading artillery was rejected. Most serious of all were the inadequate reserves. Britain, with a reserve force of 35,000, could not seriously contemplate a European war. Prussia could put a million into the field. Cardwell's army could just about cope with Zulus and Egyptians.

Entry into the civil service

Gladstone's government of 1868–74 was also at long last able to tackle civil service reform, which had surfaced as a major issue before and during the Crimean War. The driving force was Robert Lowe, the albino Chancellor of the Exchequer. In 1870 competitive examination was laid down as the normal method of entry to the civil service in place of traditional methods of patronage. It applied to all departments except the Home and Foreign Offices. When Lowe moved to become Home Secretary in 1873, entry by examination was applied there also. Only the aristocratic Foreign Office remained immune. The change certainly improved the efficiency and brainpower of the upper ranks of the civil service but there was still a clear hierarchy. British government was henceforth dominated by an upper grade of civil servants largely recruited from the best that Oxford and Cambridge could supply. They were nicknamed 'mandarins' after the traditional ruling elite of China, selected by examination for over a thousand years before the British thought of the idea. The lower clerical grade of the British civil service, drawn from the middle and even working classes, seldom found it possible to progress up to the exalted, senior posts in the various ministries.

Mary Seacole: a forgotten heroine?

The end of the Crimean War left the company of 'Seacole and Day' bankrupt and with unsaleable stock on their hands in the Crimea. Mary Seacole and Thomas Day had, however, planned ahead. They found their way back to England by way of several steam ships and on 9 July 1856 a notice appeared in *The Times* announcing their intention to set up a provisions store in the garrison town of Aldershot. On the face of it, this

Question

How far, in your judgement, did Cardwell's Army Reforms meet the British Army's problems experienced in the Crimea?

was a sensible decision. Plenty of soldiers garrisoned in Aldershot would know Mary Seacole from their time in the Crimea or would have been told about her. The 'British Hotel' had been immensely popular and there seemed no reason why a similar venture in Aldershot would not prosper. It failed within months. Pressed by creditors from the collapsed Crimean venture, unable to find suitable premises and facing competition from established traders, Mary simply couldn't cope. By October 1856 she was in London, renting rooms in Tavistock Street, close to Covent Garden. What happened to her then?

Source F

Whereas a Petition for adjudication of Bankruptcy, filed the 27th day of October, 1856, hath been presented against Mary Seacole and Thomas Day the younger of 1, Tavistock-Street, Covent-garden, and of no. 17, Ratcliff-terrace, Goswell-road, both in the County of Middlesex, and late of Spring Hill and Balaklava, both in the Crimea, Provision merchants, Traders, Dealers and Chapmen [Brokers].

From the *London Gazette* 28 October 1856

Source G

Sir

That good old soul whose generous hospitality has warmed up many a gallant spirit on the chilly heights of Balaklava has now in her turn been caught in the worst storm of all – the gale of adversity.

Where are the Crimeans? Have a few months erased from their memories those many acts of comfort and kindness which made the name of the old mother venerated throughout the camp? While the benevolent deeds of Florence Nightingale are being handed down to posterity with blessings and an imperishable renown, are the humbler actions of Mrs Seacole to be entirely forgotten, and will none now substantially testify to the worth of those services?

Part of a letter to *The Times* and printed on 24 November 1856. It was sent from the Reform Club in London and signed 'Da Meritis', which means 'A friend to merit'.

Source H

That berry-brown face, with a kind heart's trace
Impressed in each wrinkle sly
Was a sight to behold, though the snow clouds rolled
Across the iron sky.

The cold without gave a zest, no doubt,
To the welcome warmth within:
But her smile, good old soul, lent heat to the coal,
And power to the pannikin.

No store she set by the epaulette,
Be it worsted or gold lace;
For KCB [a Sir], or plain Private Smith
She still had one pleasant face.

The sick and sorry can tell the story
Of her nursing and dosing deeds.
Regimental MD never worked as she
In helping sick men's needs.

And now the good soul is 'in a hole'
What red-coat in all the land,
But to set her on her legs again
Will not lend a willing hand?

Some verses from a poem published in the magazine *Punch* on 6 December 1856

Source I

By now the subscription fund for Mary had been put on an official footing with the establishment of a committee of trustees. It asked for contributions in recognition not only of her work in the Crimea, but of valuable services rendered 'as a nurse and medical attendant in Jamaica in 1850 and 1853 when the yellow-fever and cholera committed such ravages'. The committee comprised officers and gentlemen – even royalty – who had served in the Crimea together, of course, with friend Billy [William Russell] and its simple purpose was to raise as much money as possible for Mrs Seacole, described in the Trust literature as a 'poor old soul, late in life'. After some humming and hah-ing, it was decided the best way to achieve this noble object was to hold an outrageous party, back in the Surrey Gardens, Kennington, to coincide with the publication of *Wonderful Adventures* and set her up, financially, for good. For Mary – one of life's natural extroverts – it was the perfect plan: high profile, original and flamboyant.

From Jane Robinson *Mary Seacole* published in 2005

Source J

I trust that England will not forget one who nursed her sick, who sought out her wounded to aid and succour them, and who performed the last offices for some of her illustrious dead.

The preface, written by William Russell, to Mary Seacole's book
Wonderful Adventures of Mary Seacole in Many Lands published in 1857

SKILLS BUILDER

Use Sources F–J to write a narrative summary in 200 words of what happened to Mary Seacole between her arrival back in England and the publication of her autobiography in 1857.

Perhaps it would be best to let Mary Seacole herself have the last word.

SKILLS BUILDER

How useful are Mary's memoirs to the historian attempting to research her impact?

Source K

Where, indeed, do I not find friends? In river steamboats, in places of public amusement, in quiet streets and courts, where taking short cuts I lose my way oft-times, spring up old familiar faces to remind me of the months spent on Spring Hill. The sentries at Whitehall relax from the discharge of their important duty of guarding nothing to give me a smile of recognition. Now, would all this have happened if I had returned to England a rich woman? Surely not.

From Mary Seacole *Wonderful Adventures of Mary Seacole in Many Lands*
published in 1857

And finally . . . the Victoria Cross

William Russell, as you have seen, reported much that created shock and horror back in Britain. He also reported some extraordinary acts of heroism by officers and men in the face of enemy action. Once home, Russell began to press for a bravery award that could be won by officers and men alike. At the time, bravery awards could only be awarded to officers because it was deemed that it was their skill and leadership that led the men to commit courageous acts that led to victory. The House of Commons took up the idea with enthusiasm in the face of strong opposition from senior military figures who feared, or so they said, that discipline would be lost as more and more ordinary soldiers attempted individual acts of courage that could be seen to entitle them for such a medal. However, in the face of strong support from Queen Victoria and Prince Albert, the objections of the military were summarily over-ridden.

The name of the medal, the 'Victoria Cross', was suggested by Prince Albert who also insisted that, in an age of elaborate medals, the medal should be a simple one. Queen Victoria was said to be delighted with the final design of a Maltese Cross and she herself added the phrase 'For Valour' that is inscribed on the back and the 'V' that joins the metal of the medal with the ribbon. Chinese-made Russian cannons that were captured at Sebastopol were melted down to provide the bronze for the medal. There is only enough for eighty more such medals.

The medal was to be available to all ranks. The Royal Warrant of 29 January 1856 stated:

> With a view to place all persons on a perfectly equal footing in relation to eligibility for the decoration, neither rank, nor long service, nor wounds, nor any other circumstances or condition whatsoever, save the merit of conspicuous bravery shall be held to establish a sufficient claim to the honour.

However, this was made retrospective to the autumn of 1854 in order to cover the Crimean War. Queen Victoria held the first investiture in 1857 in Hyde Park, where she pinned the medal onto the tunics of 62 of the 111 men who had been nominated for the medal by their commanding officers.

The Victoria Cross remains Britain's highest award for conspicuous courage and bravery by members of the armed forces in the face of the enemy. It is a decoration prized above all others.

3.2 Victoria Cross

What have you learned in this unit?

You have learned that the Peace of Paris did not address all the disputes with which the Crimean War began and that it was denounced by the House of Commons as being too weak. You have seen how politicians used the McNeill-Tulloch report to begin to move control of the army to Parliament and you have considered the ways in which Cardwell's Army reforms attempted to end privilege and the dominance of the aristocracy in the officer class of the armed forces as well as increase efficiency. You have learned that, despite Florence Nightingale's apparent initial reluctance, a Nightingale School of Nursing was established in the newly built St Thomas's hospital. Finally, you have looked at the ways in which Mary Seacole's life on her return to Britain was different from that of Florence Nightingale's and have considered the reasons for this.

What skills have you used in this unit?

You started by working with a poster 'Peace Rejoicings' in order to determine attitudes to the ending of the Crimean conflict and you moved on to cross-reference with information in an earlier unit so that you could reach a judgement regarding the strength of the Peace of Paris in solving the disputes with which the war began. You analysed letters from Florence Nightingale in order to determine her motives in sending one private and one public letter regarding the Nightingale Fund, and you evaluated two secondary sources (a web-site and a book) for support and challenge. Finally, you worked with a range of sources using your skills of inference making, cross-referencing, evaluation of reliability and utility in order to determine what happened to Mary Seacole on her arrival back in Britain.

SKILLS BUILDER

Working in pairs, write a character sketch of Florence Nightingale, using evidence from this unit and Units 1 and 2.

Read Source K. How would you have answered Mary Seacole?

Clive Ponting ends his book *The Crimean War* by writing:

> The Crimean War settled into the comforting mythology of the heroism of the Charge of the Light Brigade and the self-sacrifice of Florence Nightingale. Britain could begin to forget its failure in the Crimean War.

Do you agree with him? Debate this point with others in your group.

Exam style question

This is the sort of question you may find on the examination paper as a (b) question.

Source L

She kept – I will not call it a 'bad house' but something not very unlike it – in the Crimean War.

She was very kind to the men &, what is more, to the Officers – & did some good – & made many drunk.

I had the greatest difficulty in repelling Mrs Seacole's advances, & preventing association between her and my nurses (absolutely out of the question) when we established two hospitals nursed by us between Kadikoi & the 'Seacole establishment' in the Crimea. But I was successful.

Anyone who employs Mrs Seacole will introduce much kindness – also much drunkenness & improper conduct, wherever she is.

She had, then, however, one or more 'persons' with her, whom (I conclude) she has not now. I conclude (& believe) that respectable Officers were entirely ignorant of what I could not help knowing, as a Matron & Chaperone & Mother of the Army.

From a letter written by Florence Nightingale to the MP Sir Harry Verney, who was also her brother-in-law. He was involved in recruiting for nurses to provide non-partisan first-aid to the casualties of war. No one knows what prompted the letter, but it seems likely that Mary Seacole wrote to him offering her services and he asked Florence Nightingale for a reference. The letter is dated 5 August 1870. It is headed with the word 'Burn'.

Source M

A challenge to empire was that of Mary Seacole, the Jamaican nurse whose reputation just after the Crimean War rivalled Florence Nightingale's. Mary Seacole's challenge, quite simply, was to have her skills put to proper use in spite of her being black. A born healer and a woman of driving energy, she side-stepped official indifference, hauteur and prejudice; got herself out to the war front by her own efforts and at her expense; risked her life to bring comfort to the wounded and dying soldiers; and became the first black woman to make her mark in British public life. But while Florence Nightingale was turned into a legend in the service of Empire, Mary Seacole was soon relegated to an obscurity from which she has only recently been rescued.

From Peter Fryer *Staying Power: the History of Black People in Britain* published in 1984

Study Sources L and M and use your own knowledge.

Do you agree with the view, expressed in Source M, that Mary Seacole was treated differently from Florence Nightingale because she was black?

You tackled a (b) style question at the end of Unit 2. Look back to the exam tips you were given there because you will need to use them in order to answer this question. At the end of that unit you created a spider diagram as a plan. This time, use whichever sort of plan you like best and which works for you. But be sure to plan!

Exam tips

- Be very sure you know what **'view'** is being expressed in Source M.
- **Analyse** and **interpret** Source L so as to establish points that **support** and **challenge** the view given in Source M.
- **Cross-reference** between the sources by focusing on support and challenge.
- Use your **wider knowledge** both to reinforce and to challenge the points derived from the sources.
- Combine the points into **arguments** for and against the view given in Source M.
- **Evaluate** the conflicting arguments by considering the **quality of the evidence** used, involving a consideration of provenance (where appropriate) and the weight of evidence and range of supporting knowledge you can find in support.
- Present a **supported judgement** as to the validity of the stated view and/or any alternatives.

RESEARCH TOPIC

One woman who has appeared from time to time in these three units on the Crimean War is Queen Victoria.

Research Queen Victoria's role in the conflict and explain how this sheds light on the monarchy at that time.

4 The Boer War 1899–1902: how and why was it fought?

What is this unit about?

This unit serves as an introduction to the second major conflict studied in this option (the first being the Crimean War). It summarises how the Second Boer War came about in 1899, what was the nature of the British Army at the time and how well or badly it was prepared for the conflict. The unit also studies how the war proved far greater in terms of human and financial cost than was expected by either the government or the public. At the end of the unit a summary of the war is offered. There is also a focus on the conditions experienced by the soldiers in the changing nature of the conflict as the war evolved for the British from defeat and defensive sieges to triumphant offensive and a gruelling guerrilla war.

Key questions

* Why did the Second Boer War come about?
* Why did the British initially suffer military defeat?

Timeline

1815	Britain's gain of the Cape from the Netherlands confirmed by Treaty
1830s	Some Dutch settlers leave the Cape and establish the Orange Free State and the Transvaal far to the North, following the abolition of slavery by Britain
1869	Diamonds discovered at Kimberley – Cecil Rhodes becomes a millionaire
1877	Transvaal annexed by Britain with consent, in the face of that states' bankruptcy and the Zulu threat
1879	Zulu War – Zulu threat removed by Britain
1880–81	First Boer War – Battle of Majuba Hill – small British force defeated
1882–84	Britain concedes independence to the Transvaal and Orange Free State
1886	Discovery of gold in the Transvaal – Johannesburg becomes a boom town
1895	Cecil Rhodes attempts to overthrow the Transvaal Republic in the Jameson Raid which ends in fiasco
1897	Sir Alfred Milner arrives in South Africa as British High Commissioner
1899	
May	Milner and Kruger meet for negotiations on the Uitlander problem – the talks fail

August	Britain sends reinforcements to the Cape
October	Ultimatum to Britain from the Boer Republics to withdraw troops – declaration of war on refusal. Sieges of Kimberley, Ladysmith and Mafeking begin
December	British forces defeated in three battles in Black Week
1900	
January	Buller's force suffers new defeat at Spion Kop
February	Roberts relieves Kimberley and Buller finally relieves Ladysmith
March	Roberts captures Bloemfontein, capital of the Orange Free State
May	Mafeking relieved; and Johannesburg captured
June	Pretoria occupied by Roberts
November	Kitchener takes over to supervise mopping up
1901	Bitter guerrilla war and clearance of Boer civilian population
1902	
May	Peace of Vereeniging – Boers accept British Imperial sovereignty

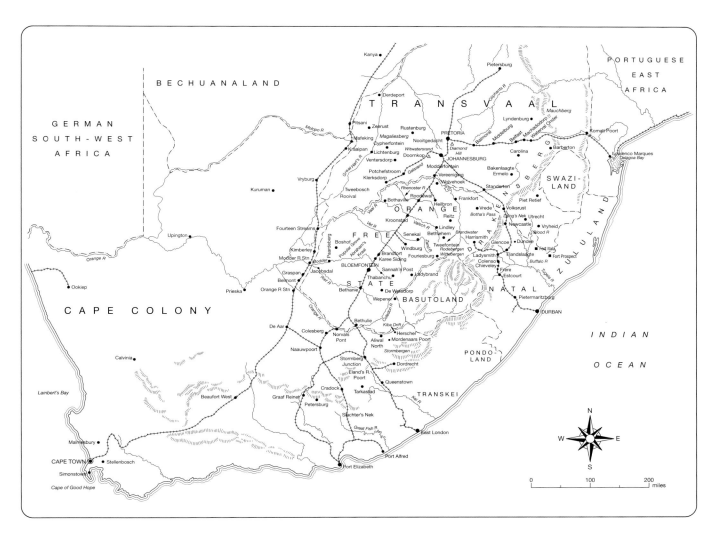

4.1 Map of southern Africa, c. 1900

Definition

Music Hall

The Music Hall was one of the most popular venues for entertainment in the late Victorian period. Dominated by popular songs and variety acts, the Music Hall gives the historian a good insight into popular culture of the time.

The Second or Great Boer War began on 12 October 1899, following the rejection by the British Government of a Boer ultimatum. The Boers demanded the withdrawal of British Troops from their borders and the redirection away from South Africa of the 50,000 British reinforcements on the high seas. Two small states of approximately 400,000 Dutch-speaking people, the Orange Free State and Transvaal Republic, had declared war on the world's mightiest imperial power, Britain.

How did the war come about?

To most of the British troops on their way to South Africa, the origins of the war which they were about to fight were unknown and not relevant. In Source A you will read a verse from a popular song of the time which makes little reference to why the war began. In Source B you will read an extract from a **Music Hall** song of the 1890s that celebrated Britain's world pre-eminence and perhaps gives us more of a clue.

Source A

Good bye Dolly I must leave you,
Though it breaks my heart to go,
Something tells me I am needed,
At the front to fight the foe.
See the soldier boys are marching,
And I can no longer stay
Hark I hear the bugle calling,
Good bye Dolly Gray

The song 'Goodbye Dolly Gray' was popular with the troops who left for South Africa in the Autumn of 1899

Source B

We are getting it by degrees, we are getting it by
    degrees,
We get a bit here, we get a bit there,
The Union Jack is everywhere,
And now and then we give it a gentle squeeze.
We haven't got quite the whole world yet – but we're
    getting it by degrees.

A verse from a popular song of the 1890s,
sung in Music Halls

SKILLS BUILDER

Study Sources A and B.

1 Explain the sentiments and tone of both sources.
2 How useful are such extracts for a historian investigating the reasons for the outbreak of the Second Boer War.

There was a certain exaggeration in Source B but Britain controlled a quarter of the Earth's land surface, ruled a fifth of humanity and largely controlled the Earth's oceans with her vast fleet. London was the financial capital of the world. Fifty per cent of the globe's merchant shipping was British. Britannia really did rule the waves. The behaviour of the Boers in

South Africa was in one sense an inexplicable and foolish impertinence given the disparity in power. Like most wars, the roots of the conflict were long, with many moral twists and turns, and yet the issues in 1899 were fairly straightforward. Was southern Africa to be part of the British Empire or part of a Dutch Republic stretching from the Cape to the Zambesi River? In July the British Prime Minister, Lord Salisbury, expressed it simply in a conversation with a colleague (see Source C).

Colonisation of southern Africa

The Dutch had seized the tip of southern Africa from the Portuguese in the seventeenth century as a key port of call on the way to the East Indies. Dutch settlers had followed throughout the next two centuries, fanning out northwards from the Cape and establishing farms. As they moved northwards they enslaved or drove off the native peoples and also encountered black Bantu tribes moving southwards and clashes occurred. During the Napoleonic Wars the Cape was seized by the British as a key strategic point, vital in safeguarding the route to British India, and in the peace treaties of 1814–15 the British possession of the Cape was confirmed. British settlers now joined the Dutch as farmers and traders in southern Africa.

In 1833 Britain abolished slavery throughout her Empire and many Boers, as Dutch farmers were known, resenting British rule in general and this reform in particular, set off northward into the interior. British power followed and in the 1840s Britain annexed the coast to the north-east of Cape Province, which became known as Natal. The voortrekkers, as the Dutch migrants were called, established two states beyond the frontiers of the British Empire, The Orange Free State, north of the Orange River and further north still, north of the Vaal River, the South African Republic or Transvaal Republic. The British authorities, aware of Dutch dependence on communication through British territory, recognised these states with the proviso that they abandoned slavery.

Zulu Wars

In the 1870s, an energetic British High Commissioner, Sir Bartle Frere, sought to tidy up British rule in South Africa by weakening the dominant native power, the Zulus, and federating the four white states of Cape Province, Natal, the Orange Free State and Transvaal into an Imperial dominion. The result was the Zulu War of 1879–80 and the annexation of the two Boer States, who reluctantly agreed in the face of Zulu power. The Transvaal had only the equivalent of 75 pence in its treasury. The war against the Zulus began with a disaster at Isandhlwana, when the bulk of one British regiment was wiped out. A shortage of screwdrivers produced delay in opening the ammunition boxes, enabling the charging Zulus to break the line of the South Wales Borderers. Days later, a company of the same regiment inflicted a terrible rebuff to the Zulus at Rorke's Drift. This time screwdrivers were available and the Martini Henry rifle was able to

Source C

[We should be prepared to make war] to make the Boers feel that we are and must be the paramount power in South Africa. The real point to be made good to South Africa is that we not the Dutch are Boss.

Lord Salisbury to the Undersecretary for the Colonies, Lord Selbourne, July 1899

do its bloody work on the Zulu warriors. Zulu power was totally destroyed at the battle of Ulundi of 4 July 1879 and Frere's scheme appeared to be working.

First Boer War

However, with the Zulu threat removed, the Boers of the Transvaal now demanded their independence back. A new Liberal government in Britain led by William Gladstone was reluctant to resist such demands and facing imperial overstretch with fighting in Afghanistan, conceded to Boer demands. Unfortunately, this came only after the Boers had inflicted a humiliating defeat on 400 British troops at Majuba Hill in February 1881 in what was known as the First Boer War. The Boers, of course, were convinced that their show of strength had paid off. In reality, Gladstone's Government had meant to grant independence anyway but this is not how it appeared to Paul Kruger, the leader of the Boer militants and, from 1883 President of the Transvaal Republic. Kruger's standing within the Transvaal rose and the belief gained wide currency that a swift blow to the Imperial British lion's nose would produce the desired results in any future conflict.

Gold

New tensions arose following the discovery of vast gold deposits on the Witwatersrand of the Transvaal in 1886. By 1898 the Transvaal produced 27 per cent of the world's gold and millions of mainly British capital had been invested there. This produced problems in two ways:

- The most high profile and the ostensible cause of worsening relations between the Boers and the British was the presence in the rand of thousands of immigrants, many of them British. These *Uitlanders* (foreigners) as the Boers called them came to the boomtown of Johannesburg attracted by the high wages. However, they grumbled continuously about the high taxes, inferior services and corruption of the Transvaal Republic. They were denied political rights. A Transvaal Republic dominated by **Calvinistic** farmers, locked in the religious mind-set of the seventeenth century, ruled a vibrant, unruly and cosmopolitan society of modern immigrants.

- The so-called Uitlanders preferred imperial rule as did the mine owners. Britain pressed for increased rights for these immigrants and tensions increased dramatically following the murder of Tom Edgar, a boiler-maker from Bootle, by a Transvaal Republic policeman late in 1898. A petition to the Queen from thousands of Uitlanders followed, and the British High Commissioner, Sir Alfred Milner, applied pressure to Paul Kruger and his government, demanding reforms and concessions of Civil Rights.

In reality Milner was using the issue of the Uitlanders to justify a takeover. As Kruger put it to Milner during negotiations – *'It is my country that you want.'* Milner's boss in London, Joseph Chamberlain, Colonial Secretary, expressed it clearly in a Cabinet Memorandum of 6 September 1899.

Definition

Calvinism

The Boers were predominately Calvinist in their beliefs. This means that they followed the strict teachings of sixteenth-century Protestant reformer John Calvin.

Source D

What is now at stake is the position of Great Britain in South Africa – and with it the estimate formed of our power and influence in our Colonies and throughout the world.

The contest for supremacy is between the Dutch and the English – the natives are interested spectators, with a preference for the English as their masters, but ready to take the side of the strongest. The Dutch desire, if it be possible, to get rid of the connection with Great Britain, which to them is not a motherland, and to substitute a United States of South Africa which they hope, would be mainly under Dutch influence. [Hence] I think the time has fully come when the troops in South Africa should be largely reinforced.

Joseph Chamberlain, Cabinet Memorandum 6 September 1899

SKILLS BUILDER

What do Sources C and D tell us about the attitudes of leading British politicians to southern Africa and the Boers?

It was not just politicians who were clear that action needed to be taken. Writers such as George Bernard Shaw saw the war as part of Britain's burden to 'civilize' the world. The following extract is taken from a book about *Fabianism and the Empire.* Fabianism was part of the Labour movement and Bernard Shaw a foremost writer of the Left.

Source E

A Great Power, consciously or unconsciously, should govern in the interests of civilization as a whole; and it is not to those interests that such mighty forces as goldfields, and the formidable that can be built upon them should be wielded irresponsible by small communities of frontiersmen.

An extract from *Fabianism and the Empire* by George Bernard Shaw published in 1900

It was in this sense that the gold discoveries of the Transvaal caused the Boer war. The vast increase in revenue to the South African Republic shifted the whole centre of gravity of South Africa north from the British Cape to the Transvaal. Instead of being poor dependants on British South Africa, the Transvaal now looked as if it could become the heart of a powerful Boer Empire. Kruger's government imported thousands of Mauser rifles and Krupp artillery from Germany and sought diplomatic help and protection from the German Empire. The vital British interest at stake was a strategic one. If the Cape and South Africa was essential to the security of the British Empire, and most commentators thought it was, then a powerful independent Transvaal could not be allowed to become the heart of an independent South Africa, hostile to Great Britain and her worldwide Empire. This helps to explain the conclusion to Chamberlain's memorandum (see Source D).

Definition

Marxist historians

Most Marxist historians emphasise social and economic factors as most important in explaining why events happen.

It was the execution of this advice that precipitated the Boer ultimatum on 9 October 1899. **Marxist historians** have often argued that it was a capitalist war waged for gold and the profits of the mine owners.

Source F

None of this means that colonies were not acquired because some group of investors did not expect to make a killing, or in defence of investments already made.

Whatever the ideology, the motive for the Boer War was gold.

A more convincing general motive for colonial expansion was the search for markets. The fact that this was often disappointed is irrelevant. The belief that the 'overproduction' of the great depression could only be solved by a vast export drive was widespread.

From E.J. Hobsbawm Age of Empire published in 1987

However, not all historians have accepted this line of argument. *The Oxford History of the British Empire, Volume III*, which is a recent and highly regarded collection of essays by contemporary eminent historians, disagrees and puts forward an alternative interpretation.

Source G

So the British government did not go to war in 1899 to protect British trade or the profits of capitalists in the Transvaal. It was not only there that capitalists suffered at the hands of an inefficient and corrupt government. Political control of the Transvaal was not sought in order to control the gold-mines, nor to secure access to the supply of gold which would continue to flow to London, as the bullion and financial capital of the world, and underpin the gold standard whether the Transvaal remained a republic or became a British Colony. It was not gold that Britain was after in 1899, but the establishment of British power and influence over the Transvaal on a firmer basis, to advance the unification of the region within the British Empire.

The Oxford History of the British Empire, Volume III, published 1999

What was the British Army like in 1899?

The British Army at the end of the nineteenth century was not vastly different from that which had gone to war with Russia in 1854. Its numbers had increased slightly and Cardwell's reforms had made it somewhat more efficient at coping with the tasks it was given. It was, however, much smaller than the conscript armies of the continental powers and, man for man, much more expensive:

- On paper the strength of the British Army was 249,466 regulars with 78,000 regular reservists, to be called up in time of war. This was a remarkably small force with which to govern the world's largest empire even with the Royal Navy.

- Between 60,000 and 70,000 were stationed in India and another 60,000 scattered in small imperial garrisons around the globe.

- In addition to the regular army there was a militia of 65,000 which did 28 days training a year attached to one of the regular regiments to which they were affiliated. Thirty-five thousand of these irregular soldiers undertook to be available for service overseas if required in return for an extra annual bounty of £1 per annum.

- There was also a large force of around 230,000 enthusiastic but poorly trained volunteers who engaged in a little drill and shooting practice. These could not be legally sent abroad. There was also the Yeomanry, volunteer cavalry, officered by the gentry and drawn from the better off farmers, numbering 10,000. Their main function, other than socialising, was the maintenance of internal security.

Tommy

The regular army was organised into closely bonded regiments, one battalion serving abroad and one training up at the regimental depot in Britain. The ordinary soldiers were drawn, as they had been at the time of Crimea and even earlier, from the poorest elements in society. A disproportionate number came from Ireland and to a lesser extent from Scotland. As the agricultural sector shrank, more and more were drawn from the ranks of the urban unemployed. The social standing of soldiers was low, as was their pay at one shilling a day, and many respectable working-class families felt ashamed of any of their number who volunteered. There were cases of soldiers being excluded from various social milieus, one being ejected from a London omnibus and three sergeants being asked to leave the Haymarket Theatre. **Rudyard Kipling** alluded to this view of military low-life in his popular poem 'Tommy'. The poem was first published under the title 'The Queen's Uniform' in 1890.

Source H

Verse 1
I went into a public-'ouse to get a pint o' beer,
The publican 'e up an' sez, 'We serve no red-coats here.'
The girls be'ind the bar they laughed an' giggled fit to die,
I outs into the street again an' to myself sez I:
O it's Tommy this, an' Tommy that, an' 'Tommy, go away';
But it's 'Thank you, Mister Atkins', when the band begins to play,
The band begins to play, my boys, the band begins to play,
O it's 'Thank you, Mister Atkins', when the band begins to play.

Continued . . .

Biography

Rudyard Kipling
1865–1936

Rudyard Kipling was an immensely popular author and poet of the period. He was born in India and made his name writing about the Raj and its army. Kipling is considered as the foremost poet of Empire. Among his most famous works are *The Jungle Book* and *Kim*. He died a few days before George V's death in 1936 and one of the papers announced that 'The King is dead and taken his trumpeter with him'.

Definition

Tommy Atkins

This was the nickname given to private soldiers serving in the British infantry. The first such known reference comes from revolt in Jamaica in 1843. It is known that there were references to British soldiers as Tommy in the American War of Independence. Many stories associate the name with the Duke of Wellington who, after the battle of Boxtel in 1794, supposedly congratulated a dying Private Tommy Atkins on his bravery to be told: 'It's all right sir. It's all in a day's work.'

Source H continued . . .

Verse 5
You talk o' better food for us, an' schools, an' fires, an' all:
We'll wait for extry rations if you treat us rational.
Don't mess about the cook-room slops, but prove it to our face
The Widow's Uniform is not the soldier-man's disgrace.
For it's Tommy this, an' Tommy that, an' 'Chuck him out, the brute!'
But it's 'Saviour of 'is country' when the guns begin to shoot;
An' it's Tommy this, an' Tommy that, an' anything you please;
An' Tommy ain't a bloomin' fool – you bet that Tommy sees!

Part of 'The Queen's Uniform' or 'Tommy' by Rudyard Kipling written in 1890

It was not just Kipling who held such views. One of the most popular magazines of the Victorian period was *Punch*. Set up in 1841 by Henry Mayhew, within a decade it had become a national institution, especially among the middle classes because it was sophisticated rather than rude in its humour. The Christmas edition of *Punch* 1890 is full of satire. At one point in the magazine, Mr Punch visits Mars where he finds 'Tommy' being really well looked after, or what he describes as being 'treated rational'. Below is a picture from 'Life on Mars'. Remember, it is satire!

Source I

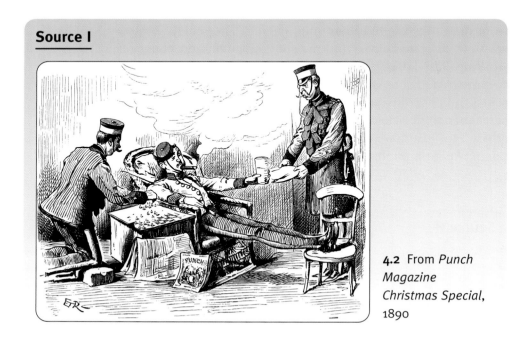

4.2 From *Punch Magazine Christmas Special*, 1890

The food allowance was generous with three-quarters of a pound of meat and a pound of bread a day provided by Her Majesty, as was a gill (a measure) of rum. It was the attractions of regular food and drink that attracted many to army life. Discipline was severe. Flogging in wartime was only abandoned in 1881 and continued in military prisons until 1907. Life was a roll call of drill, cleaning and mundane tasks. Initiative was not encouraged in recruits. In fact it was positively discouraged. Unlike the continental armies of Germany and France, the British Army still trained for close order volley firing in much the same fashion that Wellington had employed at Waterloo. Such training largely worked against the imperial enemies the British faced in the late nineteenth century. In 1898 the Dervishes in the Sudan were triumphantly crushed at the Battle of Omdurman. They very obligingly charged the British lines and were mowed down.

Source J

The British soldier, or 'Tommy', who draws a very poor daily pay, for which he has to perform a tremendous lot of work, is, if not the most capable fighter, the most willing in all circumstances to offer himself as a sacrifice at the altar of duty, or of what he considers his duty, to his country. But if 'Tommy' by any accident be asked to deviate from the usual routine in which he has been trained, he is a thoroughly helpless creature. This helplessness, in my opinion is caused by exaggerated discipline, and by a system under which 'Tommy' is not allowed to think for himself or to take care of himself, and this individual helplessness has undoubtedly been one of the shortcomings of the British soldier during the War.

From Ben Viljoen's *Reminiscences*, published in 1902. He was a leading Boer General.

SKILLS BUILDER

How reliable is Viljoen's summary of the strengths and weaknesses of the British 'Tommy'. Remember, when answering this question you should look at some or all of the following:

- the content of the source;
- the context in which it is written;
- the situation of the author;
- his purpose in writing Source J;
- the nature of the evidence.

Clearly some improvements had been made to help the military performance of the ordinary soldier. By 1899, he wore **khaki**, not the traditional red uniform when going into battle. This at least made him more difficult to see. However, brightly polished buttons or cap badges could attract attention. Most were equipped with the new **Lee Enfield magazine rifle** with an excellent range although the sights of many were defective at the start of the Boer war and needed adjusting. Improvements had been made to supply by the recent creation of the Army Service Corps

Definition

Khaki

From a Hindi word for dusty. It originated as a colour for uniforms in the British Indian Army and was generally adopted as service uniform for service overseas in the British Army from the 1880s.

Definition

Lee Enfield magazine rifle

Weighing just over 9lbs it was a very effective precision weapon with a magazine of 10 bullets.

and the engineering detachments were to show considerable efficiency as they had in the recent conquest of the Sudan. The Royal Army Medical Corps had been established in 1898 and represented a consolidation and more efficient organisation of medical support.

Officer corps

The officer corps was not very different either, from that which had conducted the Crimean War, despite the abolition of purchase of commission by Cardwell. A private income was still deemed necessary for an officer and very few, outside service in India, could manage on their pay alone. Even in the lowliest infantry regiment, it was considered necessary to have a private income of £100–£150 p.a. to cover mess bills and social life. In the smarter regiments like the Guards or, even more so the cavalry, between £600 and £1,000 per annum was advisable. In other words, the British officer corps was still drawn from traditional wealthy families. Their virtues were intense bravery and loyalty to comrades but there was an amateurishness in their approach to soldiering. Too much professional concern was bad form. Riding to hounds and sport attracted most enthusiasm and performance here won the loudest plaudits. There was little intellectual curiosity about the business of soldiering. Much time, when not engaged in sport, was given to endless form filling. The Treasury required the War Office to account meticulously for every penny of public money spent.

At the highest levels, the intellectual shortcomings of the Army were reflected in the failure of Britain to establish a General Staff, as a supreme planning department. The virtues of such a body were obvious from the successes of the Prussian General Staff. The creation in London of a British equivalent was however resisted by both Liberal politicians and reactionary soldiers. In the circumstances, the judgement in Source K on the army of 1899 appears fair and accurate.

Source K

Regarded as an institution of society the British Army of 1899 was undoubtedly a success. The numbers on its rolls were large, the uniforms most distinctive, their traditional ceremonies, known as inspections, parades, guards, elaborate and pleasing to the eye, the regulations to which they submitted infinitely complex. As a fighting machine it was largely a sham.

From L.S. Amery *The Times History of the War in South Africa, 1899–1902* published in six volumes between 1900 and 1909

SKILLS BUILDER

Given what you have already read, how accurate is Amery's judgement?

The course of the War

How was the Boer Army organized?

The two armies that confronted one another in the late autumn of 1899 (spring in South Africa) were vastly different from one another in all but numbers. The Boers could call up over 50,000 men, 21,000 in the Orange Free State and 33,000 in the Transvaal Republic. There were also 500 foreign volunteers. It was a citizen army without uniforms and unaccustomed to drill. Each man had his Mauser rifle (1896 model) and most were excellent shots. For transport they relied on their hardy little ponies for which the new veld grass was essential. Discipline relied heavily on the personality of the particular commander and each man felt perfectly entitled to a say in strategy and tactics. They were organised into Commandos drawn from a particular district. These varied from 200 to 1,000 burghers (as these ordinary citizen soldiers were known). Officers of the Commandos were elected. The plentiful revenue of the Transvaal since the discovery of gold meant that the military force was well equipped with the latest German weapons. £90,000 p.a. (per year) was also spent on intelligence gathering. This compared with the £11,000 p.a. spent by Britain for the whole of its Empire.

How was the British Army organized?

When the Boers declared war, there were only 14,750 British troops in South Africa with a further reinforcement from India about to land in Natal, bringing the total to 22,000. The new commander was the 64-year-old Sir George White. He was to be superseded by the 60-year-old Sir Redvers Buller when the full reinforcements from Britain arrived. By 1 December Buller commanded 84,000 British regulars. Most of these (around 50,000) were infantry and here lay a real problem. Movement and supply over vast distances was to be the key to success and the various British commanders constantly found themselves short of cavalry and horses. Supply depended on the four railways of British South Africa. In the west the Cape railway ran for 600 miles to the Orange River Station on the western edge of the Free State. It then ran north through the diamond mining city of Kimberley and on along the western boundaries of the Orange Free State and the Transvaal for a further 300 miles to Mafeking in the semi-desert of Bechuanaland. To the east two other railways ran north from the coast to the Free State where they joined before proceeding to Johannesburg and Pretoria in the Transvaal. In Natal another railway ran from the coastal port of Durban through Ladysmith to the western part of the Transvaal. Much of the war would hinge on these railways (see map on page 59)

How was the war fought?

The war began with three Boer offensives while they still retained superiority in numbers. These offensives resulted in three famous sieges.

- The smallest and least important of these was at Mafeking where a small British force under **Colonel Baden-Powell** held out against Boer Commandos until May 1900.

- In Kimberley, a much more important centre, British troops and the important mine owner and politician Cecil Rhodes were cut off by a Boer force under General Cronje.

- In Natal Sir George White, after suffering a series of minor reverses, managed to get himself cut off with a large British force in excess of 10,000 in the town of Ladysmith.

The Boers, after blocking the lines of attack by their offensives, settled down to besiege these centres and prepared to hold off any relieving forces. Their strategy was essentially defensive despite the initial move into British territory and perhaps their only hope of long-term success was a dramatic thrust south to the ports, as some of the younger Boers called

Biography

Colonel Robert Baden-Powell 1857–1941

Robert Baden-Powell was an experienced career soldier who served in the armed forces from 1876 to 1910. Apart from being the hero of the siege of Mafeking, he is best remembered for setting up the Boy Scouts movement. His wife, Olave, was instrumental in setting up the Girl Guides.

for, and Milner feared. Kruger hoped that after inflicting a few bloody defeats on the British they would agree to negotiate as in 1881 and recognise the full independence of the Boer States. He had misjudged his opponents.

The British repeatedly misjudged the skills of the Boers and the impact of technological developments in weaponry on tactics. The following extract is from a book by J.E.B. Seely who was a politician who also served as a volunteer Captain of Yeomanry in South Africa.

Source L

Frontal attacks in broad daylight were the recognised method of approaching the enemy. It really did not seem to have dawned on the old fashioned military mind that a complete revolution had been made in the whole science of war – strategically as well as tactically – not only by the invention of the quick firing gun, but, above and beyond all, by the discovery of smokeless powder, which clearly had made more difference than all the other inventions put together. All doctrines of superiority of fire vanished when the enemy could fire on you and still remain invisible. It became possible for ten men properly concealed to withstand effectively a hundred or more. Indeed, with my own eyes I saw this happen over and over again both in the South African and in the World War.

In the former war, the tragic failures of Graspan, Magersfontain, the Modder River, and on the Natal side, on the Tugela were striking instances of this obvious truth.

From J.E.B. Seely *Adventure* published in 1930

What was 'Black Week'?

Buller, on his arrival at the Cape, decided to divide his arriving Army Corps into three. One section under Lord Methuen he sent up the Western Railway to relieve Kimberley. A central force under Gatacre he intended to use to safeguard the North of Cape Province and the two other railway lines and he himself proceeded to Natal and thence to attempt to relieve Ladysmith and Sir George White's large force. All three met defeat; Gatacre walked into a Boer Force holding the railway junction at Stormberg and suffered 135 casualties and 561 taken prisoner on 10 December. Methuen the next day struck at Cronje at Magersfontain.

Source M

I am just broken hearted at our awful loss on the 11th. Five officers killed and 7 wounded and over 200 men killed and wounded. The loss in the Highland Brigade alone was 54 officers killed, 34 wounded, including our General killed and his ADC severely wounded. Simply terrible and all absolutely unnecessary. Our Divisional General, Lord Methuen, still sticks to his suicidal idea of a frontal attack. We got quite close to the enemy position just before daybreak and were just extending to attack when a perfect storm of bullets came into us from close quarters. The enemy were evidently prepared for us and had waited till we were within a very short distance of them. All this happened at 4 am. From then till 2pm – 10 mortal hours – about 400 of my men had to lie flat on their faces in the sun, being fired at all the time, and unable to fire back or to move. Whenever one had to rise or move he was instantly shot down.

From a letter dated 13 December 1899, by Col J.W. Hughes Hallett of the Seaforth Highlanders who had been present at the battle of Magersfontain

The attack was a disaster and the Highlanders in their kilts suffered not only from enemy fire but the myriads of ants. Methuen eventually retreated to the Modder River and gave up on his attempts to relieve Kimberly until more reinforcements arrived. In Natal Buller faced defeat at Colenso on 15 December in a very similar fashion. The three defeats constituted 'Black Week' which was a considerable blow to British power and prestige. However, Kruger was not to get his peace. When Queen Victoria was informed shortly afterwards of the unfortunate developments, she replied:

> Please understand that there is no one depressed in this house; we are not interested in the possibility of defeat. It does not exist.

Her government, to ensure ultimate victory, sought massive reinforcements and in the best Victorian tradition looked for a hero. They alighted upon 'Bobs' – **Field Marshall Lord Roberts**. To make doubly sure they resolved to send two heroes. Accompanying the 67-year-old Roberts as his chief of staff, was the latest imperial victor, **Kitchener** of Khartoum, fresh from his triumphs over the Sudanese. Roberts reached the front in early February but Buller had suffered further defeat in January at Spion Kop in a fresh attempt to reach Ladysmith. The following photograph was taken after the battle for Spion Kop. It shows the corpses of British soldiers who died fighting to gain control of the Kop.

Biography

Field Marshall Horatio Kitchener 1850–1916

Kitchener won fame by leading the re-conquest of the Sudan between 1896 and 1898 culminating in British victory in the Battle of Omdurman on 2 September 1898, Kitchener succeeded Roberts in command of British forces in South Africa in November 1900. He served in India and Egypt before being appointed Secretary of State for war on the outbreak of the First World War. He is perhaps best remembered for being the face on the 'Britons' recruitment poster. He was drowned when the cruiser carrying him on a visit to Britain's ally, Russia, in 1916, hit a mine.

Biography

Field Marshal Frederick Roberts 1832–1914

Roberts was one of the military heroes of the British Empire. He served in India during the Indian Mutiny of 1857–58 and was awarded the Victoria Cross for two acts of conspicuous bravery on one day. He fought in the Abyssinia campaigns of the 1860s and he led the force which captured the Afghan capital of Kabul during the Second Afghan War of 1878–79. He was given important posts in India and his homeland of Ireland before accepting command of British forces in South Africa in late 1899.

Source N

4.3 'Murderous Acre', the Spion Kop 26 January 1899 by an anonymous photographer

SKILLS BUILDER

Does the fact that the photographer of Source N is anonymous reduce its usefulness to the historian trying to find out about the battle for Spion Kop?

SKILLS BUILDER

Study Sources L, M and O.

How far do the three sources agree on the causes of British defeats in South Africa in 1899–1900?

Source O

You will have seen from the papers about the four days battle 20th to 24th. The last day was the worst for our brigade as we lost about a 1000 killed wounded and missing. We marched all night and got to the top of a hill on which the Boers had an outpost. They fired a few shots and then retired to their entrenchments, but at daybreak they commenced a regular storm of shot and shell until dark, men fell in all directions, and had to lie, as it was death to stand up. We got no food or drink all day, wounded men asked for water which we had not got. We have not had our clothes off this month, and do not know where we are going next. I do not think that in spite of all our troops we are making any progress towards the termination of this war. They will have to alter their tactics or they will be outwitted by the Boers who are so clever at concealment.

From a letter dated January 1900, by Private James McGowan of the Royal Lancaster Regiment, who was present at the Battle of Spion Kop

What was the extent of British success in November 1900?

In fact Private James McGowan was unduly pessimistic; for the British the tide was about to turn. More reinforcements were arriving including 30,000 from across the Empire. Many of these like the Boers were mounted infantry. Large numbers of Britons volunteered to serve and were rapidly shipped to South Africa. The eventual transportation of 448,895 soldiers half way round the globe was a remarkable achievement:

- British forces led by Field Marshal Roberts reached the Modder River in February, the Boer besiegers were rapidly out-manoeuvred and Kimberley relieved on 15 February.
- Twelve days later Cronje and 4,000 Boers were surrounded and forced to surrender at Paardeberg.
- On 28 February, Buller relieved Ladysmith after a well planned and methodical attack.

The British were learning rapidly although Buller's later successes are often forgotten. Buller's reputation in particular never recovered from the stigma of his initial defeats but over the next six months he showed real competence in out-manoeuvring the Boers in the Natal region in far more difficult terrain than Roberts was operating in further west. Nevertheless, Roberts drove on to capture the capital of the Free State, Bloemfontein, in March. There was then a pause of two months as Roberts encountered supply problems stemming from a dependence on one railway line as he prepared to head for the Transvaal. Indeed, there were serious shortages of provisions and equipment and Robert's army was hit by a devastating outbreak of typhoid which killed more troops than were killed by the Boers. The advance was resumed on 11 May and Johannesburg was captured at the end of the month. A week later Pretoria fell and the war seemed over. Roberts and Buller left in the autumn of 1900 and Kitchener took over as Commander-in-Chief in November.

What happened in 1901?

What now followed was the longest phase of the war and the one that elicited the most controversy. The loss of their major cities did not induce the Boer Commandos to surrender. They now resorted to guerrilla warfare, attacking small British detachments and in particular attacking the railways and supply lines. Kitchener responded with the ruthless logic of the engineer he was. The land was to be swept clear of food and subdivided by barbed wire and blockhouses. Farms were burnt and the Boer women and children lodged in 'concentration camps'. Source P comes from Afrikaans historian and writer Gustav Preller who served with Boer forces during the war. After the war Preller worked hard to preserve and promote Afrikaner language, identity and traditions.

Source P

At the beginning of May [1901] the English marched out again from the railway and spread over the high veld in all directions, splitting up into small columns. Fifteen to twenty independent columns systematically laid waste whatever remained. Women were taken away in open wagons and grossly ill-treated and insulted by the soldiers and officers. For example a well brought up young lady, Mrs FGA Wolmarans was called a liar by a Provost Marshal because she said she had no eggs in the house (which was the truth) and he thought otherwise.

Reminiscences of Gustav Preller, a Boer Artilleryman, 26 October 1917, from David Smurthwaite *The Boer War 1899–1902* published in 2002

Source Q

Some of our work was very unpleasant. If we found any arms or ammunition concealed on a farm we had to burn down the place and confiscate all cattle, stores, wagons etc. and as the men were usually in hiding, and we had only women to deal with you can guess how uncongenial our work was. We brought in thousands of sheep and cattle and the district appears to be fairly quietened down although one of the most hostile in the country.

Arthur Tomey, a British soldier, records his experiences, from David Smurthwaite *The Boer War 1899–1902* published in 2002

Source R

What a merciful war it was if we compare it to the wars of today. There was no firing on undefended cities. Of course there were nasty incidents but the way the reactionary Boers talk is absurd: the English did burn down farmhouses, but never shot a single one of the people in them, like the Germans did in this war, and many a time a farmhouse was burnt because some fighting Boers had fired on the English from a Koppie nearby or from the farm itself. Also the story of the concentration camps is frightfully exaggerated.

First of all, taking the women off the farms was an actual military necessity. The enemy was fighting in a country they did not know and went to the homes whenever possible. Naturally the womenfolk collected all information they could get hold of and warned our men; also they supplied them with food, and possibly ammunition. What army would have left them to do that? Of course it was terrible for us, but, anyway, though soldiers did dreadful things, as they always do in wars, no orders were given by Headquarters to shoot or kill citizens. No, it was as much a gentlemen's war on both sides as wars can be.

From the memoirs of Sophie Leviseur, *A Boer Women in Bloemfontein* published in 1982

Discussion point

This is a difficult question for you to discuss with your fellow students.

Was Kitchener right to use the tactics described in Sources O, P and Q if it meant victory in war?

To what extent did the war constitute a British victory?

Gradually the Boer Commandos were worn down and negotiations began in the spring of 1902. Kitchener and the Army were prepared to be more conciliatory than Milner. Peace was finally agreed at Vereeniging on the last day of May 1902. By the terms of the Treaty of Vereeniging:

- The Transvaal Republic and Orange Free State became part of the Empire.
- There was to be an amnesty for the Boers who had fought in the war and a grant of £3,000,000 from the British government to help repair damage.
- The prospect of self-government for the Transvaal Republic and Orange Free State was held out but without a firm date being given.

What had initially been viewed as a minor colonial conflict had cost the British government £201 million. British casualties had been high with 5,774 British troops killed by enemy action and a further 16,168 dying of disease and their wounds. Many more than this had left South Africa sick or wounded. It was a victory but an expensive one.

How the sick and wounded were treated?

Just as in the conflict in the Crimea, the British Army was fighting a war a long way from home and in difficult and often hostile conditions. Below are two pieces of evidence for us to consider.

Source S

Hundreds of men to my knowledge were lying in the worst stages of typhoid, with only a thin blanket and a thin waterproof sheet (not even the latter for many of them) between their aching bodies and the hard ground, with no milk and hardly any medicines, without beds, stretchers or mattresses, without linen of any kind, without a single nurse amongst them, with only a few ordinary private soldiers to act as 'orderlies.' There were only three doctors to attend to 350 patients. In many of the tents there were ten typhoid cases lying closely packed together, the dying with the convalescent.

Report by William Burdett-Coutts in *The Times* of conditions he witnessed on 28 April 1900 in Bloemfontein. Burdett-Coutts was a Unionist MP.

This description might be contrasted with the photograph below. East London was on the coast, far away from the fighting.

Source T

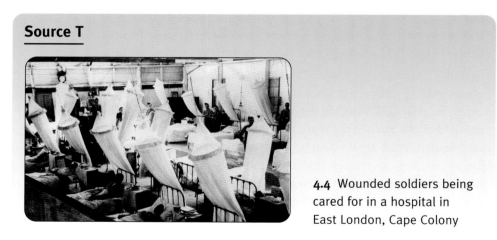

4.4 Wounded soldiers being cared for in a hospital in East London, Cape Colony

Unit summary

What have you learned in this unit?

This unit has covered a considerable amount of information. You have learned about the background to the Second Boer War, and importantly about events in southern Africa. A fair amount of the unit was focused on the reasons for the outbreak of the war and how the British armed forces fared. You have had explained the structure of the British Army and the division in experience between officer and Tommy. From the last sections of the unit you learned about how the war was fought and how the tide of war was turned in Britain's favour.

What skills have you used in this unit?

You have evaluated the utility and reliability of evidence and you have compared evidence while ascertaining the reasons for the outbreak of war. As part of your work in going through this unit you have assessed the accuracy of judgements made in the sources.

SKILLS BUILDER

1 Which of Sources S and T is more likely to provide the more accurate image of care for the wounded British soldiers during the Boer War?

2 Class debates:

Your class might want to debate one or both of the following. Alternatively, you might wish to complete one or both as a piece of written work.

Issue 1 After considering the evidence of Sources A to G and the text from pages 58 to 64, consider the following question:

A war fought for gold! Is this the primary explanation for the outbreak of the Second Boer War?

Issue 2 After considering the evidence of Sources H to R and the text from pages 64 to 74, consider the following question:

How far do you agree that the British Army in 1899 was an inadequate fighting machine?

Exam style question

This is the sort of question you may find on the examination paper as an (a) question. For general advice on how to answer the question, you need to look on page 21.

Study Sources P, Q and R.

How far do these three Sources support the proposition that the British dealt brutally with the Boer population in trying to defeat Boer guerilla fighters?

RESEARCH TOPIC

Spion Kop

The military action at the Spion Kop in January 1900 was to capture the imagination of the British public. Your research has two main points to it:

What happened at the battle for the Spion Kop in January 1900?

Why did it have such an impact in Britain?

UNIT 5 The Boer War 1899–1902: what was the impact on Britain?

What is this unit about?

The aim of this unit is to consider how the war was reported and how events in South Africa were received in Britain. This involves a consideration of the role of the press, an attempt to gauge the vast upsurge of patriotic fervour which reached a climax with the news of the relief of Mafeking in May 1900, the extent of opposition to the war and the treatment of this opposition.

Key questions

- How was the Boer War reported in Britain?
- How popular was the war in Britain?

Timeline

1886	Liberal Party split – Liberal Unionists leave over Home Rule
1895	Joseph Chamberlain, a leading Liberal Unionist, joins the Conservative government as Colonial Secretary
1896	Alfred Harmsworth establishes the *Daily Mail*
1899	
October	Outbreak of War
1900	
February	Relief of Ladysmith – outbreaks of popular rejoicing
May	Relief of Mafeking – wild rejoicing in London and other cities
October	'Khaki' election – Conservatives win a comfortable majority
1901	
January	Emily Hobhouse in Bloemfontein
June	Sir Henry Campbell Bannerman's 'Methods of Barbarism' speech
August–December	Fawcett Commission in South Africa
December	Pro-war riot in Birmingham against Lloyd George

Rudyard Kipling composed the verse in Source A in October 1899 and it was set to music by Sir Arthur Sullivan and became a popular national hit, sung in theatres and music halls. Barrel organs ground it out on street corners and it made a major contribution to raising popular support for the war. It was associated with a 'Soldier's wives and Children's fund' sponsored by the *Daily Mail*. The fund raised £70,000 by the end of January and eventually a quarter of a million pounds.

Source A

When you've shouted 'Rule Britannia,' when you've sung 'God Save the Queen,'
When you've finished killing Kruger with your mouth,
Will you kindly drop a shilling in my little tambourine
For a gentleman in Khaki ordered South?
He's an absent-minded beggar, and his weaknesses are great
But we and Paul must take him as we find him
He is out on active service, wiping something off a slate
And he's left a lot of little things behind him!
Duke's son – cook's son – son of a hundred kings
(Fifty thousand horse and foot going to Table Bay!)
Each of 'em doing their country's work
(and who's to look after their things?)
Pass the hat round for your credit's sake,
And pay-pay-pay!

The Absent Minded Beggar by Rudyard Kipling 1899

SKILLS BUILDER

1 What were the sentiments expressed in Source A?

2 Why do you think that Kipling's words might have been so effective in getting people to give money?

What was the role of the press?

The Boer War coincided with a press revolution. The mid-nineteenth century had seen the expansion of the press and the development of the penny daily symbolised by the *Daily Telegraph* launched in 1855. Others included the *Morning Post*, founded much earlier supporting the Conservatives, and *Daily News* and *Daily Chronicle* supporting the Liberals. These tended to be serious political papers with a relatively small middle-class readership. Outside London, there was still a strong regional press, pre-eminent among which was the *Manchester Guardian*. In a class of its own was *The Times* retailing at the princely sum of 3d.

The man who transformed this journalistic world was Alfred Harmsworth. In 1896 he launched the *Daily Mail*, selling at one halfpenny. It was unreservedly populist. Lord Salisbury sniffily described it as '*A paper written by office boys for office boys.*' On the other side of the political spectrum Lloyd George, the radical Liberal, said in 1900, that '*the Boers do not have the ineffable advantage of reading at breakfast every morning great works of imagination like the Daily Mail.*' Harmsworth's aim was simply to make money by maximising sales and boosting advertising revenue. Stories would be rewritten to provide spice and interest. The layout was more inviting with more headings and shorter paragraphs. It has been said that the old style dailies served their news raw. Harmsworth served it cooked. He appreciated the value of 'a good hate' and a war in selling papers. By the end of 1899, the *Daily Mail* had achieved the unheard-of daily circulation figure of 534,000. It unashamedly used the Boer War to boost sales and the special train used to carry the *Mail* outside the usual range of the London dailies was known as 'the South African train'.

The impact of the war in boosting the sales of newspapers in general is vividly conveyed in this letter of December 1899.

Source B

Our days are spent with reading our papers – ever clamouring for more, our nights in dreaming of all that is and is not to be. In my life-time this state of tension is unique. The war affects all, rich and poor alike. All have friends and relations in it and it is no exaggeration to say we are all plunged in gloom. I shall never forget last Tuesday in London, when the news of the missing battalions arrived about midday. Picture the newsboys at the corners shouting 'Terrible reverse of British Troops – Loss of 2000'. Imagine the rush for papers as we all stood about the streets . . . There was a perfect sea of newspapers and anxious faces behind.

Letter from Miss Bertha Synge, in London, to Sir Alfred Milner in South Africa, December 1899

What was the impact of Winston Churchill?

The importance attached to the war by the press is demonstrated by their desire to have their own war correspondents out in the war-zone and the salaries they were prepared to pay them. The most famous of all was the young **Winston Spencer Churchill**. Already a known author and journalist at 24, he was engaged by the *Morning Post* at the handsome salary of £250 per month. The *Daily Mail* had also shown an interest in acquiring his services and hence the very favourable pay, perhaps the modern equivalent of £170,000 p.a.

Like many war correspondents of the period, Churchill was a strange hybrid, both serving officer and employee of a newspaper. When captured by the Boers in December 1899 he claimed to be a correspondent but his actions in defending the armoured train when he was taken prisoner were those of a serving junior officer. After escaping and making his way back to Natal, Buller appointed him a lieutenant in the South Africa Light Horse but he continued to report for the *Morning Post*. There was often an engaging honesty in the reports (see Source D) and army censorship was lax. For the first time there was an official military censor but as correspondents tended to be officers and gentlemen like the young Winston Churchill or Lord Rosslyn for the *Daily Mail*, there was a tendency to trust their judgement. The denial of information or access to it was dependant on personal relationships. Churchill found Buller particularly accommodating but Roberts less so. Through Churchill's work the deficiencies of the British forces were revealed to the world in a way difficult to imagine when he was Prime Minister during the Second World War.

The papers were overwhelmingly in favour of the conflict and in this they probably reflected as much as created British public sentiment. H.W. Massingham, the radical editor of the *Daily Chronicle,* was pro-Boer and soon in trouble with the paper's proprietor.

Biography

Winston Spencer Churchill 1874–1965

Winston Churchill was the grandson of the Duke of Marlborough and the son of Lord Randolph Churchill, a famous Tory politician of the 1880s. He was well connected but not rich and made his living by writing. He had produced a bestseller called *The River War*, being an account of the conquest of the Sudan in 1898. He travelled to South Africa in 1899 to report on the war but returned to Britain and was elected Conservative MP for Oldham in 1900. His political career thereafter was extensive. In 1906 he became a Liberal Minister, and he served as First Lord of the Admiralty before and during the First World War and as Prime Minister from 1940–45 and 1951–55.

Source C

Liberals of all types are depressed and uncertain of themselves. The dismissal of Massingham from the editorship of the *Daily Chronicle* reflects the strong patriotic sentiment of its readers; any criticism of the war is hopelessly unpopular.

Extract from the diaries of Beatrice Webb in late 1899

The other Liberal paper, the *Daily News*, supported the war under its editor E.T. Cook, but early in 1901 Lloyd George helped organise a coup when he got an anti-war syndicate led by the Quaker, George Cadbury, to buy a controlling interest of the shares and the paper then adopted a pro-Boer approach, somewhat restoring balance. However, by this time there was growing sentiment against the war and the high point of patriotic enthusiasm had passed. Although the bulk of the press supported the war throughout 1899, 1900 and even after, truthful reporting was not a complete casualty. The British disasters of Black Week (see pages 70–71) were reported in mournful detail and as the following indicates the Boers were fully appreciated as soldiers.

Source D

Reviewing the whole situation, it is foolish not to recognize that we are fighting a formidable adversary. The high qualities of the burghers increases their efficiency. We must face the facts. The individual Boer, mounted in suitable country, is worth from three to five regular soldiers. The only way to deal with them is either to get men equal in character and intelligence as riflemen or failing the individual, huge masses of troops.

Part of a dispatch by W.S. Churchill sent from Durban to his paper, the *Morning Post* in January 1900

However, high standards of truth were not always maintained, as the following makes clear.

Source E

I have this morning seen an article, written by a newspaper correspondent in South Africa, stating that the 'Boers murder wounded men,' and that this is a 'frequent incident.'

I venture to ask you to publish this letter for the sake of those, tens of thousand in number, whose anxiety for their husbands, sons, brothers, is great enough already without the addition of this fresh terror. During the seventeen months that I served in South Africa, I had, perhaps, rather exceptional opportunities of learning how our wounded were treated by the Boers.

On two different occasions men under my command who were dangerously wounded were attended to by the Boers; in each case they were tended with the greatest kindness and care, and the wounded men themselves begged me to thank those who had been so good to them. I have spoken to many officers and men who have been left sick or wounded in the hands of the Boers, and in no single instance have I heard anything but gratitude expressed for the treatment they had received.

From a letter published in *The Times* in July 1901, from Captain J.E.B. Seely

SKILLS BUILDER

Study Sources C, D and E.

How far do the three sources suggest that the British press was unbiased and reliable in its reporting of the Boer War?

How extensive was the support for the war in Britain?

There seems little doubt that the war elicited widespread support and wild outbursts of popular enthusiasm. Much of the evidence for this comes from critics of the war like Beatrice Webb, quoted in Source C. Source F reveals the distaste expressed by novelist Arnold Bennett for the fervour displayed following the news of the relief of Ladysmith (it is ironic that Bennett ended up as Director of Propaganda at the War Ministry during the First World War).

However, a recent biography of Lord Salisbury makes plain the national rejoicing that the relief of Ladysmith and Mafeking induced.

Source F

I must say I have been quite unable to join with any sincerity in the frantic and hysterical outburst of patriotic enthusiasm of the last few days.

From the journal of Arnold Bennett, 4 March 1900

Source G

It took Buller's relief of Ladysmith from its four month siege on 28th February 1900 to dispel the mood of national tension which the government had been so mishandling. Church bells were rung, flags were flown, school children were given a half day off school, Stock Exchange trading was suspended, Kruger was burnt in effigy and young ladies of Newnham College, Cambridge danced and sang round a bonfire.

Such displays were surpassed in May when news of the relief of Mafeking reached London.

From *Salisbury: Victorian Titan* by Andrew Roberts, published 1999

Source H

Within five minutes of the announcement so unconventionally made by the Mansion House footman to the policeman below, the historic home of the Lord Mayor was surrounded by a crowd of no fewer than 20,000 madmen, all yelling: 'Mafeking is relieved!' Or singing 'God save the Queen' in all the notes possible in Music.

Women absolutely wept for joy and men threw their arms about each other's necks – strangers necks for the most part; but that made no difference, for Mafeking was relieved.

From a report in the *Daily Mail* on the scenes in London on the night of 18 May, published 19 May 1900

SKILLS BUILDER

1 How far do Sources F, G and H agree that there was widespread popular support for the war in 1900?

Who opposed the war?

The same patriotic excess showed itself in mass hostility to pro-Boer meetings (i.e. meetings of those who opposed the war). One of the most celebrated took place in Birmingham in 1901. The 35-year-old **David Lloyd George** had become the most notorious of the pro-Boer Liberals and his decision to address an anti-war rally in Birmingham town hall was particularly provocative. Birmingham was Joseph Chamberlain's political base and stronghold. Chamberlain as Colonial Secretary was usually seen as the architect of the war. In fact the Boer War was often referred to as 'Joe's war'.

David Lloyd George 1863–1945

David Lloyd George was one of the foremost Liberal politicians of the early twentieth century. As Chancellor of the Exchequer he introduced National Insurance in 1911 and other measures that formed the basis of the Welfare State. While in opposition, Lloyd George supported the idea of extending the suffrage to women but once in power he did little to follow this idea up and his property was a target for suffragette violence. In 1915 he became Minister for Munitions and Prime Minister in 1916, a post which he held with Conservative support until 1922.

Source J

We are told it is to spread freedom and extend the rights of the common people but it is about getting markets for goods, investors an outlay for capital and companies cheaper labour.

Keir Hardie, an Independent Labour Party MP and critic of the war. This was originally part of an article written in 1899 in the Socialist publication *L'humanité Nouvelle* and reprinted on 6 January 1900 in *Labour Leader*.

Source I

By 8 o'clock the hall was jammed full with seven thousand people, the great majority of whom were waving Union Jacks, blowing trumpets or whistles, bellowing, chanting and singing and determined that the speakers should not be heard. Lloyd George rose to his feet, took off his overcoat and beamed at his audience.

'This', he began, 'is rather a lively meeting for a peace meeting.' He talked on despite the incredible din. Within five minutes of his rising to his feet, however, the audience made a huge surge towards the stage, at which point a squad of policemen concealed beneath it rushed out of their hiding place and an ugly struggle between truncheons on the one hand and hammers and knives on the other got underway. The platform party found itself deluged with a torrent of missiles – cans, bottles, ordinary bricks and lastly bricks wrapped around with barbed wire. Lloyd George was determined to retain control of the stage rather than let his opponents take possession of it and hold a meeting of their own, but the Chief Constable eventually forced him to leave it by pointing out that other members of the platform party, including ladies, were in danger of losing their lives.

From *Lloyd George* by Peter Rowland published 1975. Here he is describing Lloyd George's experiences in Birmingham town hall in December 1901.

In an age without opinion polls, it is difficult to be precise about the degree of support for the war. Most of the anecdotal evidence points to considerable support and enthusiasm:

- It has been suggested that it was much stronger in certain areas such as London and Birmingham than others, and certainly just after the Birmingham meeting referred to above, Lloyd George held a successful anti-war meeting in Bristol in January 1902.

- On the other hand, he was roughed up at Bangor in his own North Wales heartland in April 1900.

- Chronology is clearly another factor with support being apparently at its greatest in 1899–1900 and fading somewhat after that. Some historians have suggested that enthusiasm was far greater among the middle rather than the working classes but this is difficult to demonstrate conclusively.

From its inception there were always a vocal minority of critics who felt that the war was unjust. Many Liberals to the Left of the party shared the concerns of John Morley (briefly leader of the Liberal Party in 1898) that the war was morally wrong. The leader of the recently founded Independent Labour Party, Keir Hardie, saw it as a capitalist war for the profits of mine owners (see Source J).

The Irish nationalists, who felt like the Boers that they were victims of British oppression, were perhaps the most ferocious critics carrying their opposition to actual support for the Boers and rejoicing in the defeat of

British forces in December 1899. Quakers like George Cadbury backed the opposition with money and an amalgam of different groups formed into an anti-war movement. But it was David Lloyd George whose high profile speeches brought him national celebrity or more accurately at the time, notoriety as the leading opponent of the war.

Source K

It is not President Kruger we are fighting, and we ought to consider that. Who are the men who stand, two thousand five hundred against ten thousand of the pick of our troops? They are two thousand five hundred farmers, as it were Carmarthenshire farmers from these hills, fighting for hours, retiring when they think that they have broken up and two days later fighting again. They are very ignorant, it is true. Their only book is the Bible. Morning, noon and night it is the book they read, and I would not expect the German Jews* to say much for it. But such as it is, it is the only book of the Boer, the book that made him what he is, the book his character comes from. They might be right or wrong, but they are finer, godlier men than those whom we are fighting for. We have had to put a hundred thousand men in the field – we, who have an Empire on which the sun never sets; we, who have forty millions in these islands, and scores of millions abroad, to crush a hundred thousand men, women and children.

* a reference to some of the mine owners such as Alfred Beit, of German Jewish extraction

From a speech by David Lloyd George in Carmarthen, 27 November 1899

SKILLS BUILDER

1 Summarise the arguments contained in Sources I, J and K against the war.

Biography

Alfred Beit 1853–1906

Born in Hamburg in Germany, Beit become a business partner of Cecil Rhodes. With Rhodes he came to dominate gold and diamond mining in South Africa. Not surprisingly, Beit became an ardent supporter of British imperialism.

Biography

Cecil Rhodes 1853–1902

Son of a Hertfordshire clergyman, Rhodes did perhaps more than any other to shape the development of the British Empire in southern Africa. He was the founder of the De Beers diamond company and Prime Minister of the Cape Colony. However, he is perhaps best known for the expansion of the British controlled lands northwards into the area which became known as Rhodesia, now Zimbabwe.

What was the impact of the concentration camps?

A common theme for opponents of the war was that it was a war on behalf of the rich mine owners such as **Alfred Beit** and **Cecil Rhodes** but also that it was a case of bullying a simple but decent people. Initially the focus was very much on the unjust cause of the war as indicated above but as Kitchener began to adopt new tactics to deal with the Boers' switch to guerrilla warfare, the focus of criticism moved to the methods by which the war was conducted and in particular the plight of Boer civilians herded from their farms to camps.

These were soon nicknamed 'concentration camps'. The phrase was new and had been first used in Cuba for camps set up by the Spanish authorities to hold civilians. The camps established by the military authorities in South Africa were not intended as places of punishment let alone death camps and it is a misleading accident that they share the same name with the far more horrific phenomena of Nazi Germany. Initially the camps were established in the summer of 1900 to shelter 'families of the "hands-uppers"', i.e. those Boers who had preferred to surrender and risked the vengeance of Afrikaners who wished to continue the war. More and more were added as the guerrilla war continued – inmates of farms destroyed for harbouring guns or aiding the guerrillas, families of prisoners-of-war without the means of support. Male prisoners-of-war were sent to camps in Bermuda, St Helena and Ceylon (now Sri Lanka) and were for the most part well treated and cared for.

The suffering in the civilian camps in South Africa was the result of overcrowding, supply problems and general military incompetence. More and more were sent to camps as the military drives across the veld continued and by September there were 110,000 detained in 34 camps. Six months previously there had been 35,000 in 27 camps and even then the conditions were poor. Typhoid broke out and various other diseases resulted in the deaths of 27,927 Boers, particularly children. Two women played a key part in alerting the British public to the state of things and ultimately correcting the deficiencies. The first was a well-connected Cornish spinster, Emily Hobhouse. She was Secretary of the Women's Branch of the South African Conciliation Committee and had close family relations with various leading anti-war politicians. In January of 1901 she visited one of the camps in Bloemfontein and was accorded every help by the military authorities but in a private letter to one of her family she vented her outrage:

Source L

The authorities are at their wits end and have no more idea how to cope with the difficulty of providing clothes for the people than the man in moon. Crass male ignorance, stupidity, helplessness and muddling. I rub as much salt into the sore places of their minds as I possibly can, because it is good for them; but I can't help melting a little when they are very humble and confess that the whole thing is a grievous mistake and gigantic blunder and presents an almost insoluble problem and they don't know how to face it.

From a letter by Emily Hobhouse to one of her family, January 1901

On her return to England in the spring of 1901, a report was circulated among MPs and then made public. It produced outrage. The Liberal leader, Sir Henry Campbell Bannerman, delivered a famous onslaught on the government in a speech at the National Reform Union dinner.

Source M

What was this policy of unconditional surrender? It was that now we had got the men we had been fighting against down, we should punish them as severely as possible, devastate their country, burn their homes, break up their very instruments of agriculture and destroy the machinery by which food was produced. It was that we should sweep – as the Spaniards did in Cuba; and how we denounced the Spaniards – the women and children into camps in which they were destitute of all decencies and comforts and many of the necessaries of life, and in some of which the death-rate rose so high as 430 in the 1000. A phrase often used was that 'war is war,' but when one came to ask about it one was told that no war was going on, that it was not war. When was a war not a war? When it was carried on by methods of barbarism in South Africa.

From a speech by Sir Henry Campbell Bannerman, leader of the Liberal Party, at a supporters' meeting in London, 14 June 1901

In response to growing public concern, the government dispatched an all female committee of enquiry under the formidable Mrs Millicent Fawcett, who was an active Liberal Unionist and campaigner for votes for women. After touring South Africa from August to December, her report confirmed Hobhouse's claims and made far-reaching recommendations.

Source N

The death rate was very heavy, 10 dying on one night of the Commission's visit. Though some of the houses were comfortable, others were miserable sheds or stables, and one hovel was surely meant for a pig or perhaps some poor native and yet a young girl, dangerously ill, lay in it. There is barely language too strong to express our opinion of sending of a mass of disease to a healthy camp; but the cemetery at Heilbron tells the price paid in lives for the terrible mistake.

Report of the Fawcett Commission to the House of Commons 1902. Here it refers to one camp at Heilbron, which had recently received a wave of internees suffering from measles.

Source O

The black spot – the one very black spot – in the picture is the frightful mortality in the Concentration Camps. I entirely agree with you in thinking that while a hundred explanations may be offered and a hundred excuses made, they do not really amount to an adequate defence.

Letter of Lord Milner to Joseph Chamberlain, 7 December 1901

As Mrs Fawcett and her colleagues were finishing their tour, Alfred Milner, the High Commissioner in South Africa wrote to his superior in London.

The camps were handed over to civilian administration and the death rate fell dramatically. By the time that peace was negotiated the death rate was 20 in every 1,000 refugees or 2 per cent. This was less than the average death rate in Glasgow.

What was the impact of the war on party politics?

In the autumn of 1900, the Conservative and Unionist government of Lord Salisbury sought to cash in on the patriotic fervour and its new-found popularity, following the occupation of the Transvaal. Lord Salisbury did so rather reluctantly and with a sense that it was not quite right to go to the country so much earlier than was necessary (i.e. parliaments lasted 7 years, not the 5 of today). In this sense it was a more gentlemanly world. It was Chamberlain who urged Salisbury to take advantage of circumstances and try to renew the large government majority of 1895. The government had not been popular before the war and had little to show in the way of legislative achievements. It had suffered a string of by-election defeats and had the Boer War not come along, the Liberals might have expected a sharp improvement in their fortunes compared to the drubbing they received in 1895.

In fact, the war had had a devastating effect on the Liberal Party, splitting it three ways into warring factions:

- A group of very senior figures around the former leader Lord Rosebery were dubbed Liberal Imperialists or LIMPS and these supported the war. They included the important figures of Herbert Asquith, Sir Edward Grey

SKILLS BUILDER

Study sources L, M, N and O.

1 How far do the individual natures of the four Sources strengthen the case against the camps?

and Lord Haldane, i.e. some of the most talented politicians on the Liberal front bench.

- A group of radicals like Lloyd George noisily opposed the war and were nick-named pro-Boers.
- In the middle and desperately trying to keep the party together was the rather uncharismatic figure of Sir Henry Campbell Bannerman.

In a vote in the Commons in July, 41 LIMPS supported the government, 29 pro-Boers voted against and the rest abstained. The Party was also short of cash and when the election was called the Liberals left 163 Unionist candidates unopposed. In London there were 3 paid Liberal agents compared to 30 for the Conservatives.

What was the outcome of the 'Khaki election'?

Parliament was dissolved on 18 September and the government supporters with Chamberlain in the lead made much of the war. For this reason and the fact that many Conservative candidates were serving officers, such as J.E.B. Seely (quoted above), it became known as the Khaki Election.

Source P

Chosen by Chamberlain:
'Every seat lost to the government was a seat gained by the Boers.'

Chosen by Winston Churchill
'Be it known that every vote given to the radicals means 2 pats on the back for Kruger and 2 smacks in the face for our country.'

Conservative Party slogans for the 1900 general election

The Liberals tended to concentrate their fire on Chamberlain, a hated figure since he had abandoned the Liberal Party in 1886 and fully thrown himself into the arms of Lord Salisbury in 1895. Lloyd George basically accused him of being a war profiteer. Chamberlain had family connections with the small armaments firm of Kynochs. In fact he had sold his shares in 1895 at a loss when taking office and his brother, Arthur Chamberlain, who was Chairman of the company was in fact a loyal Liberal and disliked his brother's new politics. The results justified the decision to go for an election:

- The Conservatives won 51 per cent of the vote and 402 MPs compared to 184 Liberals, 82 Irish Nationalists and 2 for Labour. They had a comfortable majority of 134.
- It was the first time since 1865 that a sitting majority government had won a second majority and it was the first time since 1832 that the Liberals had not won a majority in Scotland where the Conservative and Unionist Party did particularly well.

- In London, Lancashire and Birmingham the Conservative and Unionist Party cleaned up.

Despite the evidence of enthusiasm for the war, the turnout was low at 74.6 per cent. This is sometimes used to argue that popular enthusiasm did not really penetrate deeply into the working classes. Against this suggestion is the incontrovertible evidence of Conservative success in the large urban areas, referred to above.

Source Q

5.1 A cartoon from the *Westminster Gazette* by Frank Carruthers Gould which appeared on 18 September 1900

SKILLS BUILDER

In what ways does this cartoon display a pro-Liberal bias?

Unit summary

What have you learned in this unit?

In this unit you have learned about how the Boer War was reported and you have met a young Winston Churchill. You have studied in some detail the reaction to the Boer War in Britain. At the heart of the unit is the contrast between the feverish patriotism in favour of the war and the deep and often bitter opposition it produced. You have learned how this division had an impact on party politics, not least during the General Election of 1900.

What skills have you used in this unit?

You have evaluated source material including eyewitness accounts as part of your enquiry into the differing popular reactions to war. You have studied both primary and secondary accounts to assess the levels of support and opposition to the Boer War. In this unit you have studied and contrasted contemporary accounts of the reality of the concentration camp system in South Africa during the war.

SKILLS BUILDER

1 Arrange yourselves into groups of at least four students. Divide each group into two. After studying the evidence in this unit one team within your group is to produce a pro-Boer speech and one to produce an anti-war speech. Both speeches are to give full reasons for support and opposition.

2 Remind yourself of how the Crimean War was reported by re-reading Unit 1. Now read through the information on the reporting of the Boer War in this unit. What are the similarities and differences between the reporting of the two wars?

3 Which stance, the pro- or anti-war stance, do you most empathise with?

Exam style question

This is the sort of question you will find appearing on the examination paper as a (b) question.

Study Sources G, I and K and use your own knowledge.

Do you agree with the suggestion of Source G that there was overwhelming support for the Boer War from 1899 to 1902?

Exam tips

- Set up a spider diagram and, in the middle of the spider, explain the extent of support.
- Read Sources I and K carefully. Establish points that support and challenge the view and set those as spider 'legs'.
- Think about appropriate knowledge and add a note of this to the different spider 'legs', using knowledge to both reinforce and challenge. You are now ready to write up your answer.

Remember to:

- Combine the different points into arguments for and against the stated view.
- Evaluate the conflicting arguments by reference to the quality of the evidence used.
- Reach a supported judgement.

UNIT

6 The Boer War 1899–1902: what was its wider significance?

What is this unit about?

The aim of this unit is to consider the longer–term impact of the Boer War. The most obvious direct impact was on the army and it certainly stimulated a series of military reforms which bore fruit in 1914 when the First World War broke out. It produced sharply divergent views of empire and its value. It contributed to the 'national efficiency' debate stimulating social reform and an enhanced role for the state. By 1905 it could be seen as indirect influence, helping the Liberal Party and contributing to the Liberal election victory of January 1906. Clearly the strategic results in terms of Britain's position in the world needs some consideration and finally there is an attempt to summarise how it has been viewed subsequently.

Key questions

- In what ways and in what areas did the Boer War stimulate reform in Britain?
- What were the party political consequences of the Boer War in the years after 1902?

Timeline

1902		
	May	Peace of Vereeniging – Boers accept British Imperial sovereignty
1903		
	March	Committee of Imperial Defence established
1904		Esher Enquiry Report published and War Office reorganisation carried through
1906		
	January	Liberal landslide
1906–12		Haldane reforms of the army
1906–12		Various social reforms inspired by the concept of national efficiency
1906		Introduction of free school meals
1907		Medical inspections in schools
1911		National Health Insurance

Kipling summarised the popular perception of the War in a poem of 1902.

Source A

Let us admit it fairly as a business people should,
We have had no end of a lesson: it will do us no end of good.
So the more we work and the less we talk the better results we shall get.
We have had an Imperial lesson. It may make us an Empire yet.

An extract from 'The Lesson' by Rudyard Kipling 1902

What was the aftermath?

The lesson was perhaps expensive at 22,000 dead and over £200 million spent but it certainly induced a thorough shake-up of Britain's army:

- Heading the whole defence establishment and with the purpose of addressing the broad issues of the defence of the British Empire, the Committee of Imperial Defence was announced in March of 1903. Chaired by the prime minister and attended by both the political and service heads of the army and navy as well as the heads of the intelligence services, it was to give a much needed strategic direction to defence planning.

- To consider the lessons of the Boer War, Lord Salisbury established a Royal Commission under Lord Elgin in 1902. It reported in 1903 and recommended sweeping changes in the organisation of the army, notably the abolition of the post of Commander-in-Chief.

- One of the Royal Commission's members, Lord Esher was then appointed to make detailed recommendations on the reorganisation of the War Office. He took with him as secretary of his committee, the Royal Commission's secretary Lieutenant Colonel Gerald Ellison. Their contribution to reform of the army was considerable. Their report, known as the Esher Report, was published in February and March of 1904.

Source B

The importance of the Esher Report and its consequences can hardly be exaggerated. It coolly analysed the confusions and ineffectiveness of a military administration that had never been designed, but which had grown up piecemeal, with piecemeal demolitions and rebuilding, ever since 1660. It laid the foundations of the War Office organization and general staff system that has endured in essentials to the present time. Without the Esher report, and its acceptance by the government of the day, it is inconceivable that the mammoth British military efforts in two world wars could have been possible, let alone so generally successful.

The three essential recommendations of the Report were: an Army Council on the model of the Board of Admiralty; a general staff; and the division of departmental responsibilities inside the War Office on defined and logical principles.

An extract from *Britain and Her Army* by Correlli Barnett and published in 1970

How was the army reformed?

New administrative structures were put in place and changes were made to the way in which the army operated:

- The senior figure on the Army Council under the Secretary for War was the Chief of the General Staff in charge of planning and training. The Adjutant General was responsible for welfare and recruiting. The Quartermaster-General was responsible for supplies and transport and the Master General of the Ordnance for armaments and fortifications.
- Various changes were introduced at the same time directly affecting the life of the ordinary soldier and his capabilities. Khaki now became the standard peace-time dress instead of the Victorian scarlet and new weapons were introduced including a shortened Lee Enfield rifle and quick-firing field guns.
- Old drill books were replaced in 1904–05 and over the next few years, particularly under Douglas Haig as Director of Training, a new professionalism was inculcated in both officers and men.
- A new military base was established on Salisbury Plain and the Staff College at Camberley began to take the training of senior officers with a seriousness that matched the Prussian army.
- Various schemes were propounded for solving the crucial question of sufficient reserves and the need to produce a field force for service abroad while still retaining forces for domestic security.

It was not until the Liberals took office and **Richard Burton Haldane** was appointed War Minister that satisfactory solutions were developed and implemented. Haldane, an aristocratic, intelligent man, should rank as one of the great reforming cabinet ministers.

Source C

The National Army will, in future, consist of a Field Force and a Territorial or Home Force. The Field Force is to be completely organised as to be ready in all respects for mobilisation immediately on the outbreak of a great war. In that event the Territorial or home force would be mobilised also, but mobilised with a view to its undertaking in the first instance, systematic training for war.

An extract from a memorandum of R.B. Haldane on proposed military reform, published February 1907

So was born the British Expeditionary Force dispatched so quickly and efficiently to France in 1914 and the Territorials who were to hold the front there in 1915. The Territorials replaced the Militia and the Volunteers and were organised into field divisions complete with transport and artillery. They were still based around Cardwell's system of local regiments with the regulars normally forming the first two battalions and the Territorials, higher numbered ones. By 1910 there were 276,618 officers and men in the Territorial Army. The British Army that encountered that of the Kaiser in 1914 was incomparably superior to the one that had taken on the Boers in 1899. The lesson in this sense, as Kipling predicted 'had

Biography

Richard Burton Haldane 1856–1928

Haldane was a Liberal MP and minister. As Secretary of State for War from 1905–12 he reformed the British Army to the point that he is considered as one of the greatest military reformers in British history. He was a brilliant lawyer and amateur philosopher. It is interesting, given the debate about the effectiveness of General Douglas Haig as a military leader in the First World War, that Haldane chose him to help modernise the army.

done us no end of good'. The reform of the army was a key part of the drive for greater national efficiency which took on a broader meaning than simply national defence.

What was the drive to 'national efficiency?'

The Boer War certainly contributed to a growing sense of pessimism about Britain's position in the world in the new century. It did not create this, but underlined certain worries that had begun to emerge already in the 1890s. These worries centred on the competitiveness of British industry, the quality of education and the health of the people.

Source D

National concern for health was awakened by army recruitment during the Boer War which showed the poor physical condition of working men in towns. At Manchester in 1899 three out of five volunteers were rejected as physically unfit. Seebohm Rowntree in his study of poverty noted that of 3600 recruits seeking enlistment at York, Leeds and Sheffield between 1897 and 1900, 26.5% were rejected as unfit and a further 29% were only accepted as 'specials,' in the hope that a few months of army life would bring them up to standard – and this at a time when in order to obtain the required number of men, the army standards of health and physical development had been repeatedly lowered. These findings were confirmed by an interdepartmental Committee on Physical Deterioration which reported in 1904 and sparked off a good deal of talk about the 'decline of the race' and the need for reforms along eugenicist and social Darwinist lines. National efficiency and Britain's imperialist future were alleged to be in jeopardy.

From J.F.C. Harrison *Late Victorian Britain* published in 1990

Such concerns contributed to the spate of social reforms introduced by the Liberal governments of Campbell-Bannerman and Asquith (see timeline on page 89). It was particularly influential in securing the School Meals Act of 1906 and the provision of the medical inspection of children the next year. The National Insurance Act of 1911 with its provision of health insurance was also influenced by these concerns with the well-being of the British working class.

All three of these measures significantly enlarged the role of the state. They took some of the responsibility from the individual or the individual's family for health. The introduction of free school meals was particularly controversial and seemed to mark a seismic shift in the relationship of the state and the family. Clearly a large number of the other reforms such as the introduction of Old Age Pensions had little to do with the Boer War, except in the ways referred to on pages 94–5 of how reaction to the war helped the Liberals to take power with such a large majority.

How did the war change attitudes to Empire and Imperialism?

The Boer War produced complex and contradictory responses in terms of attitudes to Empire. On the one hand the struggle can be seen as stimulating patriotism and pride in the Empire. The war had after all been won. The great anthem of national self congratulation and trumpet blowing was composed in 1902 with words by an Eton schoolmaster, A.C. Benson, and music by Edward Elgar. It became a second national anthem.

Source E

Dear Land of Hope, thy hope is crowned.
God make thee mightier yet!
On Sov'ran brows, beloved, renowned,
Once more thy crown is set.
Thine equal laws, by Freedom gained,
Have ruled thee well and long;
By Freedom gained, by Truth maintained,
Thine Empire shall be strong.

Land of Hope and Glory, Mother of the Free,
How shall we extol thee, who are born of thee?
Wider still and wider, shall thy bounds be set;
God who made thee mighty, make thee mightier yet.

Land of Hope and Glory by A.C. Benson, 1902

Periodicals like the *Boy's Own Paper,* founded in the late nineteenth century remained popular and *Union Jack* was re-founded in 1903. They offered a diet of nationalism wedded to decency and pride in the British Empire as a force for good. The popular children's author G.A. Henty died in 1902 but his patriotic tales shaped many an Edwardian schoolboy's vision of the world and Britain's superior place in it. The poetry of Sir Henry Newbolt, who was at school with Douglas Haig, remained especially popular.

Source F

The sand of the desert is sodden red
Red with the wreck of the square that broke
The gatling's jammed and the colonel's dead
And the regiments' blind with dust and smoke
The river of death has brimmed its banks
And England's far and honour's a name
But the voice of a schoolboy rallies the ranks
Play up! Play up! And play the game.

Verse 2 of *Vitai Lampada* (They Pass on the Torch of Life), Sir Henry Newbolt, 1897

SKILLS BUILDER

What are the similarities in tone, content and implication between Sources E and F?

Newbolt published new anthologies of patriotic verse in 1904 and 1910 which were well received. Clearly there were many who shared the sentiments of heroic patriotism and belief in the civilising mission of the British Empire. The extraordinary popularity of Baden Powell's new youth movement, the Boy Scouts, might also be taken as pointing in the same direction.

Definition

Tariff Reform

Tariff Reform was the key issue in the general election of January 1906. Chamberlain won over a majority of the Conservative Party to support the imposition of duties on imported goods from outside the Empire, thus Canadian wheat would be cheaper than wheat imported from the USA. The Liberals opposed this, portraying it as an attack on the traditional cheap food policy of Britain and thus harmful to the living standards of the working classes.

SKILLS BUILDER

Summarise the main points of Source G in your own words.

Joseph Chamberlain felt that the Boer War offered new opportunities to strengthen the Empire. He, like many others, had been impressed by the support voluntarily provided by the Dominions and wished to seize the moment to bring the Empire closer together by creating a British Imperial free trade area. Hence arose his campaign for **Tariff Reform** a year after the war ended. It split the Conservative Party, driving some MPs, including the newly elected Churchill and Seely, into the Liberal Party and contributed to the Conservative election disaster in 1906.

How did the war lead to criticism of Empire?

If the Boer War encouraged greater enthusiasm for Empire in some, it also stimulated fierce criticism of Imperialism. The most important of these critics was J.A. Hobson, a Liberal writer who served as correspondent in South Africa for the *Manchester Guardian* during the Boer War. He published a highly influential book in 1902, the same year as *Land of Hope and Glory* appeared. The message of his *Imperialism: A Study* was very different to that of *Land of Hope and Glory*.

Source G

Hobson argued that mal-distribution of wealth at home meant that domestic markets were characterized by under-consumption. Since excess savings could not be profitably invested in these artificially saturated markets at home, they were forced to seek less dependable outlets overseas. This new imperialism was manipulated by parasitic interests: arms manufacturers and shippers, aristocrats anxious to find jobs for less talented sons in military or colonial civil services or as planters, ranchers, or missionaries. Co-ordinating their activities were international financiers whose interests were only indirectly responsive to British interests. But while only a narrow coterie [group] benefited from Empire, its costs were borne by the nation as a whole.

From Nicholas Owen *The Oxford History of the British Empire Volume IV* published in 1999

Hobson's interpretation that Imperialism was a by-product of capitalism was very influential among Left-leaning British writers and politicians. It had a considerable impact on a wider audience throughout the world and was adopted by Lenin, the leader of the Bolshevik Party in Russia. Hobson was eventually to argue that capitalism through Imperialism inevitably produced conflict and hence Imperialism was responsible for the First World War. While many British followers of Hobson did not go as far as Lenin in adopting such a sweeping and essentially simplistic view, the opinion became widely held that Empire brought benefits only to the few and even damaged the interests of the majority. This was to have some influence in helping to produce the electoral sea-change that took place in January 1906 when the Khaki election was totally reversed and the vast Liberal majority was elected. This is not to say that large numbers of voters had read Hobson but the ideas seeped downwards that the Boer War had cost much, gone on much longer after the government claimed that it was all over and finally led to the scandal of **Chinese slavery**.

What were the strategic results of the Boer War?

The war had been fought to ensure British control of southern Africa, the Cape being deemed vital to Imperial security. All Boer prisoners on release had to sign the following declaration (see Source H).

Source H

I . . . . adhere to the terms of the agreement signed at Pretoria on 31 May 1902, between my late government and representatives of His Majesty's government. I acknowledge myself to be a subject of King Edward VII, and I promise to own allegiance to him, his heirs, and successors according to law.

The Oath of Allegiance (to be taken by all POWs before returning to South Africa)

Insofar as it did create a loyal, British Imperial South Africa, the war was a success:

- Milner resigned in March 1905 and the new Liberal government which came to power in Britain in December of that year was anxious to promote reconciliation.
- Paul Kruger's place was taken by younger Boers prepared to work within the Empire.
- Two of their leaders during the war, Louis Botha and Jan Smuts, formed a political party entitled *Het Volk* (The People) in 1905.
- In December 1906, Campbell-Bannerman's government introduced self-government for the two conquered states and Louis Botha was elected Prime Minister of the Transvaal in February 1907.
- Two years later in 1909 the British parliament passed the South Africa Bill establishing the Union of South Africa in 1910 as a self governing Dominion like Australia and Canada.
- In the First and Second World Wars South Africa supported Britain against Germany and South African troops showed great bravery defending the Empire. The Cape was vital to British security in both wars. Jan Smuts, like Botha eventually became Prime Minister of the new South Africa. Once an irreconcilable Boer nationalist and military leader, he was to became one of Churchill's favourite and most trusted advisers in the Second World War.

Part of the price of this reconciliation was the betrayal of the hopes of the non-white population of South Africa. Non-whites were banned from sitting in the new South African Parliament and the basic civil rights of Asian, African and Coloured communities were neglected. This aspect of the Boer War and its consequences received more and more attention as the twentieth century progressed.

Definition

Chinese slavery

This became a major issue in the election of 1906. Milner approved the importing of Chinese indentured labourers into South Africa to help repair the damage done during the war. The labourers were not slaves but were bound by the terms of the contract to work off the cost of their passage. Labour and Liberal politicians likened them to slaves. British workers resented their use as being likely to under-cut wages.

Source I

Africa is still a land of surprises! I wonder what I would have said if anyone twelve years ago had predicted to me that I would, in a few year's time be a British General!

One thing I am particularly thankful for, and that is that men like Churchill and yourself, as well as myself and others who were actively engaged in the war, have been given an opportunity of healing the wounds then inflicted and of preparing the way for a cordial understanding between the races on a basis of mutual respect and confidence.

You would be surprised to see the effects of my conciliation policy and witness the cordial cooperation between Briton and Boer today.

An extract from a letter from Louis Botha, a former Boer Commander and now Prime Minister of South Africa, to Colonel Seely, Secretary of State for War in Asquith's cabinet, 6 September 1912

SKILLS BUILDER

Study Sources H and I.

1 How far do these two sources suggest that the British were successful in winning the loyalty of the defeated Boer population in the ten years after the Boer War?

2 Which of the two do you consider the more useful for a historian investigating the impact of the Boer War?

How has the Boer War been judged?

Almost from the first studies of the war, such as the *The Times History of the War in South Africa, 1899–1902* by L.S. Amery published between 1900 and 1909, the focus tended to be on British military incompetence and the need for reform. This has tended to produce some distortion and some unfairness to the reputation of soldiers such as General Sir Redvers Buller. He certainly made mistakes initially but he learned from them and, as indicated above, finally conducted an almost text-book campaign in Natal and the eastern Transvaal in 1900, ending in victory, which has been largely overlooked. The press and even historians like to divide humanity into heroes and villains, the competent and the incompetent, rather than accept the muddy mix of the two which tends to be reality. A highly influential book on military incompetence written by Norman Dixon, a Professor of Psychology, and published in 1976 has a unit on the Boer War. Dixon's analysis tends to reflect the prevailing view although there are those who disagree.

Source J

Never has a nation been more wrong-headed in its selection of a general. Never has a general been more disastrous in the execution of his duties. Like Raglan, Buller had no experience of commanding a large body of men. For the previous decade he had held a number of different posts in the War Office. According to contemporary accounts he was bereft of creative imagination and totally lacking in discrimination. He was also without the gift of intuition which impels a good general to choose the right course of action.

From Norman Dixon *On the Psychology of Military Incompetence* published in 1976

Source K

Lessons were learnt the hard way, Buller's final attack over the Tugela at Colenso providing a model which unfortunately was seldom followed in the First World War. In spite of justified criticism of his conduct of the previous battles, Buller deserves more credit as a commander than he has generally received.'

From Field Marshall Lord Carver *Britain's Army in the Twentieth Century* published in 1998

SKILLS BUILDER

Study sources J and K.

In what ways do the two opinions of Buller differ and what might explain these differences?

More recently there has been a shift away from the military debate or even the moral debate concerning the concentration camps to a concern for the impact on the majority black population of South Africa. As early as 1979, a major study of the war drew attention to this phenomenon.

Source L

What of the black majority? Perhaps the worst legacy of the war was the political price it exacted from Africans to pay for white unity.

Bringing two new states into the Empire made urgent the need to reconcile the white communities. The war made that process a great deal more difficult. It has taken seventy six years and is not fully accomplished. And, in the end, the grand design defeated itself. The two half-reconciled communities left the Empire. And the price of trying to reconcile the whites was paid by the blacks and browns. In fact, the end result of Milner's destruction of the old republics was not only to lose the two old colonies, too, but to cast away that priceless Liberal legacy: the no-colour bar tradition of the Cape.

From Thomas Packenham *The Boer War* published 1979

Conclusion

Undoubtedly the Boer War contributed to a major fault line in British attitudes and prejudices. It either created or reinforced the intellectual contempt and disdain displayed by the left-wing intelligentsia for the military. They in consequence returned the disdain and contempt with a belief that those not involved at the sharp end could not understand the practical problems of war, much of which turned on feeding and moving large bodies of men. The impact of the war, in terms of practical changes and in changing and reinforcing attitudes should not be underestimated.

Unit summary

What have you learned in this unit?

You have learned that the Boer War had a considerable impact politically and otherwise. It very much influenced the course of general elections in Britain, both in 1900 and 1906. The administrative and organisational changes introduced in the wake of war were to have an important impact on the effectiveness of Britain's military. Perhaps above all else you have learned that the Boer War was to have a profound impact on attitudes to Empire, both in Britain and South Africa.

What skills have you used in this unit?

You have used a range of source material to explore the issues surrounding the impact of the Boer War. The evaluation of a range of primary and secondary sources will have led you to understand that the impact of the Boer War was immediate and far reaching. You will have used sources dealing with the differing attitudes to Empire. A study of sources relating to the reputation of the British military will have helped you understand differences in interpretation.

Exam style question

Study Sources A, B and D and use your own knowledge.

How far do you agree with the opinion that the Boer War acted as a spur to much needed reform in Britain?

SKILLS BUILDER

1 Class debate. Given all of the information studied in this unit and previous units, would you consider Sir Redvers Buller to be an essentially competent or incompetent General?

2 Discussion point. You have dealt with quite a few secondary sources in this unit some with conflicting interpretations. Why and how do some of the sources in this unit give such differing opinions?

3 Essay question. To what extent was the reorganization of Britain's armed forces the most significant consequence of the Boer War?

Exam tips

The structure of the question is different from the (b) questions you have worked on previously in the 'exam style question' sections. This time the 'view' isn't contained in one of the sources but is given in the question.

You will see that the two sources (B and D) are quite densely written. This means that they will need very careful reading.

Think carefully about what each source says about the impact of the Boer War and jot this down. You will need to refer to these notes when you make your plan. Now draw up your plan.

Analyse all three sources for points that support and points that challenge the view that the Boer War acted as a spur to much needed reform in Britain. Cross-reference between the sources for points of agreement and disagreement.

Use your wider knowledge both to reinforce and to challenge the points you have derived from the sources.

Combine the points into an argument for or against the view given in the question.

Evaluate the conflicting arguments by considering the quality of the evidence used.

Reach a balanced, supported conclusion.

7 The First World War 1914–18: how and why was it fought?

What is this unit about?

The purpose of this unit is to try to explain why and how Britons fought the First World War on land in Europe, on what became known as the Western Front between August 1914 and November 1918. The difficulty of this lies in achieving brevity in a task of such complexity. Thereafter, a summary of the war is offered with a focus on a series of key questions.

Key questions

- How did a war of movement change in 1914 into trench warfare?
- How did the rapidly expanding British Army seek to defeat the Germans in the great positional battles of 1916 and 1917?
- What contribution did the British Army make to the defeat of Germany in 1918?

Timeline

1914

August	Britain declares war on Germany and sends over the BEF to France
September	The Miracle of the Marne – Paris saved – war of attrition begins
October	First Battle of Ypres virtually destroys old regular units

1915

April	Build up of BEF – supporting battles fought to assist French offensives
	Second Battle of Ypres
	First successful gas attack
May	Shell shortage scandal
September	Battle of Loos

1916

February	German attack on Verdun begins
1 July	First day of the Battle of the Somme
September	Tanks first used at Flers

1917

April	Battle of Arras – Canadians capture Vimy Ridge
June	Capture of Messiness Ridge by 2nd Army
July	Opening of Third Battle of Ypres
November	Capture of Passchendaele Ridge ends Third Ypres
	Battle of Cambrai – use of massed tanks

1918

March	First of German offensives strikes British 5th Army
April	Second German offensive on the Lys near Ypres
May	Third German attack – from the Aisne to the Marne
August	Battle of Amiens – 'the Black Day of the German Army'
September	Break through the Hindenburg Line
November	Armistice

For many the outbreak of war in 1914 was a release. The following extract comes from a poem written by Rupert Brooke. Brooke saw action at Antwerp in 1914 as a member of the Royal Naval Division. He died in April 1915 on the way to Gallipoli.

Source A

Now, God be thanked Who has matched us with His hour,
And caught our youth, and wakened us from sleeping,
With hand made sure, clear eye, and sharpened power,
To turn, as swimmers into cleanness leaping,
Glad from a world grown old and cold and weary,
Leave the sick hearts that honour could not move,
And half-men, and their dirty songs and dreary,
And all the little emptiness of love!

Oh! we, who have known shame, we have found release there,
Where there's no ill, no grief, but sleep has mending,
Naught broken save this body, lost but breath;
Nothing to shake the laughing heart's long peace there
But only agony, and that has ending;
And the worst friend and enemy is but Death.

From Rupert Brooke 'Peace' written in 1914

SKILLS BUILDER

What are Brooke's attitudes to war and peace as represented in this poem?

What were the causes of war?

Reasons why Britain did not go to war

Perhaps it is convenient to start by dealing with some widely believed but essentially wrong-headed notions of why Britain went to war in August 1914.

- War was not an antidote to domestic pressures in Ireland or arising from industrial disputes which had been such features of 1912 and 1913. The wave of strikes was dying down and far from the government seeing war as a solution, they feared that interruption to food supplies might intensify class struggle. Two divisions were held back in Britain in case of unrest.

- Nor was war urged on the government by capitalists who saw it as a means of profit. The City of London panicked at the prospect of war and the Governor of the Bank of England pleaded with David Lloyd George to keep out of the coming conflict.

- Nor was it a result of German economic competition. Britain was Germany's best customer but Germany was Britain's second best and taking financial services into account, Britain had a favourable balance of trade. The growth of the German economy had benefited Britain and in particular the City of London.

- Nor was war caused by Imperial rivalry, the cause made so much of by Lenin. All Imperial disputes with Germany had been peacefully settled as they had been for the past thirty years. In one important sense it was the ending of Imperial competition that brought attention back to Europe and it was here that the trouble lay.

Why go to war?

Rightly or wrongly, by 1914 many influential Britons in the Foreign Office, parliament and elsewhere had come to believe that Germany was bidding for European domination:

- If France were to be defeated, Germany would accomplish European domination and British interests would suffer. Germany's behaviour over the previous decade had given rise to this perception.

- Aggressive diplomatic initiatives and speeches by the Kaiser, the building of a large navy when Germany already possessed the strongest army in Europe, all contributed to this impression.

- War was not inevitable but the crisis of July/August 1914 was badly handled, particularly by Germany, who added to the impression of aggression. Germany declared war on Russia and then declared war on France, Russia's ally.

- To get at France, the one military plan the Germans had (the Schlieffen Plan) dictated that they should first march through neutral Belgium. This enabled the British government to carry an almost united country into war. To hard-headed calculations about the balance of power in Europe, which probably meant little to most people, there could now be added the emotional issue of 'Gallant little Belgium' standing up to the bullying German. Britain also had a legal fig-leaf in a treaty of 1839, in which she had guaranteed Belgium's neutrality. On 4 August Britain declared war on Germany.

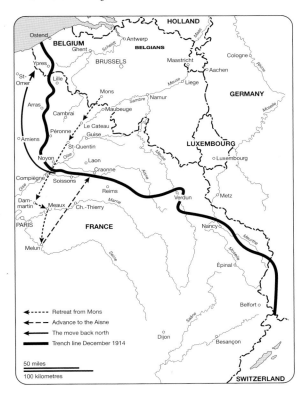

7.1 Map of the Western Front in 1914

Sir John French
1852–1925

Sir John French was a cavalry officer who had made a reputation for himself in the Boer War as an aggressive column commander. He was not a success in commanding a much larger body of troops in France where he was often timid and uncertain. He enjoyed atrocious personal relations with one of his Corps commanders, Sir Horace Smith Dorrien, who might have been a better choice as Commander in Chief. French had Smith Dorrien sacked in 1915. The result of this was that when French himself was replaced in December 1915, it was by the other Corps commander Sir Douglas Haig.

How and why did trench warfare evolve in 1914?

The scene is set

Four British infantry divisions and a cavalry division, 80,000 men, 30,000 horses and 315 guns were rapidly dispatched to France. It became known as the British Expeditionary Force, or BEF for short. Transporting ships sailed at ten-minute intervals from Portsmouth and Southampton. The whole army under **Sir John French** concentrated around the town of Maubeuge near the Belgian frontier on 20 August. It was placed on the left of the much larger French forces under General Lanrezac. Facing the British and the French were three enormous German armies which were the swinging hammerhead of the German attack through Belgium. Heading straight for the British was the German 1st Army of Von Kluck, composed of 320,000 men. Von Kluck did not know the British were in his path and the British did not appreciate the scale of the forces they were about to encounter. The neighbouring German 2nd Army under Von Bulow crashed into Lanrezac's forces on the Sambre River and as a third German army began to threaten its eastern flank, Lanrezac decided to retreat.

Mons

As the French began to retreat the British had nudged forwards into Belgium, and around the coal-mining town of Mons fought their first battle of the war against the vastly superior forces of Von Kluck. The battle was a replay of the early battles of the Boer War with this time the British playing the part of the sharp-shooting Boers.

Source B

Well entrenched and completely hidden, the enemy opened a murderous fire. The casualties increased, the rushes became shorter and finally the whole advance stopped. With bloody losses the attack gradually came to an end.

From *Die Schlacht bei Mons* (The Battle of Mons) published by the German General Staff 1919

Source C

Reports coming back along the column seemed to confirm the fact that the English were in front of us. English soldiers? There was much joking about this and about Bismarck's well known remark (back in 1864) of sending the police to arrest the English army but by the end of the day the men were chilled to the bone almost too exhausted to move and with the depressing consciousness of defeat weighing upon them. A bad defeat, there could be no gainsaying it; in our first battle we had been badly beaten and by the English – by the English that we had laughed at a few hours before.

From Walter Bloem *The Advance from Mons 1914* published in an English translation in 1930. Bloem was a Captain in the Imperial German Army and wrote this memoir after the war.

SKILLS BUILDER

1 What are the strengths and weaknesses to an historian investigating the Battle of Mons of using German sources such as Sources B and C?

The BEF paid a price. There were 1,600 casualties and as it became clear that the French were retreating on their right the British Army began to pull back too in what became part of a general 150-mile retreat to the River Marne where a new French Army was beginning to form. Morale inevitably began to suffer but on 5 September, the miracle of the Marne began when the French Commander-in-Chief, Field Marshal Joffre, launched a counterattack.

What was the 'race to the sea'?

The Germans had advanced with their strongest forces into a growing bulge in the French line but the line had not broken and as the Germans passed east and south of Paris they were open to a flank counterattack from the capital:

- Fearing encirclement, the German Commander-in-Chief, Field Marshal Von Moltke lost his nerve and ordered his armies to pull back to a defensive line to the north on the River Aisne.

- The BEF now began to advance after the retreating Germans but neither they nor the French could push them back from their new positions on the Aisne. Here trench warfare began.

- The Allies tried to outflank them by moving round the German's right wing. The Germans responded by trying to outflank the French and the line of conflict slowly snaked north-westwards towards the south-west corner of Belgium, where the remnants of the Belgian army was holding out.

- The decision was taken to move the BEF by rail northwards to the Belgian city of Ypres, where it could assist the small Belgian army to cling on to a corner of their country and the BEF would be closer to the channel ports and easier to supply.

- Reinforcements had been sent over to France from England and the year ended with a struggle around the city of Ypres. The German high command decided to throw everything into a last ditch push to reach the channel ports and, on 20 October 1914, launched the First Battle of Ypres. The battle was a bloodbath: many of the German troops were composed of newly enlisted enthusiastic students. First Ypres came to be known in Germany as *Kindermord vom Ypern* (the Massacre of the Innocents at Ypres). The BEF held on to Ypres but at a terrible price of over 50,000 casualties.

The British losses at the First Battle of Ypres are summarised by Sir Anthony Farrar-Hockley in the following source. Farrar-Hockley was a senior British officer of much experience in the Second World War and a noted author on military history.

Source D

The 8th Division arrived and with the 7th, reconstituted IV Corps under Rawlinson. Soon the whole Expeditionary Force was settled in behind the line from Ploegsteert wood to La Bassee. No; not the whole Expeditionary Force. It would never be whole in the original sense again. Typical of its battalions, 2nd Highland Light Infantry was relieved on November 16th by the French. Out of all the officers and men mobilised at Aldershot a bare three months before, there were now scarcely thirty left.

From A.H. Farrar-Hockley *Ypres 1914: Death of an Army* published in 1967

By the end of the year, the German thrust into France had been held but much of northern France and most of Belgium was occupied by the Germans. A line of trenches, increasingly complex and fortified with barbed wire, stretched from the Channel just north-east of Dunkirk to the Swiss border. There was now no possibility of turning a flank. A head-on assault was the only option. The BEF had expanded despite the casualties and by the end of 1914 numbered 245,197 men and in addition there were divisions from the Indian Army.

What happened in 1915?

The Second Battle of Ypres

Despite the expansion, the British Army was still very much the junior to the French throughout 1915. It continued to expand steadily but there were acute shortages of shells and heavy guns. The new armies raised at the start of the war took time to train and prepare and British Secretary of State for War, Lord Kitchener was determined not to use them too soon:

- Territorial divisions arrived in France and a Canadian Division. These were to hold the Germans in the Second Battle of Ypres in the spring.
- Poisoned gas added a new unpleasant way of dying and nearly enabled the Germans to break through but the line held around the shattered remnants of the old Belgian town.
- The British assisted the French in their costly assaults on the German trenches and Festubert and Loos added new roll calls of the dead and missing.
- Troops were required for new theatres of war, Gallipoli, Iraq and Egypt, against the Ottoman Empire which had joined Germany. By January of 1916 there were 60 infantry divisions overseas, 12 regular, 17 Territorial,

30 New Army and a Royal Naval Division. Britain had become a major military power and in 1916 would begin to take the lead in the assault on Germany.

Perhaps the most famous poem of the war appeared in 1915. It had been written during the Second Battle of Ypres, in the spring, by a Canadian doctor John McRae. It was published in *Punch* magazine in December 1915.

Source E

In Flanders fields the poppies blow
Between the crosses, row on row
That mark our place; and in the sky
The larks, still bravely singing, fly
Scarce heard amid the guns below.

We are the Dead. Short days ago
We lived, felt dawn, saw sunset glow,
Loved and were loved, and now we lie
In Flanders fields.

Take up our quarrel with the foe;
To you from failing hands we throw
The torch; be yours to hold it high.
If ye break faith with us who die
We shall not sleep, though poppies grow
In Flanders fields.

'In Flanders Fields' by John McRae, 1915

SKILLS BUILDER

1 How does the impression of war given by McRae compare with that given by Rupert Brooke in Source A?

2 Suggest some reasons for why the impressions of war might differ in the two poems.

What were the issues facing the British Army in 1916?

In December, a new commander-in-chief of the BEF had been appointed. General Sir Douglas Haig had replaced Sir John French, who had paid the price for the costly failure at Loos. Haig had worked closely with Haldane in shaping the reformed British Army after the Boer War, and now commanded the largest military force Britain had ever sent overseas. Before any educated judgement can be made as to Haig's qualities it is essential to appreciate the problems he faced.

Logistics

Haig eventually commanded five armies, each composed of hundreds of thousands of men. These needed feeding, moving, welfare and leisure provision and medical services. Vast munitions dumps had to be created and supervised. In one 24-hour period in 1918, in a small area on the Western Front, 943,947 shells were fired. In 1915 there had been severe shortages of both shells and heavy guns and even in 1916 there were still far too few of the really heavy calibre guns and howitzers. Haig was a cavalry officer in origin but he fully appreciated the vital role of artillery and eventually produced the most sophisticated and massive artillery corps that was to crack the German lines. In 1916 this was in the process of creation.

Defeating the Germans

The blood-letting on the Western Front was primarily the result of advances in the technology of war. No General in any army had a ready solution to the problems that had been thrown up:

- Smokeless powder, machine guns, rapidly firing, accurate artillery all gave an advantage to the defence. A machine gun could fire a hundred thousand rounds in less than the summer hours of daylight.

- By the end of 1915, the Germans had constructed an increasingly complex series of trench fortifications across northern France and southern Belgium. These could be several miles in depth and studded with strong-points at strategic locations.

- The Germans were on the defensive, occupying much of industrial France. To win, they only had to stay there. The French and British had to attack and attacking cost lives.

- A whole series of interlocking problems presented themselves to the attacker. How to cut the barbed wire so plentifully in use? The answer was the high explosive shell that exploded as it struck the ground. The invention of fuse 106 was crucial in enabling this to happen. Unfortunately most of the shells in 1916 were not equipped with fuse 106, but were of small calibre and filled with metal fragments designed to kill troops in the open.

- Another problem was that the enemies' artillery had to be silenced, first finding it, miles behind the front line, and then accurately hitting it. Eventually flash spotters and microphones were used to fix the enemy using sound waves. A young Nobel Prize winning physicist, Lawrence Bragg, played a useful part in achieving this, but this solution lay in 1917.

- The artillery had to be used to silence machine gun posts and suppress the fire from enemy trenches but as the bombardment ceased the enemy knew an attack was coming and rushed from their places of shelter, setting up their machine guns before the infantry could over-run them. The answer was to be the creeping barrage with the infantry advancing closely behind a wall of shells but this took incredible sophistication to perfect, requiring excellent observation and communication. It was the latter which was the real bane of First World War commanders. Telephone lines were used but were constantly being cut by shell fire. Runners were killed and the result was that commanders at all levels operated in a fog that meant that control of the situation was usually impossible. Eventually radio communication would vastly improve the situation but this was not widely in use in 1916.

Wherever technology appeared to offer a promising solution to the multitude of problems, Haig embraced it, whether this was fuse 106, the tank or the aeroplane. There were however, no easy solutions. Newly trained soldiers would have to learn with their commander how to discover answers.

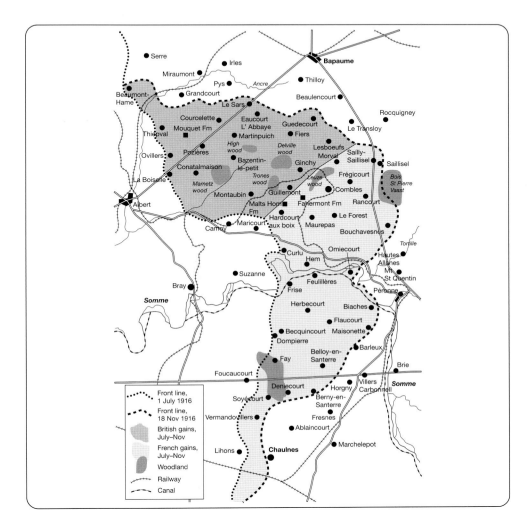

7.2 Map of the Somme in 1916

What happened on the Somme, 1916?

In 1916 the allies determined to coordinate their attacks on Germany. Russia, France and Britain would attack at the same time to prevent the German High Command moving reserves from one threatened area to another.

- The British and French decided on a joint offensive and this determined the place, the Somme, near the city of Amiens, where the two armies met. But the Germans struck first at the French around the ancient city of Verdun. From February they launched a murderous assault on the French **salient** with the primary object of bleeding France to defeat. The effect was to reduce the French contribution to the Somme offensive, which now became a primarily British affair.

Definition

Salient

A salient is a military term for a part of the line which juts into enemy held territory so that it is semi-surrounded and vulnerable to attack. The two most famous salients were Verdun, held by the French and Ypres held by the BEF.

- However, it became all the more urgent to launch the attack to relieve pressure on the French at Verdun. Haig placed General Rawlinson of the 4th Army in charge of the attack, which was to be along a 27,000 yard front and involve 14 divisions. Many of the units were New Army divisions, filled with enthusiastic volunteers.

The first day

For seven days before the attack there was a massive bombardment of the German lines, the theory being that this would cut the wire and eliminate any effective resistance. One and a half million shells were fired but one million of these were shrapnel, not high explosive and not effective at killing or immobilising men in sheltered dug-outs. In addition, many of the shells were duds with poor fuses. The result was that 1 July, the day of the infantry attack, was largely a disaster. This was particularly true at the northern end of the battlefield. The assault on the German-held village of Beaumont Hamel became the stuff of tragic legend. The 1st Battalion, Essex Regiment, was virtually wiped out in the initial early morning attack at 7.30 a.m. The supporting 1st Newfoundland Regiment was also destroyed suffering a 91 per cent casualty rate.

Source F

We knew at 7.30 that the assault had started through hearing the murderous rattle of German machine guns, served without a break, notwithstanding our intense bombardment which had been expected to silence them. The fire from these guns periodically sprayed the crest above our head. Towards 7.45 the West Yorkshire began moving forward down the gentle slope into the furnace. Apparently they advanced across the open – I saw those near me climb out of their trench. The enemy's machine guns, some 1400 yards from my position, now swept the crest like a hurricane and with such accuracy that many of the poor fellows were shot at once. This battalion had 280 casualties in traversing the 600 yards to our front line.

A little after 8 o'clock it became our turn to go forward. I decided that we had better go by the shell blasted communication trenches rather than across the open ground. Round one traverse I came on three Yorkshiremen, two of them shattered, the third sitting quite naturally, but dead. About 8.30 a.m. I reached the front trench, then occupied by various parties belonging to the battalions preceding us, and by one company of the West Yorkshire, together with wounded who had been able to return from the hellish area ahead. From the news I could glean it appeared to be highly improbable that any of the Middlesex, Devons or West Yorks were in action beyond No Man's Land. No communication with them, however was possible.

The sun had now dispersed the morning haze and the day promised to be warm. On the upward slope behind us lay many bodies of the West Yorkshire. No Man's Land was strewn with prone forms; up against the hostile wire they showed thickly. Not all of these were casualties, however; among them were men driven out of the German trenches and taking what cover they could in the shell holes amid the long grass decked with sunlit scarlet poppies on our side of the enemies' wire entanglements. These men remained still as the dead to avoid drawing fire till darkness should screen their escape; others not so patient would make a dash singly or crawl patiently towards our trenches sniped at on the way.

From J.L. Jack *Trench Diary* published after his death in 1964. Jack was a company commander and second in command of the 2nd Battalion Cameronians. Here he is writing about the events of 1 July 1916 when his battalion was in a supporting role for the assault towards La Boiselle, just south of Beaumont Hamel.

It has been described as the worst day in British military history. Yet further south the British XIII and XV Corps were more successful as were the French. Out of the 120,000 British troops taking part, over 57,000 were casualties and over 19,000 died. The first day came to embody the whole Somme battle although this was to last until well into November.

Source G

To the British, it was and would remain their greatest military tragedy of the twentieth century, indeed of their national military history. The regiments of Pals and Chums which had their first experience of war on the Somme have been called an army of innocents and that, in their readiness to offer up their lives in circumstances none anticipated in the heady days of volunteering it undoubtedly was. Whatever harm Kitchener's volunteers wished the Germans, it is the harm they thereby suffered that remains in British memory, collectively but also among the families of those who did not return. There is nothing more poignant in British life than to visit the ribbon of cemeteries that mark the front line of 1 July 1916 and to find on gravestones, the fresh wreath, the face of a Pal or Chum above a khaki serge collar staring gravely back from a dim photograph, the pinned poppy and the inscription 'to a father, a grandfather and a great-grandfather.' The Somme marked the end of a vital optimism in British life that has never returned.

From John Keegan *The First World War* published in 1998

What were the successes of the Somme battle?

The Somme battle continued on after 1 July and the British struggled forward with renewed assaults. The infantry learned new tricks and the integration of weapons systems with tactics. On 15 September, Haig employed a surprise, the tank. It had enormous local success with an advance of 3,500 yards achieved. However, most tanks broke down that day and at 2 miles per hour were not as yet 'war winning' weapons. The Royal Flying Corps had rapidly expanded and achieved a superiority over the German air-force during the Somme battle. The Germans counter-attacked every allied gain and lost vast numbers of men in the process. Although the whole assault finally ground to a halt in November in appalling weather and mud without any breakthrough, some historians view the overall conflict in a positive light for the BEF although German losses on the Somme were roughly equal to the combined British and French losses, i.e. c.600,000 casualties. Two-thirds of these casualties on the allied side were British.

Source H

Haig's initial attempt to achieve a breakthrough on 1st July was a failure. The battle that developed was nonetheless a success for the British Army. In February and March 1917, the Germans abandoned their positions on the old Somme battlefield, methodically carrying out a scorched earth policy as they did so. This was in part an acknowledgement of British success on the Somme; the German army was not prepared to endure another such defensive battle on that ground.

While the Somme weakened the German army, the BEF gained experience and improved its tactics. Commanders at all levels could certainly have conducted the battle more effectively and thus saved lives. Yet unpalatable as it may seem, it is difficult to avoid the conclusion that the Somme was an essential precondition to success in the last two years of the war

From Gary Sheffield *Forgotten Victory: The First World War – myths and realities* published in 2001

It is interesting to view the battle through German eyes.

Source I

The gigantic dimensions of the Battle of the Somme have put the events of the war before 1 July 1916 so much in the shade that in Britain they reckon that the real war began only from that time. The main reason is that it was the time when Britain first came to grips with its real enemy, Germany. Most of the front-line soldiers too are extremely proud of what they have achieved so far. Again and again we hear from prisoners the self-satisfied question; 'Don't you think we have done very well?'

From a German intelligence report on the Somme published in January 1917 and quoted in C. Duffy *Through German Eyes: The British & the Somme 1916*, published in 2006

SKILLS BUILDER

1 Compare the accounts of the Somme battle given by Sources F and G.

2 Suggest reasons for the differences in interpretation between the sources.

3 Study Sources G, H and I and use your own knowledge.

How far do you agree with the opinion that the Battle of the Somme in 1916 was a total disaster for Britain and her army in France?

Source J

7.3 Ypres landscape

SKILLS BUILDER

1 How useful is this one photograph for a historian investigating the events on the Western Front?

What were the major British offensives of 1917?

The Battle of Arras

Allied plans were rather thrown into confusion by the German withdrawal from the old Somme battlefront in March and April 1917. In April the British gained four miles of territory in the Battle of Arras but failed to break through German lines. This started with an exceptional set-piece attack by the Canadians, who seized the strongpoint of Vimy Ridge. British tactics showed improvements on 1916 but there were still problems of exploiting local success due to communications difficulties and movement beyond the range of artillery support. Although gains were made the battle was allowed to go on for too long with diminishing results and increasing losses. The French Chemin des Dames offensive in April and May also failed to break through. The French army, after three years of unrelenting attacks, now experienced widespread mutinies. The situation meant that the initiative on the Western Front was thrust even more upon the BEF.

Haig planned his major assault around Ypres. The Germans held higher ground curving round the town in an arc. An advance of seven miles would push them off the ridge and threaten their control of the railway junction at Roulers. If that could be seized the whole German position on the Flanders coast would be threatened and withdrawal forced. There were powerful arguments for pursuing this strategy:

- Germany's hopes against Britain in 1917 were centred on the U-Boat campaign. They had launched unrestricted submarine warfare in the hope of starving Britain into submission. For this the Belgian coastal ports were vital.

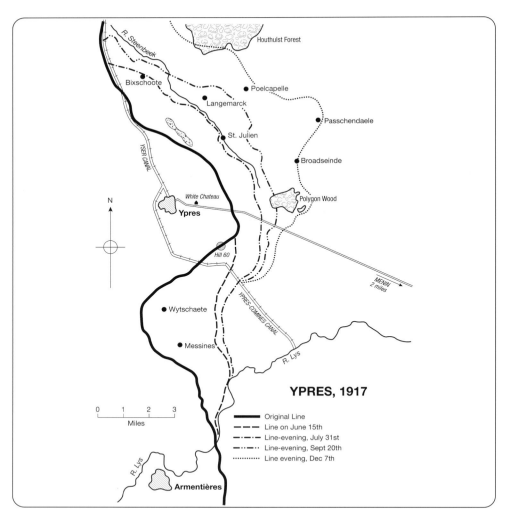

YPRES, 1917

——	Original Line
– – –	Line on June 15th
–·–·–	Line-evening, July 31st
–··–··–	Line-evening, Sept 20th
·········	Line evening, Dec 7th

7.4 Map of the Flanders front

- Haig hoped to combine a push north and east from Ypres with an amphibious landing behind the Germans on the coast.

As a preliminary to the main attack which began at the end of July, there was a brilliant set-piece battle to seize the Messines Ridge running to the south of Ypres. The planning and execution was by General Plumer and his 2nd Army. There was a massive artillery bombardment involving three and a half million shells and then on 7 June, just before the attack went in, the exploding of 19 mines that had been produced by secret tunnelling beneath the German defences. The explosions were heard in England. The ridge was successfully gained.

The main attack began on 31 July. There was a skilfully orchestrated creeping barrage and in most places there was considerable penetration of the enemy position. But weather intervened and it began to rain forcing the abandonment of planned assaults. The whole low lying area depended on a sophisticated and ancient drainage system. The rain plus the pounding of the ground by the heavy artillery shells reduced the whole area to swamp. Death by drowning in glutinous, clinging mud became the dreaded fate. Fresh attacks began on 16 August and continued until November. The battle became a chaotic watery hell.

Source K

The country resembles a sewage-heap more than anything else, pitted with shell holes of every conceivable size, and filled to the brim with green slimy water, above which a blackened arm or leg might project. It becomes a matter of great skill picking a way across a network of death traps, for drowning is almost certain in one of them. I remember a run I had at the beginning of the week – for dear life, if you like. Five of us had spent the night patrolling and were returning to Brigade HQ when the enemy sighted us and put a barrage along the duckboard track we were following. Early dawn broke in the east, and a grey light filtered through dim cloud masses to a desolate world of brown, touching skeleton woods strangely, and blackening the edge of the ridge where the German trenches lay. First one shell dropped 10 yards behind us then one came screaming so close we dropped in our tracks and waited for the end. I got right under the duckboard track, and the hail of shrapnel and mud on it was thunderous enough to frighten the most courageous. Then we stood up, all safe but muddy and with a 'Run like hell boys,' went off in a devil's race with shells bursting at our heels for half a mile, dropping at last in complete exhaustion in a trench out of range.

From a letter home, written on 17 September 1917 by Hugh Quigley of the 12th Royal Scots

Passchendaele

With painful slowness and at great cost Gough's 5th Army and then Plumer's 2nd Army ground their way outwards from Ypres. The weather improved in September and by 4 October the British had established a dominance on the battlefield that was deeply worrying to the German High Command. Haig determined to press on but the weather deteriorated again and the last phase of the assault towards the ridge on which the village of Passchendaele stood became synonymous with futility and suffering. The ground on which the village had been, for it was now but a smear of brick dust, was taken by the Canadians at the end of the first week in November. The British had advanced seven miles. The whole campaign had cost both sides roughly 260,000 casualties.

Not surprisingly there are very varying views of the campaign.

Source L

Notwithstanding the many difficulties, much has been achieved. Our captures in Flanders since the commencement of operations at the end of July amount to 24,035 prisoners, 74 guns, 941 machine guns and 138 trench mortars. It is certain that the enemy's losses considerably exceeded ours. Most important of all, our new and hastily trained Armies have shown once again that they are capable of meeting and beating the enemy's best troops, even under conditions which favoured his defence which it required the greatest endurance, determination and heroism to overcome.

General Sir Douglas Haig *Official Dispatch*, reviewing the recent operations in Flanders, published 25 December 1917

Source M

The fighting on the Western Front became more severe and costly than any the German Army had yet experienced. I myself was being put to a terrible strain. The state of affairs in the west appeared to prevent the execution of our plans elsewhere. Our wastage had been so high as to cause grave misgivings and had exceeded all expectation.

From General Von Ludendorff's War Memoirs *published in 1919. Ludendorff was the effective director of the German war effort from 1916 to 1918. Here he is writing about the Flanders offensive of 1917.*

Source N

Hindsight teaches me that Haig is to be blamed for failing to know when he was beaten, not by the Germans but by the Flanders mud. We came out of the battle confident that we could capture any thousand yards of Flanders if we paid the price, and could balance the account by killing more Boches than they killed of us, but we had begun to realise that we should never get to Berlin by that technique. As we used to sing, to the cheerful tune of an Irish jig.

Oh what with the wounded and what with the dead,
And what with the boys who are swinging the lead,
If the war isn't over, and that bloody soon,
There'll be nobody left in this bloody platoon.
Tra la la . . . .

Taking the shorter view we should not even get to the Flanders coast before winter at this rate.

From Charles Carrington Soldier from the Wars Returning *published in 1965. Carrington was a company commander in the Royal Warwickshires, who experienced fighting in the Third Battle of Ypres.*

SKILLS BUILDER

Study Sources L, M and N.

1. How far do the three sources suggest that 'much was achieved' by the Third Battle of Ypres, July–November 1917?

2. What are the strengths and weaknesses of these three sources in weighing up the significance of the Third Battle of Ypres? Please refer to all three sources in your answer.

Battle of Cambrai

Before the year ended there was to be one more British attack. On 20 November, the British 3rd Army launched a surprise attack at Cambrai using 476 tanks. The artillery was used in a different and more effective manner than on the Somme; 1,003 guns opened up at 6.20 a.m. as the tanks began to roll forward. There was no lengthy warning bombardment or range-finding shots. Targets had been pre-selected and guns carefully calibrated to ensure accuracy. Artillery, infantry and tanks worked together. The result was an advance of five miles. Unfortunately there were problems in positioning reserves to follow up effectively and the Germans counterattacked on the 30th using new techniques of infiltration involving storm troopers, hurricane bombardments and aircraft. Place the British and German innovations together and add effective radio communication and the result was tactics of 1940 rather than 1917.

Why was 1918 a year of crisis and victory?

In 1918, the German commander, Ludendorff, decided that it was the turn of the Germans to go on the offensive:

- As a result of the Bolshevik Revolution in Russia in November 1917, the German High Command was able to transfer fresh troops to the Western Front from the east, giving them a temporary superiority by early 1918 of 192 German divisions against 156 British and French.

- However, this superiority was temporary; as a result of the **unrestricted submarine campaign** begun by the Germans against Britain the USA had declared war on Germany in April 1917. The result was a growing number of American troops in France in 1918, which would ultimately make Germany's position impossible.

21 March, 1918

The German attack was towards Amiens across the Somme battlefields. Its aim was to punch in the most southerly of the British armies and then curl round to the north rolling up the British forces who would be separated from the French. The main blow would fall on Gough's 5th Army of only 12 divisions, withdrawn from the Ypres salient after the battering of the previous year. Gough had to cover 42 miles of front with his 12 divisions. He faced an attacking force of 43 German Divisions. To his north the 3rd British Army under Byng held 28 miles with 14 divisions. To Byng's north lay the even stronger 1st and 2nd armies and the bulk of the reserves. Haig reckoned that he could concede ground in the south away from his supply points and had concentrated his forces in the north where the German front was closer to the Channel ports.

For the attack Ludendorff concentrated half of Germany's guns; 6,473. Gough had only 976. The German storm broke on the morning of 21 March with a 5-hour bombardment, scientifically constructed like a music score, now high explosive, now gas, now on the gun positions, now on the front line, back to gas on the gun emplacements. Much of the 5th Army disintegrated and the front collapsed. The British began to pull back and the Germans achieved a remarkable breakthrough into the area behind the battle zone. The British 3rd Army held on more effectively, threatening the Germans with a battle of attrition they did not want. The result was that Ludendorff reinforced success against Gough, pressing on to try and seize Amiens. His forces were stopped 10 miles short. French and British reserves were rushed in and even the cavalry played a heroic part in halting the grey tide.

Definition

Unrestricted submarine warfare

Unrestricted submarine warfare is a term applied to the German naval strategy of abandoning the accepted rules of trade war. These had evolved to relate to commerce raiding by surface ships and involved stopping a merchant ship and searching it before either sinking it or taking it as a prize. It was almost impossible for submarines to do this. The Germans, after much internal debate, decided to sink merchant ships on sight in a zone around the British Isles. The danger was that it would bring the USA into the war, which it helped to do.

Source O

I saw at once that the position was desperate, if not fatal. If the enemy captured the ridge (the Moreuil Ridge commanding a view of Amiens) the main line from Amiens to Paris would be definitely broken, and I knew already that when that happened the two armies – the French and the British – would be compelled to retire; the French on Paris, and our Army on the Channel ports. All that we had fought for, and bled for, for nearly four years would be lost.

As I rode through our front line, who were lying down and firing, I said to a young Captain; 'We are going to re-take the ridge. Fire on both sides of us, as close as you can, while the rest of us go up.' He knelt up and shouted: 'Good luck to you, sir.' Our infantry opened a glorious fire on both sides of us as we galloped on. Five out of about twelve of my signal troop were shot by the enemy, but the remaining seven reached the wood, jumped off and opened fire. My orderly jammed the red flag into the ground at the point of the wood, I looked back to see my gallant brigade galloping forward by the way I had come.

I went with Flowerdew (commanding the leading squadron of Strathcona's Horse) to where we could see round the corner of the wood. He had lost comparatively few men up till then. He wheeled his four troops into line and with a wild shout, a hundred yards in front of his men, charged down on the long thin column of Germans, marching into the wood. A man with him told me his last words as he and his horse finally crashed to the ground – he had two bullet wounds through the chest and was shot through both thighs, but he still had strength to shout loudly, 'Carry on boys. We have won'. And so they had.

A short time later, when I arrived on the eastern face with the supporting squadron, I found the survivors of this desperate charge in a little ditch, which bordered the wood, in twos and threes, each with a German machine gun and with three or four Germans lying dead by their side. It was recorded that seventy Germans were killed by sword thrust alone outside the wood. I saw perhaps another two or three hundred lying there, who had been killed by machine-gun fire. In those brief moments we lost eight hundred horses, but only three hundred men killed or wounded. The fanatical valour of my men on this strange day was equalled by the Bavarian defenders now surrounded in the wood.

From the Memoirs of Major General J.E.B. Seely, commanding the
Canadian Cavalry Brigade, published 1930

SKILLS BUILDER

1 How does the tone of Source O compare with that of Source F?

2 Suggest reasons for these differences.

Flowerdew was awarded the Victoria Cross and Seely himself was gassed shortly afterwards but his Brigade clung onto the ridge. The German offensive ended. The Germans had lost heavily and further progress towards Amiens proved impossible.

Ludendorff decided to launch a second offensive in the north near Ypres on the River Lys. Here Haig could not afford to give much ground. The German attack initially fell on a Portuguese division and broke through to a depth of over three miles. The attacking troops eventually reached nearly to the walls of Ypres, the British losing all the gains of the previous year.

The seriousness of the situation was underlined by Haig's issuing of the following Special Order.

Source P

TO ALL RANKS OF THE BRITISH ARMY IN FRANCE AND FLANDERS

Many amongst us now are tired. To those I would say that Victory will belong to the side which holds out the longest. The French Army is moving rapidly and in great force to our support.

There is no other course open to us but to fight it out. Every position must be held to the last man: there must be no retirement. With our backs to the wall and believing in the justice of our cause each one of us must fight on to the end. The safety of our homes and the Freedom of mankind alike depend upon the conduct of each one of us at this critical moment.

From Field Marshal Douglas Haig *Special Order of the Day*, 11 April 1918

The position was held, just. German losses began to mount and Ludendorff called off the attack. A third drive in May from the Aisne reached the Marne and almost seemed to threaten Paris but again ran out of steam and was stopped by the French reserves and the Americans. Two minor offensives in June and July signalled the exhaustion of the German Army. It had suffered in excess of 800,000 casualties since 21 March. The trench lines had been broken and great advances made but the war had not been won. The attacks had shown tactical brilliance but were a strategic disaster.

The allied counter-offensive

The weakened German army was left holding an extended front and highly susceptible to counterattack. By 1918, Haig commanded a highly skilled mass army. He now had the artillery in sufficient quantity that he required, a large air-force, increasing numbers of tanks and well trained infantry who could be increasingly controlled on the battlefield. The lesson had been learned that after initial success the engagement in an attritional slogging match was not the most profitable way of proceeding. One offensive could be closed down as penetration lessened and a new point of impact adopted. The British began their assault near Amiens on 8 August. General Rawlinson, who had commanded in the same area two years before, was in charge once again but the results were profoundly different:

- At 4.20 a.m. 2,000 guns opened up in a controlled artillery barrage. Aerial photography, sound ranging, calculation of temperature and its effects on explosive propellants were all used to ensure accuracy and the elimination of the German guns capable of damaging tanks.

- A creeping barrage by the lighter field artillery advanced at the same speed as the infantry and tanks, 100 yards every 3 minutes.

The result was a devastating breakthrough by the Australian and Canadian corps: 18,000 German troops were taken prisoner and 9,000 killed or wounded. Four hundred guns were captured from the German Army on 8 August alone. Ludendorff pronounced it the 'Black day of the German Army.'

Source Q

The real achievement of Amiens had been the triumphant coordination of an all arms attack. It was the first truly modern battle.

It was also the beginning of the 'hundred days' in which German forces in the West were driven back and brought so close to total destruction that on 11 November their government was forced to ask for an armistice. The BEF was the main engine of this offensive, which in terms of scale remains the greatest campaign in British history. As Professor Harris has argued, it is also probably the campaign in which forces under British command exercised the most influence on the history of the world in the twentieth century. After Amiens, blow after blow forced the Germans back. Not even the mighty Hindenburg Line could protect them: it was penetrated by British divisions largely without the help of tanks. Armies of tradesmen, office clerks and factory workers had come of age. The Battle of Amiens was the beginning. From the 8 August onwards they took on and defeated the best army in the world, bringing to an end what had been the most terrible war in history.

From Peter and Dan Snow *Twentieth Century Battlefields* published in 2007

In September the old battlefield of Ypres, won in 1917 and then lost in April 1918, was recaptured.

Source R

28 September 1918
The day's success has been astonishing; an advance of over five miles (more than in four months' bloody fighting last year). No doubt the hostile shelling has been less severe than formerly. And his infantry, behind ample defences, have not put up their wonted resistance. Nevertheless, allowing for every mercy (including our smoke screens), the good leading and drive of all our ranks from sunrise to sundown, through this bullet swept wilderness, has been admirable, hustling the enemy off his feet.

The Brigade casualties are 306; the Fusiliers have lost 12 out of 22 officers. We have taken several hundred prisoners and some guns.

29 September 1918
The dismal belt of land devastated by four years of war lies behind. In front and slightly below us is spread a flat unshelled plain, intersected by winding brooks and dotted with undamaged farms, hamlets and a few trees.

From J.L. Jack, DSO *Trench Diary* published after his death in 1964

On the same day that Jack records breakout from the trench battle-zone in Belgium, one of the most remarkable military achievements of the war took place to the south. The 46th (North Midland) Division, a Territorial unit, broke the Hindenburg Line, crossing the formidable obstacle that was the St Quentin Canal. Once again it was a triumph of coordination of different arms, good planning and courageous skill. Unlike the first day of the Somme, few today have ever heard of it; yet it is a superb testimony to what the BEF had become, a formidable military machine.

Conclusion

It is worth leaving the conclusion of this unit to one of the most respected historians on war on the Western Front, Gary Sheffield.

Source S

The victory of 1918 was a coalition effort, and although this book has concentrated on the efforts of the Anglo-American armies, the contributions of the French and Belgians and other allies should not be forgotten. The burden of fighting the German army fell mainly to the French and Russians in the first two years of the war, but in 1918 it was the turn of the BEF. Between them, the French, Americans and Belgians took 196,700 prisoners and 3,775 guns between 18th July and the end of the war. With a smaller army than the French, Haig's forces captured 188,700 prisoners and 2,840 guns in the same period. This was, by far, the greatest military victory in British history.

From Gary Sheffield *Forgotten Victory: The First World War – myths and realities* published in 2001

Unit summary

What have you learned in this unit?

It has not been possible in such a short space to give anything but general detail as to the fighting experience of the British Army on the Western Front. However, you have learned that the BEF adapted to the type of warfare to the point that, by 1918, it had become a highly efficient military force. You have learned in this unit about the main British military engagements on the Western Front.

What skills have you used in this unit?

You will have used a range of evidence to explore the issues relating to the war on the Western Front. You will have used evidence from participating soldiers as part of your enquiry primarily to inform about those aspects of war reported in diaries and journals. You have tested a number of sources through evaluating their reliability and you will have cross-referenced sources for information.

SKILLS BUILDER

1 Debate: you are to debate one or both of the following motions in your group or in your class. Both motions are bound to raise emotions and you may well need to do some further research before the debate to ensure that your argument is as strong as it could be.

> Motion 1 'Haig: Bloody Butcher or Great Military Commander?'
>
> Motion 2 '29 September 1918 deserves to be remembered as much as 1 July 1916.'

2 Make a list of the reasons why the British Army was so much more effective in July–November 1918 compared to the same period in 1916.

3 The historian Jay Winter once wrote that while the Battle of the Somme was 'a tragedy, one that no one had ever seen before, but the Battle of Passchendaele was a crime'.

How far do you agree with this statement?

Exam tips

- Get underneath the sources and make inferences from them.
- Compare the sources by analysing their similarities and differences.
- Contextualise the sources, giving weight to the significance of their origin, nature and purpose and integrate them with relevant wider own knowledge.
- Reach a judgement on 'how far' by using both all the sources and relevant own knowledge.
- Remember, there is the Exam Zone section at the end of the book to help you further.

Now plan an answer to this question and write a response.

Exam style question

This is an example of a (b) question that you might encounter in your examination.

Use Sources Q, R and S and your own knowledge.

How far do you agree that the British Army was remarkably successful between August and November 1918?

RESEARCH TOPIC

The First World War generation

The First World War generation has now died out but the aim of this research topic is for you to find out as much as is possible about the First World War generation. Much can still be found out about your family's involvement in the First World War. However, you do not have to research your family's involvement, you can research the story of someone from your locality or from a friend's family. You should try to find out as much detail as possible about an individual who was involved in some way in the war.

Where can I find information?

- Ask your parents, grandparents or your guardian.
- Log on to the Commonwealth War Graves website at www.cwgc.org.
- Go to your local library.

8 The First World War 1914–18: what was army life like?

What is this unit about?

The purpose of this unit is to try to explain something of military life in France between August 1914 and November 1918 for the soldiers of the BEF when not engaged in major conflicts. Battles and 'going over the top' formed a very small part, although possibly the most important and adrenalin charged part of army life. It is important to realise the nature of trench warfare in other than periods of intense conflict.

Key questions

- How was the BEF organised and equipped?
- How was discipline and morale maintained?
- What were the medical facilities and treatment of the wounded like?

Timeline

1914
- August–December   1.2 million volunteer for the army to form Kitchener's new armies

1914–15
- Winter   First cases of trench foot recorded in France

1915
- January   First official investigation into the newly-named condition of 'shell shock'
- March   First two Territorial Army divisions arrive in France
- May   First Kitchener division, 9th Scottish, arrives in France

1916
- December   First time an officer shot for desertion

1917
- October   Trench Fever Commission of enquiry set up – discovers lice as the cause

1918
- May   Delousing pits widely establish results in improved hygiene

Much time was spent not in trenches but in rear areas undergoing training or simply trying to keep boredom at bay. W.J. Turner, an Australian who served in the Royal Artillery from 1916–18, captures some of the essence of training in his poem, 'Death's Men' (see Source A).

Source A

Under a grey October sky
The little squads that drill
Click arms and legs
   mechanically
Emptied of ragged will.
'Click, clack, left, right,
   form fours, incline,'
The jack-box sergeant
   cries;
For twelve erect and
   wooden dolls
One clock work doll
   replies

Death's Men by
W.J. Turner, published
in 1939

How was the British Army in France organised?

Structure

There were four types of British soldiers serving in France between 1914 and 1918. Initially there were the regulars dispatched in 1914. These were increasingly supplemented by Territorials in 1915 and the first of the new army, composed of volunteers. A last resort in dealing with wartime manpower shortages was the introduction of conscription in 1916. All the infantry however were drafted into the existing British regimental system organised on a regional basis. The number of battalions in a regiment expanded rapidly. The first two being regulars, the next two Territorial and later ones being New Army. George Coppard, a New Army volunteer, who wrote his memoirs in 1968 from notebooks kept during his time in the trenches, introduces the reader to the structures of the BEF in the following passages.

Source B

By the end of October (1914), with the steady arrival of recruits, the battalion strength was nearly completed. Number 701 was my regimental tag, and my official address was 13 platoon, 'D' Company, 6th battalion, The Queen's Royal West Surrey Regiment. We were part of the new army being formed throughout the country, Kitchener's army. The Co's name was Lieutenant-Colonel Warden, a regular army officer. 'A' Company Co and second in command of the battalion was Major Watson, also a regular. I regret that I cannot remember for certain the name of 'B' Company's Co but I think it was Captain Butler. Captain Rolls was of 'C' Company and a regular officer. My own Co was Captain Hull, a regular too. It is a pity I cannot supply the initials of these gentlemen.

By May of 1915, with basic training over, they were ready for departure to France. Sergeant Morgan of 13 platoon now left us, as he was too old for overseas service. His place was filled by Sergeant Fulbrook from the 2nd Battalion the Queen's, another fine-looking soldier. Any drum major would have envied his proud strut. Very soon he became 'D' Company sergeant major.

There was great activity going on in Aldershot and we soon heard that our destination was France as part of the 37th Infantry Brigade. The other three battalions were the 6th Battalion, Royal East Kents, commonly known as the Buffs, the 6th Battalion, Royal West Kents, and 7th Battalion East Surreys. The Brigade formed part of the 12th Division, the other two brigades being the 35th and 36th. According to an old notebook I still have, a division consisted of headquarters, 3 infantry brigades, 3 Royal Field Artillery brigades, 1 howitzer brigade, 1 heavy battery and ammunition column, 3 field companies of Royal Engineeers,1 signal company of Royal Engineers, 1 cavalry squadron, 3 field ambulance units and 1 divisional train. The GOC of the 12th Division was Major-General F.D.V. Wing, CB CMG.

From George Coppard *With a Machine Gun to Cambrai* published in 1969

SKILLS BUILDER

1 Use Source B to construct a diagram showing the organisation of the army with the appropriate rank of the officers in charge at each level.

2 Why is Coppard such a useful source of evidence in finding out about a soldier's life on the Western Front?

A British infantry division was normally composed of 19,600 men, although in practice there were often considerably less than that this in view of casualties and shortage of replacements. Divisions were organised into Army Corps under a Lieutenant General and two or more corps were grouped into armies. There were eventually five of these in the BEF as a whole. Divisions could be moved from corps to corps and both armies and corps were remote organisations for most soldiers, with which they would find it hard to identify.

Which weapons were used?

The weapons issued to British soldiers were thoroughly serviceable for the tasks.

Lee Enfield rifle

The basic weapon for the infantry was the short, magazine Lee Enfield rifle introduced in 1903. It proved an excellent weapon; regular soldiers could fire 15 rounds of .303 bullets a minute which could penetrate a helmet at 400 yards and pass through two thicknesses of sandbags at 200 yards. It has been described as the best combat rifle issued to any army during the war.

Source C

8.1 Vickers Machine Gun

SKILLS BUILDER

Why might the Vickers Machine Gun not fit with a war of movement?

Vickers Machine Gun

Much appreciated by the troops, although underestimated initially by generals who thought in terms of a war of movement was the Vickers Mk1 Machine Gun. It had been introduced in 1912. Two were issued to each battalion and George Coppard writes of it as 'A wonderful weapon.' It fired 450–550 rounds a minute to a range of approximately 3,000 yards. The numbers of Vickers guns were steadily increased as their value became clear. In 1915 each battalion was equipped with four machine guns and then special machine-gun companies were attached to each division and the heavy machine gun withdrawn from battalion control to be replaced by the light machine gun. By 1918 these had been raised to 64 machine guns per division.

Lewis gun

The light machine gun or Lewis gun had just been developed in the USA and, when war broke out, the British began manufacture under licence. Initially there was no German equivalent. It proved wonderfully useful in trench warfare. It was lighter than the Vickers, being air cooled. Martin Pegler, historian and Western Front expert, describes the Lewis gun below.

Source D

When it worked, the Lewis was a fine weapon, but technically it was a complex gun, prone to a bewildering number of stoppages – one manual lists thirty-one.

Despite this the gun was much appreciated by the Germans who paid it the compliment of using as many as they could capture, sometimes adapting it to fire German calibre bullets. From late 1915, each battalion was issued with eight Lewis guns and a further eight in 1916. This meant that each platoon had its own machine gun by the time of the Somme Battle.

From Martin Pegler *Attack on the Somme* published in 2006

Stokes Mortar

Other weapons were added to the soldier's armoury as time went on. Initially the BEF had no trench mortars but eventually a very effective design was accepted, and named after its inventor, Wilfred Stokes. The following two historians describe the strengths and weaknesses of the Stokes Mortar.

Source E

Costing only £40 per weapon, the mechanism was supremely simple. All a man had to do was to select a shell with a ballastite cartridge of the right colour, green for 300 yards and red for 450, drop it onto the spike at the base of the firing tube and his job was done. Such was the speed of fire that twenty-two shells could be fired in a minute, with eight in the air at any moment – pocket artillery indeed.

From Denis Winter *Death's Men* published in 1978

Source F

[It was] the most effective mortar produced during the war. The three-inch Stokes was sited in the firing or support line, dug into pits so that no part projected above ground level. It was unfortunate that the Stokes mortar pit was very much the same dimension as a latrine, and German artillery, firing at targets identified from air photographs, spent much time shelling the British latrines, thus increasing the incidence of constipation amongst soldiers in the firing line.

From George Corrigan *Mud, Blood and Poppycock* published in 2003

SKILLS BUILDER

1 Using Source E, descide what the strengths and weaknesses of the Stokes Mortar were.

Grenades and shells

Grenades hardly existed in the BEF in 1914 and, as trench warfare evolved, were improvised from jam jars and cans. Eventually in 1915 the Mills bomb was developed and could be considered by 1918 the most effective in use in any army.

The great killer for most infantrymen was not the bullet, whether fired from rifle or machine gun but shellfire. Here again the BEF started with very inadequate numbers of guns and ammunition, although the 18 pounder was an excellent field gun. There was a particular shortage of 'heavies', i.e. artillery pieces firing much bigger shells such as the 6 inch howitzer, but this deficiency was made good in 1916–17, as indicated in the previous unit. Likewise the improvement in types of shells and fuses made the British artillery of 1918 formidable and much feared by the Germans. The British Tommy had gone to war in 1914 with a soft cap but this was replaced in 1915 by the steel helmet. This could not protect from bullets but it offered some protection from shrapnel and flying debris. Overall a British infantryman could feel that he was increasingly as well equipped for conflict as his highly industrialised country could manage and certainly he did not suffer by comparison with his German opponent or his French ally.

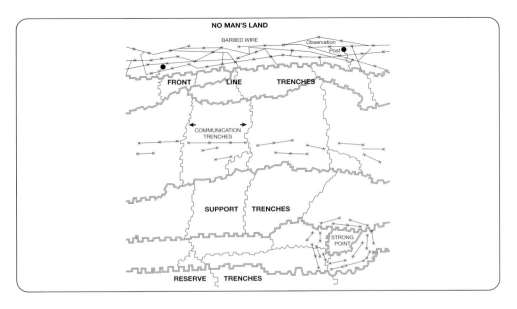

8.2 Diagram of a British trench system

How were morale and discipline maintained?

Post and leave

Among the most important factors here was contact with home. In one respect this was excellent. The arrangement of postal and parcel deliveries was outstanding. Before the war the Royal Engineers had established a postal section, sufficient for six divisions. As the BEF expanded so did REPS (the Royal Engineers Postal Section) and men were kept in touch with their loved ones in a very effective fashion. Letters home were censored but contact was remarkably speedy. One soldier over Christmas 1914 records receiving three letters on 30 December posted on 26 and 28 in England and Ireland. Parcels likewise poured into France. By April 1917, 125,000 letters a day were being handled. Physical contact via leave was less satisfactory but it did improve. In summer 1917, there were 100,000 who had not been home for 18 months and 400,000 who had not been home for a year. A year later every man was getting home leave after six months.

Food was the other key ingredient in maintaining morale.

SKILLS BUILDER

Summarise the points made in Source G.

Source G

The British Army aimed to give its soldiers at the front a daily intake of 4193 calories. This was less than the French and more than the Germans, who aimed for 4466 and 4038 calories respectively. The difference was that the French ration, despite including almost a pint of wine daily, was of such poor quality that it was one of the causes of the mutinies of 1917. The Germans, however hard they tried, rarely managed to provide the laid down ration once the blockade of the Royal Navy began to take effect. British soldiers hardly ever went without.

From George Corrigan *Mud, Blood and Poppycock* published in 2003

Source H

8.3 Rations dump

There could be complaints about monotony or the absence of some favourite food but in general British soldiers were well fed and in the case of many from poor homes, better fed than at any time during their life hitherto. The daily tot of rum in the trenches introduced in October 1914 was also much appreciated. It was at the discretion of the battalion commander to counter inclement weather but he usually found the weather justified this remedy. Tobacco was widely and cheaply available and there were many frequent issues of free cigarettes and pipe tobacco.

Pay

Pay was not generous but the British Tommy was paid better than the French **Poilu**, and an agricultural labourer was certainly no worse off soldiering and, taking food into account, probably better off:

- The lowest rate was one shilling a day (5p) but for most soldiers this was increased by proficiency payments (extra allowances for acquired skills) and the average pay was at least 50 per cent higher than the lowest rate. Promotion brought higher rates. It may not sound very much but a shilling could buy a soldier 70 Woodbine cigarettes in the army-run canteens.
- Food and clothing was free and payments were made to dependants back home. These payments were partially paid for by small stoppages from the soldiers' weekly pay but they were also enhanced by the government.
- A serving British soldier in France was paid 10 Francs a week. Egg, chips coffee and a roll could be had for 1 Franc and wine and watery beer for a few sous a glass (1 Franc = 100 sous).
- It was probably only the presence of the better paid colonial contingents of the BEF that excited temporary discontent over pay.

This said, George Coppard, mentioned in Source B as a member of the New Army, records his sense of poverty as a young 17-year-old soldier, but he adds the explanation that most of his pay went rapidly in one of the many gambling games that filled a young soldier's spare time.

What was life like behind the lines?

Perhaps equal to the food and the mail services in maintaining morale was the regular rotation of units from the front line to reserve positions and then back to billets behind the battle zone. This process involved considerable staff work and tended not to be practised in the French and German armies in such a calculated and methodical fashion. It had its disadvantages from a military perspective insofar as units would not get to know their section of the trenches as well but the British staff was firmly convinced that this was more than outweighed by improved morale. Most units spent no more than an average of 8 days in the trenches in any one month and usually no more than 2 days in the firing line, i.e. the front-line trench. Thereafter there was the march back to billets where warm food and baths were waiting.

Definition

Poilu

Poilu literally means 'hairy one', the term Poilu was affectionate slang to describe a French infantryman.

Source I

In the evenings there were Housey-Housey sessions outside an estaminet [café] in the middle of the village with crowds of Tommies sitting on the ground knocking back wine and beer. The game – called Bingo today – was the only game of chance allowed in the army then. Those in the mood for more serious gambling games, such as Crown and Anchor, Banker or Pontoon, slunk off to lonely spots, away from the vigilance of the military police.

From George Coppard *With a Machine Gun to Cambrai* published in 1969

Source J

The march from the zone of destruction was the first part of the cure. Men came into areas of trees with branches and turf without shellholes. There was no need to strain the ears for shell sounds nor was stooping a condition of survival. The hushed wariness of the trenches merged into bustle, which became noisier all the time, with blacksmiths' shops, horse lines, supply depots and motor repair shops roaring with sound. All this hit the tired men hard. They were blind men recovering their sight, normalcy growing by degrees, and feeling coming in gradually from extremities of sensation. It was just like a man on night sentry slowly thawing out after sunrise.

From Denis Winter *Death's Men* published in 1978

Back in billets was a round of training and fatigues but there was also a morale-boosting programme of entertainments and diversions. Cinemas were established in rear areas and band concerts were regularly performed in many localities. Entertainments were sometimes provided by the officers for the men. One soldier recalls his memoirs below.

Source K

Colonel Portal gave a realistic impression of George Robey and brought the house down with a spirited rendition of 'The flowers that bloom in the spring, tra, la' with dance accompaniment. One man remarked to me with surprise, 'Who'd have thought that the old man was such a decent old bugger?' The star of the show was the company officer, Captain Hazlitt, made up as a fetching young lady. Several satirical sketches poked fun at military regulations, **brass hats**, politicians, including one which depicted a draper's shop run on military lines after the war.

From F. Noakes *The Distant Drum: The Personal History of a Guardsman in the Great War* published in 1952

Definitions

Brass hats

Brass hats is a rather derogatory term for very senior officers, so-called because of their extensive gold braid.

Batman

Batman was a soldier from the ranks who acted as a servant to an officer.

In addition there were inter-company football matches and athletic competitions up to Divisional level. George Coppard would turn his hand to anything in the name of competition.

Source L

Company sports took place and I picked up second prize in the **batman**'s race. I knew next to nothing about horses or mules but allowed myself to be kidded into competing in the mule race. My mount, named Norman, was generally regarded as one of the most recalcitrant of the stubborn bunch . . . [In the race] Norman shot ahead and cunningly suggested that I was on my way to an easy victory, but he veered sharply and deliberately bucked me off.

From George Coppard *With a Machine Gun to Cambrai* published in 1969

How harsh was army discipline?

Army discipline is a subject of much controversy, particularly the use made of the death penalty and field punishment number one. The traditional flogging, in use in the Crimea, had been abolished, yet the problems posed of disciplining thousands of young men were very real. It is important to judge the army by the standards of its own time, not the late twentieth or the twenty-first century.

The death penalty was in use in civilian life and very widely accepted and supported. Around 5,700,000 men served in the British Army during the First World War and of these 346 were executed; 322 of those executed were serving in France or Belgium. The others were serving in other theatres of war, such as the Middle East. Of those executed, 266 were killed for desertion and 37 for murder. Many were repeat offenders, 91 of those executed were under suspended sentence. In other words the army did not resort to the death penalty readily. From 1917 special Court Martial Officers, drawn from the legal profession, were attached to every corps. The author of the following source, John Nettleton, served in the ranks before becoming an officer and as such then served on a number of court martials.

Source M

I was impressed with the general fairness of the court martial procedure. The commander of an army in the field has to be given wide powers to deal with a variety of offences, but in the actual trial a great effort is made to give the prisoner every possible assistance and he is given the benefit of any possible doubt. In fact, everyone leans over backwards to make sure that the prisoner's case is not prejudiced.

From John Nettleton *The Anger of the Guns: An Infantry Officer on the Western Front* published in 1979

SKILLS BUILDER

In what ways might Nettleton's account in Source M be regarded as a reliable source for the fairness of court martials?

Field punishment

Field punishment number one causes nearly as much controversy as the death penalty. This involved the miscreant being tied for a period of up to two hours to a stationary object, traditionally a gun wheel. Two old soldiers disagree almost totally on its appropriateness.

Source N

A lot of hot air has been talked about the iniquity of [field punishment number one], but I cannot see that it was so terrible. You were not lashed tightly to the wagon wheel; you were never kept there for longer than an hour at a time; you were loosed if it got too hot or too cold or if it rained, so there was little physical discomfort. Presumably, it was the moral effect that was supposed to be the deterrent.

From John Nettleton *The Anger of the Guns: An Infantry Officer on the Western Front* published in 1979

Source O

One fine evening, with a big crowd all set for a game, two military policemen appeared with a handcuffed prisoner, and, in full view of the crowd and villagers, tied him to a wheel of a limber, cruciform fashion. The poor devil, a British Tommy was undergoing field Punishment number one, and this public exposure was a part of the punishment. There was a dramatic silence as every eye watched the man being fastened to the wheel and some jeering started. The game got underway. An hour passed and suddenly a scuffle started, with a couple of Tommies rolling on the ground and making a great show of pummelling each other. The military policeman ran over to separate them, but the two frolickers assured the police that the scramble was just a friendly caper. In the meantime the prisoner had gulped down several swigs from a bottle of red wine neatly produced by other conspirators. Lashing men to a wheel in public in a foreign country was one of the most disgraceful things in the war. Troops resented these exhibitions.

From George Coppard *With a Machine Gun to Cambrai* published in 1969

SKILLS BUILDER

1 In what ways do Sources N and O disagree about field punishment number one?

2 What might explain the disagreement?

The commonest punishment was being confined to barracks or 'Jankers' for a few days. This involved loss of pay and unpleasant jobs like cleaning the latrines. It might be meted out for having a dirty rifle. There was widespread disagreement at the time about army discipline and its effects, as the following passage based on German interviews with British prisoners makes clear.

Source P

Three Kitchener men of the Leeds Pals testified that 'the discipline is not really harsh, but you have to remember that the battalion consists mainly of volunteers from the better middle class, who have the necessary self-discipline. Punishments are therefore rare. In the view of twenty one men of the 4/Royal Berkshire Regiment, all of them neighbours, 'there is not a great deal of punishment', and they considered Field Punishment No. 2 a reasonable penalty for having a dirty rifle. Elsewhere in the unhappy 2/Border Regiment, 'the discipline is extraordinarily strict, even by the standards of Regular units. The punishments are frequent and severe, evidently to bring the young recruits up to the military mark as soon as possible.'

From C. Duffy *Through German Eyes: The British & the Somme 1916* published in 2006

Whatever the strictness of the discipline, which clearly varied from unit to unit and time to time, morale for most part remained high and as Coppard points out the men showed 'an ingrained sense of duty and obedience, in keeping with the times'. This was important. There was a widespread acceptance of hierarchy and authority. Coppard writes of men being 'wholly loyal to their officers based on trust and comradeship founded on the actual sharing of dangers together.' What is beyond dispute is that the British Army never displayed that collapse of morale that took place in the French and Russian armies in 1917 and in the German army late in 1918.

There was grumbling a plenty but they were well fed, well equipped and possessed a fundamental belief in victory and their ultimate superiority over the enemy.

How effective were the health and medical services?

Given the sheer scale of the problems and the level of medical skill and knowledge, the achievements in terms of health, both preventative and remedial were outstanding. This was to be the first British Army in history where more men died from enemy action than from disease. In this respect it stands in sharp contrast to both the Crimean and the Second Boer Wars.

Latrines

The lessons from the development of public health in urban Britain were applied. First and foremost was the struggle with the soldier's own waste products. The digging and positioning of latrines was crucial.

Lice

Life in the trenches produced many problems even without the daily hazards offered by German action. Intermittent bombardment and snipers killed and wounded the odd unlucky individual but lice affected all. They were almost impossible to remove and as well as the obvious irritation were a cause of what became known as trench fever, with recurring flu-like symptoms. Delousing stations were established in rear arrears and a campaign launched on the insects as protracted as that against the Germans. The lice survived.

Trench foot

Standing in the cold mud and water, combined with tightly laced boots which restricted circulation, could induce trench foot. This involved the painful swelling of the feet and in a secondary phase the development of gangrene. This condition necessitated amputation. Every effort was made to keep it at bay. Whale oil was issued to rub into the feet before going up to the trench line and men were ordered to take a dry pair of clean socks with them. Officers carried out regular inspections. The incidence of trench foot in a unit became a measure of that unit's efficiency. Its incidence was reduced but never eliminated.

How were the wounded treated?

The treatment of the wounded was in the hands of the Royal Army Medical Corps numbering 1,509 officers and 16,331 other ranks in 1914. Like all other sections of the military establishment it had to undergo a massive expansion. There was an inevitable shortage of doctors even though 25 per cent of all doctors had joined up by July 1915. Large numbers of volunteers were taken from the USA to help the shortfall. As in so many other respects the organisation of the service was in the circumstances impressive. There was one hospital ship and one hospital train allotted to each division and a network of ambulances, field dressing stations and base hospitals established. The great curse in the treatment of the wounded was infection. Source Q is from the memoirs of Arthur Osburn who was a leading military doctor during the war.

Source Q

We soon learned, however, of the differences between wounds sustained on the clean South African veldt and those contaminated by European mud. Anaerobic bacteria lurking in the soil were responsible for the gas gangrene which proved to be one of the chief causes of death among those who reached a base hospital alive.'

From Arthur Osburn *Unwilling Passenger* published in 1932

SKILLS BUILDER

How far does Source Q support the impression given in Source R about the level of medical knowledge and competence?

Source R

Looking back today on the treatment received at the various stages of the process, one can only wonder at the high rate of success. The general level of medical knowledge was distinctly Victorian. Quite apart from these gaps in knowledge was a backwardness in medical technology. Since there were no practical X-rays for hospital use, battle hardware was likely to remain in the body with all its possibilities for septicemia later. Haemorrhages were always likely to be fatal, since blood transfusion was in its infancy, although Keynes was pioneering a transfusion apparatus which would remain standard for twenty years. Blood groups were discovered by trial and error, with donors sufficiently traumatised to merit 14 days of Blighty in return. The lack of antibiotics was even more damaging. Nearly all field wounds went septic within six hours. The knife or packing with lime chloride were the only specifics and the wound had to be kept unstitched, filled with gauze and drained regularly to allow slow healing from the bottom up. If there was arterial damage and gangrene set in, washing with peroxide might be tried but the prognosis was gloomy. In the American expeditionary force (British figures don't survive) 44% of those contracting gangrene died. Osburn remembers the smell of gangrene in the Boulogne hospital train lasting several days after disinfection, he and the nurses vomiting continuously.

From Denis Winter *Death's Men* published in 1978

Source S

It was the First World War which decisively advanced skin transplants. Confronted by horrific facial injuries, Harold Gillies (1882-1960) set up a plastic surgery unit at Aldershot in the south of England. He was one of the first plastic surgeons to take the patient's appearance into consideration. After the Battle of the Somme in 1916, he dealt personally with about 2000 cases of facial damage.

From Roy Porter *The Greatest Benefit to Mankind: A Medical History of Humanity* published in 1997

Where technology and medicine could assist it was readily employed. Every company commander was given a stock of morphine tablets. Inoculation was widely used against typhoid, which had been the great killer of the Boer War and this plus greater hygiene resulted in the incidence being only 2 per cent of that in the former conflict. Nervous strain and disorders were little understood and often went under the general term 'shell shock'. The army authorities could not make up its mind if this should count as sickness or being wounded but did not ignore it. A consultant neurologist, Lieutenant Colonel W.A. Turner was ordered by the War Office to investigate the condition in January 1915. The Mental Health Bill of 1915 provided that anyone suffering from mental disorder as a result of the war could be treated for six months in specially appointed mental institutions. As in so many areas there were no easy answers but neither the army nor the government were guilty of indifference to suffering.

Enormous strides were made in key areas. Blood transfusions have been mentioned above. The American surgeon Harvey Cushing, serving with the British Army, gained valuable experience dealing with head wounds and much advanced the cause of brain surgery in the process. Artificial limbs were improved and became more widely available and the following source draws attention to another beneficial development.

Conclusion

The picture that emerges of the British Army in France is one of a massive triumph of organisation. A huge army, the largest in the country's history, was improvised. There were inevitable mistakes and considerable suffering but it was on the whole well fed, increasingly well equipped with weapons and increasingly cared for in terms of both preventative and curative medicine. Morale was maintained by various strategies, not least the sense that it was winning and it did eventually win. There was never the collapse in morale in the British Army that occurred in the French, Italian and Russian armies in 1917 and in the German army in the summer and autumn of 1918. Britain created and maintained a formidable fighting machine.

Unit summary

What have you learned in this unit?

You have learned about the detail of the soldiers' experience of life on the Western Front. You should have picked up from the unit that all was not death and destruction although life was by no means easy. You have learned that good morale depended on regular food and communication with home. As the war continued so the technology of warfare improved as did the medical care to look after the troops.

What skills have you used in this unit?

There has been a great emphasis in this unit on war memoirs. You have used these memoirs to gain a snapshot of what life was like on the Western Front. However, in evaluating these memoirs you should have come to realise the limitations of using this type of evidence to draw general conclusions. As in the previous unit, you have looked to explain the different interpretations of contemporaries and historians.

SKILLS BUILDER

1 Go through the unit again, listing the ways in which discipline and morale were maintained. After considering the text and the evidence in the unit answer the following question, either on paper or in discussion.

2 To what extent was the British Army successful in maintaining the morale of its troops throughout the First World War?

3 Research a particular case of either the treatment of an injured soldier or the serious punishment of a soldier.

Exam style question

This is the sort of question you will find appearing on the examination paper as a (b) question.

Study Sources G, O and R and use your own knowledge.

Do you agree that, on the whole, the soldiers in the British Army were well looked after and treated fairly by the military authorities?

Exam tips

You have worked on (b) style questions at the end of other units.

You have experimented with different sorts of plans and considered different styles of question.

You should now have a good idea of the way in which you prefer to plan your answer. So go ahead and plan an answer to this question.

Now test yourself! Look at your plan and check what you have drawn up.

Have you:

- Analysed the sources for points that support and challenge the view that the soldiers in the British Army were well looked after and treated fairly by the military authorities?
- Shown how you will cross-reference between the sources for points of agreement and disagreement?
- Shown where you will use your wider knowledge both to reinforce and challenge the points you have derived from the sources?
- Thought about how you will combine the points you have made into an argument for or against the view that the soldiers in the British Army were well looked after and treated fairly by the military authorities, and noted this on your plan?
- Shown how your evaluation of the points you have used in argument has considered the quality of the evidence used?
- Noted what your conclusion will be, and how you will ensure it is balanced and supported?

RESEARCH TOPIC

Medical and surgical developments

The First World War led to the speeding up of medical and surgical developments. Your task is to find out about developments in the following areas:

- X-rays

- blood transfusions

- brain surgery

- skin grafts.

You can find your information from books or on the Internet. The more detail you find out the better.

UNIT 9

The Home Front 1914–18: how was a fighting force mobilised?

What is this unit about?

This unit focuses on the ways in which a fighting force, sufficient to supplement the regular army, was recruited from the British civilian population and on the personal and social impact this recruitment had on that population. It addresses the reasons why **voluntaryism** was not enough to meet the demands of a war of attrition and explains the need for conscription. It considers the position of those who were unwilling, because of the dictates of their consciences, to become combatants and on the attitudes of society towards them. Finally, the significance of the changing role of women behind the front line in support of the armed forces is considered, as well as the prevailing attitudes to women's involvement in elements of warfare.

Key questions

- To what extent were civilians effectively recruited both into the armed forces and to support the armed forces?
- How were conscientious objectors treated?

Timeline

1914
4 August	Great Britain declares war on Germany
5 August	Kitchener appointed Secretary of State for War
7 August	Government-driven recruitment drive begins. Kitchener calls for the 'First 100,000' volunteers for his 'New Armies'
3 December	No Conscription Fellowship formed

1915
15 July	National Registration Act passed, requiring the registration of anyone who might be eligible for military service
11 October	Derby Scheme begins

1916
9 February	First Military Service Act introduces conscription for unmarried men
March	Formation of Non-Combatant Corps
2 May	Second Military Service Act introduces conscription for married men
1 December	Formation of WAAC

1917
29 November	Formation of WRNS

1918
1 April	Formation of WRAF

Definition

Voluntaryism

Voluntaryism is relying on people to volunteer rather than forcing them to contribute.

What was the challenge of the home front?

The outbreak of war in August 1914 launched the British people into a period when their lives would be shaped by the demands of total war. For the first time, civilians and armed forces would be called upon to commit hearts, nerves and sinews, money, time and their lives to the conflict. This war, because it was fought between highly industrialised nation states, demanded the total commitment of the political, economic and social resources of the countries involved. The national resources – and this included people – of all the combatants had to be mobilised on an unprecedented scale over a period of four years. The efforts of the armed forces would come to nothing if they could not be backed by a civilian population capable of sustaining a high level of industrial output. In order to wage total war, the whole adult population of Britain had to be mobilised effectively and efficiently. How was this done?

Patriotism or propaganda?

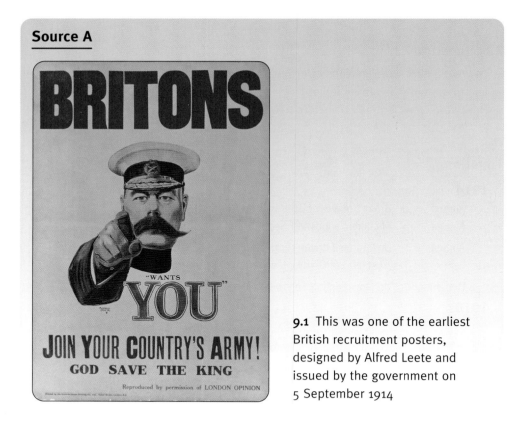

Source A

9.1 This was one of the earliest British recruitment posters, designed by Alfred Leete and issued by the government on 5 September 1914

SKILLS BUILDER

1 How does this poster try to persuade men to join up?

2 Would the poster have persuaded you to enlist if you had been of the right age to fight in 1914?

Now look at these next two recruitment posters.

Source B

9.2 A First World War recruiting poster, issued by the government in 1915

Source C

9.3 A First World War recruiting poster, issued by the government

Why was civilian recruitment into the Armed Forces necessary?

At the outbreak of war on 4 August 1914, Britain had a small, highly skilled, professional army consisting of some 247,432 officers and men. Of these, around 8,000 could expect to be in India at any one time. The British Expeditionary Force took a further 80,000 men to France (see pages 102–3) and it very shortly became clear that the regular army was incapable of waging war in continental Europe.

Enter Lord Kitchener

The Secretary of State for War, Colonel Seely, resigned from the government shortly before war broke out and the post was temporarily taken over by Prime Minister Asquith. Clearly a new Secretary of State was urgently needed. One obvious candidate was Lord Kitchener. He had successfully commanded the British troops during the last two years of the Boer War (see page 71) and because of this was a hero in the eyes of a large section of the public. Confident that Kitchener would command the respect and confidence of the people, the press waged a campaign calling for him to be seconded to the War Office. A vacillating government, with no better candidate in mind, on 5 August appointed him Secretary of State for War. It was not an altogether happy appointment. At age sixty-four, Kitchener was past his prime; much had changed in the twelve years since the ending of the Boer War, and he was no politician. Summoned to the Cabinet, he warned that the war would last for at least three years and that he would need at least one million fighting men. He was received in silence. The Foreign Secretary, Edward Grey, said afterwards that he thought the prediction 'unlikely, if not incredible'. Even so, on 6 August parliament authorised an increase in the army of 500,000 men and the first recruiting drive began the following day, with Kitchener calling for the 'First 100,000' volunteers to form his 'New Armies'.

Source D

YOUR KING AND COUNTRY NEED YOU
A CALL TO ARMS

An addition of 100,000 men to His Majesty's Regular Army is immediately necessary in the present grave National Emergency. Lord Kitchener is confident that this appeal will be at once responded to by all who have the safety of our Empire at heart.

TERMS OF SERVICE

General service for a period of three years, or until the war is concluded. Age of enlistment, between 19 and 30.

A recruiting appeal published in *The Times* on 7 August 1914

SKILLS BUILDER

To what extent does this appeal differ from that of the posters?

Recruiting offices, set up in almost every town and city, were swamped as young men, in a fever of patriotic enthusiasm, volunteered to fight for 'King and Country'. The first 100,000 had enlisted by 25 August; on 28 August the government authorised the recruitment of a further 100,000 men, raised the age-limit to 35 and began an appeal to married men. By 25 September, after a further 500,000 recruits had been authorised, well over half a million young men had enlisted. Recruitment targets of another million were authorised in November and by December 1915, a third and then a fourth million had been sanctioned.

What were the Pals' battalions?

Pals' battalions, formed on the basis of 'those who joined together should serve together', proved to be an enormously popular move. All kinds of companies and businesses, towns and cities formed their own battalions.

- Hull raised four battalions; Glasgow, three.
- Accrington, a small cotton town in Lancashire, raised one batallion in only ten days of recruiting.
- In Liverpool, the White Star shipping line formed its own platoon as did the Cunard line and the Cotton Exchange.

There were artists' battalions and battalions raised by orchestras and other cultural groups. Friends joined up together: whole football teams, young men from the same back streets, factory floors and offices. They were trained together, usually by elderly officers and sergeant majors, and they served together. Over 300 battalions, some 250,000 men altogether, were raised in this way. What was little talked about was that joining together, training together and serving together also meant possibly dying together. Whole towns were devastated in this way. Ellis Dawson, who lived in Radcliffe, Manchester, told his daughter that as a boy aged 11 (in 1916) he walked with his father into central Manchester and every house they passed had its blinds pulled down as a sign of mourning. Every single household had lost a son, a brother, a father, a husband. This was after the first battle of the Somme.

Discussion point

1 What use could an historian make of this photograph?

  For a hint: think of 'witting testimony': that which the photographer intended to show think of 'unwitting testimony': that which the photographer didn't set out to show, but which is there, nonetheless.

2 What questions does this photograph raise in your mind – and how would you set about finding answers to them?

Source E

9.4 The formation of Pals' Battalions provided a perfect occasion to express civic pride and many towns and cities competed with each other to produce the most, or the best, battalions. One of the largest landowners in the country of Lancashire was the Earl of Derby. On 3 September he held a meeting in the Lancashire glass-blowing town of St Helens, where he and other religious and political leaders appealed for local men to form a local battalion. This is a photograph of some of the men who volunteered for the St Helen's Pals' Battalion, marching to war in February 1915.

Why did men volunteer to fight?

We know now about the horror of trench warfare and the needless loss of thousands of young lives. But then, back in 1914, there was hope and optimism. The war, after all, would be over by Christmas. To join up was a chance to see the world, to get out of dead-end jobs and to have a bit of an adventure. Let the volunteers talk for themselves.

Source F

Everybody was terribly excited, and there was nobody more excited than my elder brother George. He was going, he said, 'first thing tomorrow morning'. Dad didn't want him to enlist. He tried to persuade him against going so soon – stop to see the harvest in. But George was keen to go and here was his chance, and he went into my mother's bedroom – she was not very well at the time – and he picked up a stick which she used to rap on the floor if she wanted anything. 'This is how I shall strut about the London parks,' he said, jokingly, of course. It was the glamour of it all, nobody sort of gave it a second thought that they might never come back.

One of the first to enlist was George Whitehead, a farmer's son.
His younger brother, Len, remembers what it was like.

George was killed on the Western Front.

Source G

George Pulley (son of our local butcher) and I attended our first and last recruiting meeting. A leather-lunged gentleman was urging the crowd to throw up their jobs and fight. The way he spoke, it was just a matter of coming up, drawing a rifle, and ammunition and proceeding straightaway to France. The sergeant already had his eagle eye upon George and I and he was most pleased to greet us, possibly because of all the crowd we were the only ones to join up that night. When I got home, my poor aunt and Gran could scarcely believe their ears. Hardly waiting to close the door, I called out 'I've joined the army!' 'Oh dear! Oh dear!' said Gran. 'My poor boy.' Neither of them were at all demonstrative, but when I sat down, Gran put her old arm around me for a moment. My aunt shed a tear and then said, 'Well, I suppose you'd like a cup of tea now.'

Vic Cole enlisted on 5 September 1914.

Vic survived the war and was one of the first soldiers to be discharged from the army and to begin working again in civilian life.

Source H

In the evening, my father called me in and said he'd got to go back to Kidderminster, back to barracks. 'Will you walk with me a little way, just up the hill, will you come with me?' Of course I would. He said goodbye to my mother, who was crying, and we went off down the road and then up this long hill. It was a ten-minute walk, I suppose, but we didn't hurry, we just walked slowly up the hill and I really can't remember what we talked about, we must have talked, I think. I held on to his hand so tight, and when we got to the top, he said, 'I won't take you any further, you must go back now and I'll stand here and watch you until you're out of sight,' and he put his arms around me and held me so close to him that I remember feeling how rough the khaki uniform was, and he said 'Now I want you to promise me three things. You'll look after your mother, and I want you to go to church because I bought you that nice new prayer book and I would like to think you were going to use it, and then the last thing I want you to promise me is that you'll grow up to be a good girl.'

He picked me up against him and put his arms round me and held me tight to him and he kissed my cheeks and put me down and he said 'You must go now. Wave to me at the bottom, won't you?' And I went, I left him standing there and I went down the hill, waving, and he was still there, just standing there. I got to the bottom and then I'd got to turn off to where we lived, so I stopped and waved to him and he gestured as much as to say, 'Go on, you must go home now', sort of thing, ever so gently gestured, and then he waved and he was still waving when I went. And that was the last I ever saw of him.

Ten-year-old Lucy Neale remembers her father Harry's departure.

Harry died from dysentery while serving with the British Army in Africa.

SKILLS BUILDER

1 Take each source in turn. What attitudes towards enlisting can you find?

2 What similarities and what differences can you find?

3 How can these similarities and differences best be explained?

Voluntary or 'voluntary'?

'Voluntary' usually means that of your own free will you have agreed or decided to do something. So it was for thousands of volunteers. But it was a bit different for some of them. One man remembers travelling to his depot with eight servants of a peer who had been told that they ought to 'volunteer'. The Nestlé company announced that it expected all single male employees between the ages of 18 and 30 to 'volunteer'.

Recruiting, too, had its shady side and this was connected to volunteering. Early on in the war, those who recruited were paid 2s 6d (two shillings and six pence) for each man who enlisted, those recruiters who were less than honest turned a blind eye to, for example, age. In October 1914 the payment was reduced to 1s, so recruiters had to work harder or become more dishonest. It was not unknown for recruiters to prey on the drunk at public house closing time. In the autumn of 1914, medical officers had to examine some 200 men per day and were paid 2s 6d for every man they passed as 'fit'. Abuse of the system was common.

What was the 'Derby Scheme'?

Over one million men had volunteered to fight by the end of 1914 and altogether, throughout the whole war, some 2.5 million men enlisted voluntarily. However, initial enthusiastic patriotism faded and, as the losses on the Western Front mounted, numbers of those volunteering understandably dwindled. By the spring of 1915, it became clear that voluntary recruitment was not going to provide the numbers of men wanted. A war of attrition needed more victims than volunteering could provide.

As the prospect of conscription loomed, the Liberal-dominated coalition government, seeing in conscription the death of everything liberalism stood for, made one last-ditch attempt to avoid compelling men to join the armed forces:

- On 15 July 1915, the National Registration Act was passed by parliament in an attempt to stimulate recruitment by discovering how many men there were between 15 and 60, and the occupations they followed. All those in this age range who were not already in military service were obliged to register. This 'census' revealed that approximately 5 million men of military age were not serving in the armed forces and of these, 1.6 million were in 'starred' occupations – highly skilled work important to the national economy.

- On 11 October 1915 Lord Derby (the same man that has urged the men of St Helens to form a Pals' Battalion) was appointed Director-General of Recruiting. He immediately came up with a scheme which for ever afterwards was known as the Derby Scheme. Lord Derby invited all men between the ages of 18 and 41 to attest their willingness to serve if they were called upon to do so. They were to attest in age groups and by occupation; and a pledge was given that married men would not be called up until the pool of the unmarried was exhausted. Men who attested under the Derby Scheme were sent back to their homes and jobs until they were called up, and were given a grey armband with a red crown as a sign that they had so volunteered.

Discussion points

1 Why do you think men who had attested were given special armbands?
2 Should those in 'starred' occupations have been given something similar to wear?
3 How valid was the voluntary system as a method of recruitment?

The Derby Scheme was a failure: 215,000 men enlisted while the scheme was operational, and another 2,185,000 attested for later enlistment. However, 38 per cent of single men and 54 per cent of married men who were not in 'starred' occupations failed to come forward.

Source I

As it affected society, the Derby Scheme was a gigantic engine of fraud and moral blackmail, but, given that the Government had to find soldiers somehow, it was a very astute piece of political tactics. If it succeeded, well and good – the sanctity of voluntaryism had been maintained; if it failed, the case for conscription would be well nigh irresistible.

From Arthur Marwick *The Deluge: British Society and the First World War*
published in 1965

Discussion point

Why do you think the Derby Scheme failed?

Question

Do you agree with Arthur Marwick's view of the Derby Scheme?

Conscription!

The government bowed to the inevitable and decided to introduce conscription:

- In January 1916 the Military Service Act was passed by parliament. All voluntary enlistment was stopped. All British males were deemed to have enlisted – that is, they were conscripted – if they were aged between 18 and 41 and resident in Great Britain (excluding Ireland) and were unmarried or a widower on 2 November 1915. Conscripted men were no longer given a choice of which service, regiment or unit they joined, although if they asked to go in the navy, they normally could.

- In May 1916 the Act was extended to include married men. The only exceptions were those in **reserved occupations** or **conscientious objectors**. A series of tribunals were set up to hear appeals from men who believed that they should not be called up.

Definitions

Reserved occupations

These were occupations that the government thought were so important to the war effort that the workers could not be released for military service.

Conscientious objectors

These were people whose consciences would not let them fight.

Were enough men found to fight?

The short answer to this question is 'only just':

- The poverty and poor nutrition of industrial workers in pre-war Britain meant that large numbers of men failed to reach the minimum standard for military service. In some industrial areas, 70 per cent of men were rejected as unfit.

- Thousands were excluded from conscription on the basis that they were doing important work on the home front, such as engineering, mining and munitions work.

Source J

Army recruiting in the First World War

Year	Total joining the armed forces	Fighting strength of the British Army on 1 October every year
1914	1,186,357	1,357,372
1915	1,280,000	2,475,764
1916	1,190,000	3,343,797
1917	820,000	3,883,017
1918	493,562	3,838,265

The huge losses of 1916–17 meant that the size of the army was barely increasing. The German offensive in the spring of 1918 caused 300,000 British casualties and seriously damaged the British Army's ability to conduct the war. Desperate measures had to be adopted, including sending 18-year-olds to the trenches in northern France, something the government had previously promised not to do. Indeed, by the end of the war, half the British infantry in France was under 19 years old.

What happened to those who opposed the war?

There was a considerable amount of opposition to the war on both moral and practical grounds. While a lot of opposition was limited to the personal and local, for example making jokes, grumbling and defacing posters, some of the opposition became organised nationwide.

The No Conscription Fellowship

In the autumn of 1914, two **pacifists**, Clifford Allen and Fenner Brockway, formed the No Conscription Fellowship (NCF), an organisation dedicated to support those who objected to fighting. These men became known as 'conscientious objectors' and their reasons for refusing to take up arms were many and varied.

Definition

Pacifist

A person who rejects war and violent action as a means of solving disputes, especially international disputes between nations.

Source K

A month ago Europe was a peaceful group of nations: if an Englishman killed a German, he was hanged. Now, if an Englishman kills a German, or if a German kills an Englishman, he is a patriot. We scan the newspapers with greedy eyes for news of slaughter, and rejoice when we read of innocent young man, blindly obedient to the word of command, mown down in thousands by the machine-guns of Liege. Those who saw the London crowds during the nights leading up to the declaration of war, saw a whole population, hitherto peaceable and humane, precipitated in a few days down the steep slope to primitive barbarism.

Part of a letter sent by Bertrand Russell to the magazine *The Nation* on 15 August 1914.
Bertrand Russell was a philosopher and a pacifist who campaigned against the war.

Source L

We are all young men, and life is a precious thing to such men. We cherish life because of the opportunities for adventure and achievement which it offers to a man who is young. They say our country is in danger. Of course it is, but whose fault is that? It will be in danger in fifty years' time, if our rulers know they can always win support by hoisting danger signals. They will never heed our condemnation of their foreign policy if they can always depend upon our support in time of war. There is one interference with individual judgement that no state in the world has any sanction to enforce – that is, to tamper with the unfettered free right of every man to decide for himself, the issue of life and death.

In 1916 Clifford Allen was conscripted, but refused to serve. This is part of his statement to the Military Tribunal convened to hear his case.

Source M

Every individual gives loyalty to something which counts more than anything else in life. In most men and women this supreme allegiance is inspired by national patriotism; if their government becomes involved in a war, as a matter of course they will support it. The socialist conscientious objector has a group loyalty which is as powerful to him as the loyalty of the patriot for his nation. His group is composed of workers of all lands, the dispossessed, the victims of the present economic system, whether in peace or war.

Fenner Brockway explains why he is opposed to the war in 1914. At the beginning of the war he was editor of the **Independent Labour Party**'s journal *Labour Elector*. Arrested because he refused to serve in the armed forces, he spent the rest of the war in prison.

SKILLS BUILDER

What different reasons can you find in Sources K–M for refusing to fight?

Discussion point

Is it ever valid to refuse to fight for your country?

Definition

Independent Labour Party

Established at a conference in Bradford in 1893, the ILP included a number of socialist organisations, among them the Scottish Labour Party. In 1900 the ILP took the initiative in forming the Labour Representation Committee and linking in with the trade unions. The general election of 1906 saw 29 LRC MPs elected to parliament, most of whom were members of the ILP. By 1910 the ILP had over 28,000 members. Membership split over the First World War, with a significant number becoming pacifists. After 1918, mainly because of the rise of the Labour Party, the ILP became more and more of a left-wing pressure group under the organisation of Clifford Allen.

How did the law treat conscientious objectors?

Largely due to pressure from the NCF, MPs agreed that the first Military Service Act should include a clause that continued the use of tribunals that had been set up under the Derby Scheme. Under the Derby Scheme these tribunals heard representation from men who wanted to be considered for exemption from military service for personal and economic reasons. The remit of the tribunals was now to be extended so that they could hear appeals that were based on 'a conscientious objection to the undertaking of combatant service'. This, of course, left a loophole whereby conscientious objectors could be sent out to the front to undertake, say, loading or cleaning. The NCF weren't totally happy with this as some of their members didn't want to have anything whatsoever to do with the war. The second Military Service Act made it clear that in certain cases, absolute exemption from any work to do with the war would be permitted.

What happened in practice?

It is one thing to lay down, by law, that something *can* happen, but quite another to make sure that it *does* happen. Historian Arthur Marwick explains why.

Source N

Made up of solid local worthies, the tribunals could scarcely be expected to treat the claims of conscientious objectors with sympathy: hatred, fear and horror at the mounting slaughter on the Western Front could be vented vicariously on such 'shirkers', the exposure of whom seemed a patriotic duty. A few tribunals did comport themselves with scrupulous attention to the letter and spirit of the conscience clauses of the Military Service Acts, but all found great difficulty in comprehending the attitude of the young man who declared he could play no part at all in the national effort and demanded absolute exemption.

From Arthur Marwick *The Deluge: British Society and the First World War* published in 1965

Definition

Non-Combatant Corps

This was set up in March 1916 as part of the army and was run by its regular officers. The conscientious objectors assigned to it had the rank of army private, wore army uniforms and were subject to army discipline, but they didn't carry weapons or take part in battle. Their duties were mainly to provide the physical labour of building, cleaning, loading and unloading in support of the military.

What happened to the men who came before a military tribunal?

- If the tribunal refused their conscientious objection they were sent to France to fight. When they refused to obey an order (as, of course, they did) they were court-martialled and sentenced to death. A horrified government issued Army Order X, which laid down that court-martialled conscientious objectors had to be handed back to the civilian authorities where they would be imprisoned. In June 1916 the government set up the Pelham Committee which offered work, such as road building within the UK, to those who had been imprisoned in this way.
- If their conscientious objection was upheld in whole or in part, men could serve in the **Non-Combatant Corps** – driving ambulances, for example – or could work under the direct supervision of the tribunals, or could accept work from the Pelham Committee.
- Absolutists, those who wanted absolutely nothing to do with the war, were imprisoned.

How did the numbers stack up? Of around 16,500 men who claimed conscientious objection to the war and appeared before the tribunals, approximately:

- 3,300 served in the Non-Combatant Corps;
- 3,000 did various forms of ambulance work (often run by **Quaker** organisations) or worked under the direct supervision of the tribunals;
- 4,000 accepted work directly from the Pelham Committee and a further 3,750 did so after having been imprisoned;
- 1,500 absolutists were imprisoned.

How was the No Conscription Fellowship organised?

Nearly 300 men joined the NCF as soon as it was founded, far more than Fenner Brockway and Clifford Allen had anticipated. Initially, the administration was undertaken by Lilla Brockway, Fenner Brockway's wife, working from their cottage in Derbyshire. However, as numbers of groups formed throughout the country and membership grew, with some 61 branches by November 1915, it became clear that the administration and organisation of the Fellowship ought to be placed on a more professional basis. Consequently, a London office, run by Clifford Allen, was opened at the beginning of 1915. It was at this point, with losses on the Western Front mounting, that it became clear that conscription would be one of the options open to the government. The NCF immediately utilised their growing countrywide network of branches to fight against the threatened Military Service Bill and in November 1915 held a national convention in London. All this was to no avail (see page 143). However, once conscription was introduced, the NCF:

- kept meticulous records, documenting the experiences of every conscientious objector;
- maintained contact with conscientious objectors in camps, barracks and prisons across the country;
- set up a press department that aimed to keep the treatment of conscientious objectors in the public eye by publishing leaflets and pamphlets;
- began publishing a weekly newspaper *The Tribunal* with its first issue in March 1916;
- briefed MPs and set down questions for ministers.

The final convention of the NCF took place in November 1919 and was attended by 400 delegates from branches all over the country.

How did people react to conscientious objectors?

The men and women who supported conscientious objectors (nicknamed 'conchies') and those who were sympathetic to their views even if they didn't share them were, however, in a minority. It was common, for example, for men dressed in civilian clothes to be jeered at in the streets

(see page 143)

Discussion point

1 Why might a conscientious objector have problems joining the Non-Combatant Corps?
2 The Non-Combatant Corps was nicknamed the 'No Courage Corps'. How fair was that?
3 How should the law treat conscientious objectors?

Definition

Quaker

A member of the Society of Friends, a Christian movement founded by George Fox c.1620. Quakers are dedicated to pacifist principles.

and for them to be handed white feathers as a sign of cowardice by those who believed they were shirking their duty. Government propaganda encouraged this, though subtly, as Source O shows.

Source O

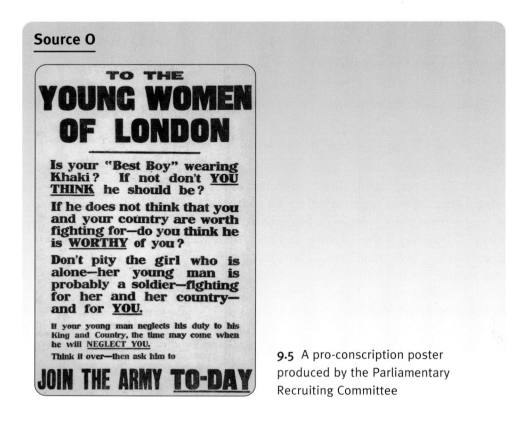

9.5 A pro-conscription poster produced by the Parliamentary Recruiting Committee

Source P

Sir

What right have 'conscientious objectors' to live in this country whose existence is only maintained by the fighting men of our Army and Navy?

G. Moor, Silver Fields, Harrogate

A letter written to the *Daily Mail* newspaper and published on 10 January 1916

Source Q

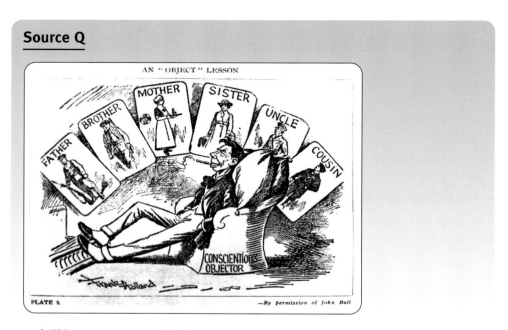

9.6 This cartoon was published in the magazine *John Bull* in May 1918

SKILLS BUILDER

1 What is the hidden message of Source O?

2 Could Source O have any relevance to conscientious objectors and their supporters?

3 How useful is Source P as evidence of hostility to conscientious objectors?

4 How does Source Q show that the cartoonist was hostile to conscientious objectors?

Keep the notes you made when answering these questions. You'll need them when you tackle the exam style question at the end of this unit.

How did conscientious objectors cope with people's reactions to them?

Source R

On my way from a No Conscription meeting, I was pushed off my bike and arrested by two policemen. At the local police station, my clothes were taken from me and I slept the night on a hard board in a cell.

In the morning I was taken before a magistrate and a military escort took me to barracks. Here khaki clothes were forced upon me. There were about twelve of us, including my brother. We refused to drill properly. For this we were sentenced to 28 days tied spread-eagled to the wheel of a gun. I was court-martialled and sent to Newcastle prison. This old prison was a great shock, rows and row of cells, and when the door of my cell slammed on me the bottom seemed to fall out of my little world and I wondered if I would survive. I was in this cell 23 hours out of every 24. There was a tiny window high up, a hard wooden plank bed, a bucket for a toilet and terrible food. We met other COs [conscientious objectors] only in the exercise yard and we were forbidden to talk.

Len Payne remembers how he was treated during the 1914–18 war

Source S

The field court-martial seemed to have an atmosphere of hostility, but I heard in a side-room as we were waiting, one officer say to another 'You know it would be monstrous to shoot these men.'

We were taken to one side of the parade ground, then, led out one by one in front of over 1,000 soldiers. I was the first of them.

An officer in charge read out my various crimes: refusing to obey a lawful command, disobedience at Boulogne, and so on, then: 'The sentence of the court is to suffer death by being shot.' There was a pause. I thought, 'Well, that's that.' Then he said 'Confirmed by the Commander-in-Chief.' 'That's double sealed it now,' I thought. Then, after a long pause: 'But commuted to penal servitude for ten years.' And that was that. What was good was that we were back in England and out of the hands of the army.

Part of an account given by Howard Marten who was a Quaker. The tribunal that heard his objection forced him to join the Non-Combatant Corps. He was sent to France, where he refused to obey orders and so was court-martialled.

Source T

It was right at the beginning that I learnt that the only people from who I could expect sympathy were soldiers and not civilians. I was waiting in the guard room when five soldiers under arrest came in. When they asked me what I was in for, I was as simple as possible 'I am a Quaker and I refused to join the Army because I think that it is murder.' 'Murder?' one of them whispered, 'it's bloody murder!' As they went away they each came up to me and shook me by the hand. 'Stick to it, matey,' they said, one after the other.

From an account given by a conscientious objector who was a Quaker

SKILLS BUILDER

1 What similarities, and what differences, can you find between Sources R, S and T?

2 How far does Source T challenge Sources R and S about attitudes towards conscientious objectors?

What about the women?

The First World War opened up new opportunities (albeit frequently only temporary ones) and new horizons for women. The new situations in which they found themselves, or created for themselves, helped to bring about change in the ways in which society viewed women's role. Women were, explicitly and implicitly, challenging the '**separate spheres' philosophy** that had so shaped nineteenth-century thinking. You will read more about this in the next unit, but for now the focus is on women's direct involvement with the armed services.

Nurses, VADs and FANYs

Florence Nightingale (see pages 31–8) had done much to make nursing a respectable occupation for women. She had, too, given nurses their uniform, which was an outward symbol of their individual personal and professional dedication that was recognised and accepted as such by the general public. Perhaps as importantly, she had set the precedent for women's involvement close to front-line warfare.

Nurses

The Army Nursing Service was established in 1884 and received royal patronage in 1902, becoming the Queen Alexandra's Imperial Military Nursing Service. Two reserve services were also created: Princess Christian's Nursing Reserve in 1894, which became Queen Alexandra's Imperial Military Nursing Service Reserve in 1908; and the Territorial Force Nursing Service in 1908. Even so, by 1914 there were only 700

Definition

'Separate spheres' philosophy

The philosophy that maintained that men and women occupied 'separate spheres' in society. The woman's sphere was the home and all things domestic; the man's sphere was the world of work, finance and government.

trained nurses employed in War Office, Admiralty and Territorial hospitals. By 1918 this number had grown to 23,000.

VADs

Since 1910, the regular army nurses had been supplemented by the War Office Scheme for Voluntary Aid Detachments to the Sick and Wounded (VADs). Members of these detachments, because they were voluntary and therefore unpaid, had to be financially self-sufficient or supported by their families. Consequently, recruitment tended to be from the middle and upper classes only. By July 1914, around 5,300 women had volunteered to help in hospitals, and some 2,500 VAD branches had been established throughout the country. During the four years of the war, following a huge recruitment drive, some 38,000 VADs worked as assistant nurses, ambulance drivers and cooks, and VAD hospitals were opened in most English towns. At first, the military authorities were unwilling to allow the VADs anywhere near to the front-line troops. However, this restriction was removed in 1915, and women volunteers over the age of twenty-three and with three months' experience, were allowed to go to the Western Front, Mesopotamia, Gallipoli and, later, the Eastern Front.

FANYs

The First Aid Nursing Yeomanry (known as the FANY) was different again. Founded in 1907 as a mounted nursing corps with the somewhat romantic notion of bringing wounded soldiers from the battlefield on horseback (something they never in fact ever did!). By 1914 they had adapted their horse-riding skills to car, truck and ambulance driving. The FANY comprised mostly of upper class young women, fired with the patriotism shown by their fathers and brothers and they projected a dashing, daring image of themselves. They remained a small but exclusive group: by 1918 there were only some 116 FANYs working in France.

> **Discussion point**
>
> What tensions could you see developing between the trained nurses and the VADs when they had to work together close to the battlefield?

Source U

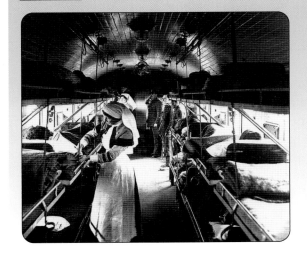

9.7 A photograph showing the interior of a British ambulance train near Doullens, France, 27 April 1918

> **SKILLS BUILDER**
>
> What image of nursing was the photographer trying to portray?

Source V

I am a Sister VAD and orderly all in one. Quite apart from the nursing, I have stoked the fire all night, done two or three rounds of bed pans, and kept the kettles going and prepared feeds on exceedingly black Beatrice oil stoves and refilled them from the steam kettles utterly wallowing in paraffin all the time. I feel as if I have been dragged through the gutter. Possibly acute surgical is the heaviest type of work there is, I think, more wearing than anything else on earth. You are kept on the go the whole time but in the end there seems to be nothing definite to show for it – except that one or two are alive that might otherwise have been dead.

The picture came back to me of myself standing alone in a newly created circle of hell during the emergency of March 22nd 1918, gazing half hypnotised at the disheveled beds, the stretchers on the floor, the scattered boots and piles of muddy clothing, the brown blankets turned back from smashed limbs bound to splints by filthy bloodstained bandages. Beneath each stinking wad of sodden wool and gauze an obscene horror waited for me and all the equipment that I had for attacking it in this ex-medical ward was one pair of forceps standing in a potted meat glass half full of methylated spirit.

From Vera Brittain *A Testament of Youth* published in 1933. Here she remembers her experiences as a VAD in a field camp hospital in the town of Étaples, France, in 1918. Her fiancé, Roland Leighton, and her brother Edward were both killed on the Western Front.

SKILLS BUILDER

1 Both Sources U and V are describing situations in 1918. Why, then, are they so different?

2 How far does the evidence of Source V challenge that of the photograph, Source U?

WAACS, WRNS and WRAF

Beyond nursing, the government was most reluctant to allow women anywhere near the front lines. However, the mounting losses on the Western Front caused the government to re-think. Women were doing sterling work on mainland UK, replacing men who had enlisted or been conscripted, so why not at the front? Lieutenant General Sir Henry Lawson suggested to Brigadier General Auckland Geddes, Director of Recruitment at the War Office, that far too many soldiers were employed doing 'soft' jobs. After talks with the government, it was decided to use women to replace men in administrative work, thus releasing the men to fight:

- In January 1917, the government announced the formation of a new voluntary service, the Women's Auxiliary Army Corps. These women undertook a wide variety of army work in Britain and in France, for example working as clerks, telephonists, cooks, and instructors in the use of gas masks, thus releasing men to fight. By the time the armistice was signed in 1918, over 57,000 women had served in the WAAC.

- Heavy naval losses in 1916 and the resulting loss of manpower for active sea service led to the formation of the Women's Royal Naval Service in November 1917. The aim was the same as that of the formation of the WAACs – to release men from 'soft' administrative duties so that they could go to sea. Initially, the Admiralty decided to recruit no more than 3,000 women (with the slogan 'Free a man for sea service') but eventually over 6,000 women worked as WRNS. Although they never got to go to sea, there were units based overseas, the first one being in Gibraltar.

- By the end of 1917, the Royal Flying Corps had all-female companies where the women lived at home and worked alongside the men who were training them to take over their jobs. The amalgamation of the Royal Flying Corps and the Royal Naval Air Service into the Royal Air Force in April 1918 affected the role of women workers. Under new terms of service, volunteers from the WAACs and other all-female voluntary organisations were encouraged to join the newly formed WRAF. The aim of the new organisation was to 'train women to take over the work of home-based mechanics and so to free them for service in the combat areas'. The numbers of recruits increased rapidly, as this offered an opportunity to learn new and previously inaccessible skills. Over 2,000 women were trained in some 43 trades, working, for example, as armourers, radio operators, parachute packers and flight and instrument mechanics.

So, in the end, why did men and women, and particularly young men, risk their lives to place themselves at the forefront of the conflict? Historian Gerard J. DeGroot has part of the answer.

Source W

This innocent, gullible generation still believed in heroes, duty and the glory of war. War was not a disaster, but an opportunity, a chance to prove oneself and do one's bit.

From Gerard J. DeGroot *Blighty: British Society in the Era of the Great War* published in 1996

Discussion point

Do you agree with DeGroot?

What have you learned in this unit?

You have learned how a fighting force, sufficient to supplement the regular army, was recruited from the civilian population, first by voluntary enlistment and finally by conscription. You have found out how conscientious objection to the war was organised and supported, how conscientious objectors were treated and about the reactions to conscientious objectors. You have explored the role played by women behind the front lines in nursing and in the WAAC, the WRNS and the WRAF.

What skills have you used in this unit?

You have used source material to evaluate the effectiveness of recruiting posters and their role as propaganda and you have considered primary source material as evidence of why men volunteered for the armed services. You have utilised your empathetic skills to explore the motives of those refusing to fight, and the attitudes of those around them to this refusal. Finally, you have worked with source material to evaluate apparently different experiences of women working close to the front line.

SKILLS BUILDER

1 To what extent do you regard civilian recruitment into the armed forces as being driven by government propaganda?

2 Were conscientious objectors treated appropriately?

3 Think about the reasons why women become involved in supporting the armed services. How far would you agree with the view of one such woman who said that 'It was insulting, really. We were wanted only so that men could be freed to fight. If the killing hadn't been so dreadful, no one would have thought of involving us.'

Exam style question

This is the sort of question you will find appearing on the examination paper as an (a) question.

Study Sources O, P and Q.

How far does Source O support the attitudes to conscientious objectors shown in Sources P and Q?

Look back to page 149 and to the notes you took when you did the Skills builder exercise. You'll need them now to help construct an answer to this question.

You tackled (a) style questions at the end of Units 1, 4 and 7. Now let's develop what you learned there about approaches to the (a) question.

Exam tips

- What is the question asking you to do? It is asking **how far** Source O **supports** Sources P and Q.
- Consider the sources carefully and make **inferences** and **deductions** from them rather than using them as sources of information. You might put these inferences in three columns.
- **Cross-reference** points of evidence from the three sources by drawing actual links between evidence in the three columns. This will enable you to make comparisons point by point and so use the sources as a **set**.
- **Evaluate** the evidence, assessing its quality and reliability in terms of how much weight it will bear and how secure are the conclusions that can be drawn from it.
- Reach a **judgement** about how far Source O can be said to support Sources P and Q.

RESEARCH TOPIC

There were women who really pushed at the boundaries of what it was considered possible for women to do behind the front lines.

Three such women were Edith Cavell, Mairi Chisholm and Flora Sands.

- What did they do that was difficult, dangerous or downright outrageous?
- Do you consider them to have been brave or foolhardy?

10 The Home Front 1914–18: how were people's minds mobilised for total war?

What is this unit about?

This unit focuses on the ways in which propaganda was used by Britain during the First World War. It considers the role and purpose of the government in both creating and disseminating propaganda, and on the ways in which rumour and gossip gained their own momentum as the war progressed and how these in turn created myths and developed into atrocity stories. The role of Germany itself in creating propaganda opportunities for the British government and people is considered. The ways in which fear of the 'enemy within' developed and expressed itself are addressed, as are the role of the press, film and the cinema in mobilising people's minds for total war. Finally, the unit ends with asking whether it was all worth it: were people effectively turned against the enemy?

Key questions

- To what extent was propaganda managed by the government?
- How effective was propaganda at changing people's attitudes?

Timeline

1914	British government set up its own propaganda bureau in Wellington House under Charles Masterman
	Russians reportedly seen marching through England 'with snow on their boots'
	'Angel of Mons' story first surfaces
	'Priests as bell clappers' story develops
	German shelling of Hartlepool and Scarborough used in anti-German propaganda
1915	Sinking of the *Lusitania* by German U-boats creates propaganda opportunity for Britain
	British propaganda turns Edith Cavell into a martyr after the Germans shot her for espionage
	Official film unit permitted to work on the Western Front
1916	Film *Battle of the Somme* shot mainly using scenes that might have been from the battle, but weren't
1917	Government sets up Department of Information led initially by C.H. Montgomery and then by Colonel John Buchan
	'Corpse Conversion Factory' becomes the most notorious atrocity story of the war
	War Aims Committee set up
1918	Government sets up Ministry of Information headed by Lord Beaverbrook

Source A

10.1 A First World War poster

Source B

It refers solely to the control of opinion by significant symbols, or to speak more concretely and more accurately, by stories, rumours, reports, pictures and other forms of social communication. Propaganda is concerned with the management of opinions and attitudes by the direct manipulation of social suggestion, rather than by altering the conditions in the environment.

From H.D. Lasswell *Propaganda Technique in the World War* published in 1927

Definition

Propaganda

One of the best definitions of the propaganda used during the First World War was made shortly after that war as historians debated the nature and impact of propaganda; see Source B.

SKILLS BUILDER

1 Look back at the recruitment posters on pages 136–7.

2 Using the definition in Source B, do you think they are propaganda posters?

3 Using the definition in Source B, do you think that Source A is a propaganda poster?

4 What conclusions can you draw about the differences and similarities between these posters?

How was propaganda managed on the home front?

What was the role of government departments?

In 1914, the government set up its own propaganda bureau in Wellington House in London under the Liberal politician Charles Masterman. It was so secret that most MPs did not even know it existed, operating as it did behind the front of a non-existent government agency, the National Insurance Department. This was supplemented by the War Office's Directorate of Military Operations and the Foreign Office's News Department, but with no one department or person in overall control the result was chaotic and sometimes contradictory.

It wasn't until early in 1917, with war weariness permeating both the military and civilian population, that the government decided to take control of the situation in a far more positive way than previously. David Lloyd George, now Prime Minister, set up the Department of Information. The function of the Department was to supervise four sub-divisions:

- Wellington House, which continued to provide material for home consumption and for the consumption of neutral countries;
- a Cinema Division devoted to using this new media to good effect;
- a Political Intelligence Division, which worked to discover the state of public opinion throughout the world;
- a News Division, whose work was concerned with filtering war news through to the British public.

The Department was led initially by C.H. Montgomery of the War Office, then by Colonel John Buchan. Subsequently, Sir Edward Carson was given a supervisory role over all propaganda matters. The Department was aided by an Advisory Committee consisting of three prominent newspapermen:

- Lord Northcliffe, a newspaper baron who owned, among other publications, the *Daily Mail* and who was later replaced by Lord Beaverbrook, owner of the *Daily Express*;
- Robert Donald, editor of the *Daily Chronicle*;
- C.P. Scott, owner of the *Manchester Guardian*.

Finally, further re-organisation in early 1918 led to the creation of a Ministry of Information, headed by Lord Beaverbrook. Beaverbrook, Rothermere* and Northcliffe were drafted into the Cabinet.

Source C

There was no blueprint to work on; no experience to guide the new department. There was no office, no staff. There was nothing but a decision of the War Cabinet that such a Ministry should be created, and that I should be the Minister.

From Lord Beaverbrook *Men and Power* published in 1956

* Co-founder, with his brother Lord Northcliffe, of the *Daily Mail* and owner of the *Daily Mirror*.

In point of fact, by the time the Ministry was established, there was considerable experience in the propaganda field and considerable thought had been given to its function and purpose.

Source D

The function of propaganda is the formation of public opinion. The method is to tell the truth, but to present it in an acceptable form. It is useless to imagine that the mere existence of a fact will penetrate everywhere by its own weight, or that facts themselves do not require treatment according to the audience to which they are to be presented.

From an anonymous memorandum in the House of Lords Record Office of March–July 1918

SKILLS BUILDER

1 How would you account for Beaverbrook's description of his new job, given in Source C?

2 How far does Source D support Source B in its definition of propaganda?

The establishing of government departments and agencies was one thing: getting them to work effectively was quite another. It is clear that, in the early years of the war, when patriotism was riding high and the war would be over, if not by this Christmas then by the next, government initiatives were few and far between and then in a limited and surreptitious fashion. The government preferred, in the first years of the war, to let the propaganda machine roll of its own accord and under its own momentum. There were definite advantages to this approach. The people, it was argued, would be more likely to listen to, and act upon, blandishments from individuals, the press and other private sources than they would to government directives. It also enabled the government to distance itself from the more distasteful elements of propaganda. On the other hand, with no real propaganda programme, different exhortations and initiatives could be counter-productive. Assurances that all was well on the front could lead to a fall-off in recruitment; the press elevation of Kitchener to hero status made his dismissal almost impossible when, in the government's eyes, his deficiencies had become apparent.

How was the war reported?

Despite the influence of the Lord Northcliffe-dominated press the War Office and the army were slow in learning to utilise it. It was accepted that there would be a number of correspondents but they were regarded as something of a nuisance and to be kept quiet.

Source E

Each correspondent was only allowed to take one servant and one horse with him. His personal baggage was not to exceed more than 110lb and they could draw the ordinary army rations, which was all at their own paper's expense. Correspondents were not allowed runners or dispatch riders and were banned from bringing motor vehicles. Any communications would have to be submitted in duplicate to the Press Officer who would accompany the correspondents, and he in turn submitted them to the Chief Field Censor for authorisation. There were strict rules about what could and could not be included in a correspondent's dispatch. No reference could be made to the morale of troops, casualties, troop movements, their strength, location or composition and criticism or praise of a personal nature was also forbidden. Once on the register and licensed, the correspondent had to wait in London, horse and servant at the ready for his call-up by the War Office.

From Martin J. Farrar *News From the Front: War Correspondents on the Western Front 1914–18* published in 1998

Source F

The principle which guided me in my work was above all to avoid helping the enemy. This appeared to me more important than the purveyance of news to our own people. I tried to tell as much of the truth as was compatible with safety, to guard against depression and pessimism and to check unjustified optimism which might lead to relaxation of effort.

From E.D. Swinton
Eyewitness
published in 1932

Until May of 1915 the prevailing approach was one of trying to muzzle the press. Some correspondents, tired of waiting for official accreditation by the military authorities, decided to risk trying to get to the front themselves without the army's approval. They risked arrest or worse, being shot as spies. There was a dearth of reliable reports and there were complaints about this in parliament. Kitchener, the Secretary of War, under pressure to do something to increase the flow of news, appointed an officer from the railway branch of the army, Colonel Swinton, to reside at GHQ in France and send back dispatches of the front-line action. After vetting by Kitchener, these would be published under the title *Eyewitness*. Swinton later wrote his memoirs in which he tried to defend and explain his role.

Complaints about the lack of accurate information continued to grow, with Swinton's reports often referred to as 'eye-wash'. Questions were asked in parliament and the *Daily Mail* and other papers campaigned for greater access to the front. The army felt it had to relax somewhat and four leading correspondents were invited to GHQ in France in the spring of 1915. There was still considerable suspicion among the senior military figures, like Haig, who saw war correspondents as just another problem, not as potential allies. *The Times* military writer, Colonel Repington, was a personal friend of Sir John French, the Commander-in-Chief, and used his friendship to evade the usual controls. He published his famous articles on shell shortages in May 1915 (see page 181), much to the embarrassment of the government. It tended to confirm the distaste that Haig felt for journalists. However, as in so many other ways, Haig was to learn and adjust. The May Crisis (see Unit 11) illustrated the power of the press. It became increasingly clear that working with correspondents was more effective than simply frustrating them. Swinton's accounts were dropped in July 1915 and during the battle of Loos, in September of that year, war correspondents were allowed close to the front line.

War correspondents fully cooperated with the army in reporting the Battle of the Somme in 1916.

Source G

British offensive – At about 7.30 o'clock this morning a vigorous attack was launched by the British Army. The front extends over 20 miles north of the Somme. The assault was preceded by a terrific bombardment, lasting about an hour and a half. It is too early to as yet give anything but the barest particulars, as the fighting is developing in intensity, but the British troops have already occupied the German front-line. Many prisoners have already fallen into our hands, and as far as can be ascertained our casualties have not been heavy.

Report sent to the *Daily Chronicle* at 9.30 a.m., 1 July 1916 and published in that paper on 3 July

SKILLS BUILDER

Compare the dispatch in Source G with the information provided in Unit 7 on the first day of the Battle of the Somme (pages 107–10), including Source F of that unit. What explains the discrepancies?

Source H

The war correspondents had become a valuable asset to the military, communicating directly with the home front and deflecting difficult criticism. During this time the British press had demonstrated its full support of the military and they were fighting for the same goals and aims. They had surrendered their press freedoms to censorship and even turned a blind eye to the true reality of war, and now the military was ready to fully embrace the correspondent within its inner organisation.

From Martin J. Farrar *News From the Front: War Correspondents on the Western Front 1914–18* published in 1998

Source I

The weather changed for the worse last night although fortunately too late to hamper execution of our plans. The rain was heavy and constant throughout the night. It was still beating down steadily when the day broke chill and cheerless, with a blanket of mist completely shutting off the battlefield. During the morning it slackened to a dismal drizzle, but by this time the roads, fields, and footways were covered with semi-liquid mud, and the torn ground beyond Ypres had become in places a horrible quagmire.

It was pretty bad in the opinion of the weary soldiers who came back with wounds, but it was certainly worse for the enemy holding fragments of broken lines, still heavily hammered by the artillery and undoubtedly disheartened by the hardships of a wet night after a day of defeat.

From a dispatch by Percival Phillips published in the *Daily Express* on 2 August 1917. He is writing about the new British offensive around Ypres.

After the war, five accredited war correspondents were rewarded with knighthoods. They and their fellows have been criticised since the ending of the war for not reporting the full horrors of the extensive casualties and the suffering, and therefore in some way contributing to that suffering. Some, like Philip Gibbs, who thought of refusing his proffered knighthood, clearly felt guilty about this and helped to ensure in their memoirs and later writing, that the First World War was not remembered as a glorious victory but a national agony. In a sense this has produced as distorted a vision as their portrayal of events during the conflict. Philip Gibbs tries to offer a balanced assessment of his and fellow journalists' role in Source J.

Source J

On the whole we may claim, I think, our job was worth doing, and not badly done. Some of us, at least, did not spare ourselves to learn the truth and to tell it as far as it lay in our vision and in our power of words. During the course of battles it was not possible to tell all the truth, to reveal the full measure of slaughter on our side. But day by day the English-speaking world was brought close in spiritual touch with their fighting men, and knew the best, if not the worst of what was happening in the field of war, and the daily record of courage, endurance, achievement, by the youth that was being spent with such prodigal unthrifty zeal.

From Philip Gibbs *Adventures in Journalism* published in 1923

The press had clearly made a contribution to the war effort by their reporting and exercised a major influence on British society. Horrors had been downplayed and success emphasised to keep the home front working at turning out the necessary weapons. Siegfried Sassoon did not disagree about its influence, but bitterly criticised the role of the press (see Source L).

Source K

The press reached perhaps its highest point of influence during the First World War. Radio was in the future. Newspapers were the only source of news and their circulation rose still more when the casualty lists began to appear. With the politicians almost silent, the newspapers provided opinions as well. Lloyd George said in 1916: 'The press has performed the function which should have been performed by Parliament and which the French Parliament has performed.'

From *English History 1914–18*
by A.J.P. Taylor published 1965

Source L

I wonder why it was necessary for the Western Front to be attractively advertised by such intolerable twaddle. What was this camouflage which was manufactured by the press to aid the imaginations of people who had never seen the real thing?

From Siegfried Sassoon *Memoirs of an Infantry Officer* published in 1930. Siegfried Sassoon, a decorated soldier, became a bitter critic of the war by its later stages.

What was the role of the press in stirring up trouble at home?

Anti-German attitudes were driven largely by the press, aided by an increasingly literate population, eager to believe that what was in print had to be true. With the national newspapers being mainly controlled by three powerful press barons, Northcliffe, Rothermere and Beaverbrook, there was virtually no room for an opposing voice. Cynicism was to come later. Initially, these men's views prevailed and their ability to mould and control public opinion was enormous.

The government needed the press; indeed, newspapers were essential to government policy, particularly in the early years of the war. In a country with no large standing army, rapid dissemination of propaganda through the medium of daily newspapers was essential if civilian recruitment was to stand any chance of success and if the country as a whole was to be prepared for total war.

One of the most colourful and notorious figures to influence public opinion in the early years of the war was Horatio Bottomley, a former Liberal MP who owned a publication *John Bull* that sold between one and two million copies an issue:

- Bottomley regularly warned the public against the 'enemy within', calling Germans 'the Hun' and assuring a gullible readership that a German invasion would be facilitated by thousands of 'Huns' living in Britain, quietly waiting for their time to come. 'I call for a vendetta', said Bottomley, 'against every German in Britain, whether naturalised or not. As I have said before, you cannot naturalise an unnatural abortion, a hellish freak. But you can exterminate it. And now the time has come.'
- In this the *Daily Mail* agreed, demanding a boycott of restaurants employing Germans. 'Refuse to be served by a German waiter. If your waiter says he is Swiss, ask to see his passport. The naturalization form is just a scrap of paper. Once a German, always a German.'

There were, however, Germans who escaped what seems to have been persecution on a fairly massive scale. In Sussex, for example, a German Dr Steinhauser continued to work, visiting his patients and holding the usual surgeries with no signs of any animosity towards him; in south London, a German husband and wife who ran a local bakery were protected by local people. The wife had readily given credit and even free bread to help poorer members of the community, and now the community rallied round her when the authorities threatened the couple with internment.

The enemy within?

It was, as you have seen, but a short step from overt morale building to morale building of the covert sort: by raising worries about the Germans, and people who could be Germans, living in the midst of 'ordinary' British people.

That there were German spies living in Britain prior to, and during the war was undoubtedly true. Many of them were known to British Intelligence and when war was declared, twenty-two were arrested immediately, followed quickly by another fourteen. Some were imprisoned for the duration of the war; eleven were shot in the Tower of London. None of them had come to the attention of the authorities because of the diligence of the public. Of the first 9,000 'spy cases' that had been investigated by the police by September 1914, not one had led to an arrest. Nevertheless, 'spy-spotting' became a national sport.

Source N

It was just people panicking. Mr Schiffler, the pork butcher, he was taken away and his shop was all boarded up too. I think he was interned. I was vexed about them because I liked Mrs Schiffler, she was a nice old lady, but typically German. She'd lived there for years but she couldn't speak very good English. Mr Schiffler had the German band, they played oompah music – on a Saturday night outside the railway station. They used to sit with Mr Schiffler with his Tyrolean hat on and play. It was such a happy town at the time, before the war started.

Maud Cox was eight years old in 1915 and lived in Methil, Fifeshire. This is part of what she remembered.

Source M

Everything associated with Germany was attacked or rejected. Dachshunds were kicked or abused in the street, and in one or two cases, even burnt alive. German shepherd dogs were renamed Alsatians, and German measles 'Belgian flush'. There were elaborate explanations at Boots the Chemist that eau de cologne had nothing to do with the city but was entirely British, as were traditional German sausages and sauerkraut, which suddenly acquired English names. Perrier, which advertised itself as the 'table water of the Allies', asked in adverts 'Are you drinking German water?' Apollinaris water came from Germany, whereas Perrier water was from France. German music was no longer played, nor were many Steinway pianos, the lids of which were shut for the duration of the war. Then people began changing their names: Prince Louis of Battenberg resigned as First Lord of the Admiralty and changed his name to Mountbatten, and, most famously of all, the royal family was re-named in July 1917, losing Saxe-Coburg-Gotha and gaining Windsor.

From Richard van Emden and Steve Humphries
All Quiet on the Home Front published in 2003

SKILLS BUILDER

Study sources M, N and O.

How far do these sources suggest that everything associated with Germany was attacked or rejected?

Source O

10.2 German shops were frequent targets for mob violence, particularly after the sinking of the *Lusitania* in May 1915. This German shop in Poplar, east London, is being looted in that month.

Myths, rumours and just plain gossip

Initially, most of the morale boosting was carried out by ordinary people, repeating and embellishing what they heard down the pub, over the garden fence, in the queue and wherever two or more people gathered together. The most popular rumours were those that inspired optimism:

- Russian soldiers, presumably heading to the Western Front, were seen in various parts of Britain, marching with snow on their boots. Some reported having actually shovelled the snow away to help their progress – and this in August 1914.

- The story of the Angel of Mons spread like wildfire through troops and general population alike. In the period of hectic retreat from Mons (23 August 1914) when British troops would be at their most vulnerable from German attack, something extraordinary happened. Three angelic figures appeared in the air and warded off the attacks of the enemy.

Source P

I could see quite plainly in mid-air a strange light which seemed to be quite distinctly outlined and was not a reflection of the moon, nor were there any clouds in the neighbourhood. The light became brighter and I could see quite distinctly three shapes, one in the centre having what looked like outspread wings, the other two were not so large but were quite plainly distinct from the centre one. They appeared to have a long, loose-hanging garment of a golden tint. They were above the German line, facing us.

From Harold Begbie *On the Side of the Angels* published in 1915. Here he quotes an eyewitness account told to him by a lance-corporal who was involved in the retreat from Mons. Begbie was renowned for his patriotic poems.

SKILLS BUILDER

Read sources P, Q and R.

How do you account for the 'Angel of Mons' story?

Source Q

A fictional story of mine, *The Bowmen*, published on 29 September 1914, served as the inspiration for the Mons legend. In this story, a group of beleaguered British soldiers, in a moment of desperation, call on St George for help. A troop of ghostly archers promptly appears in the sky above them, raining deadly fire upon the enemy.

From Arthur Machen *The Bowmen and Other Legends of the War* published in 1915

Source R

There is the story of the 'Angel of Mons' going strong through the 2nd Corps, of how the angel of the Lord on the traditional white horse, clad all in white with flaming sword, facing the advancing Germans at Mons and forbade their further progress.

From a letter written by Brigadier-General John Charteris in early September 1914. He was involved in many propaganda exercises.

How far did Germany provide propaganda opportunities for the British?

A population ready to believe that Russians marched through Britain with snow on their boots and that every German name concealed a spy with evil intent, was more than ready to believe stories of German atrocities. These were usually concerned with innocent children, young women, nuns and members of the clergy, and involved severed hands, sliced breasts, the impaling of children and rape.

Where did the stories begin?

The most common ones seem to have originated early on in the war, beginning with the German invasion of Belgium. Here, with a mainly conscript army operating in enemy territory, soldiers did occasionally run amok. The Belgian resistance to invasion was intense and sometimes vicious; German officers ordered their men to respond with brutality. Rape was committed; human shields were used and between 20,000 and 30,000 buildings were maliciously burned to the ground. The Germans never denied their involvement, and were surprised to discover later that these acts of war were labelled atrocities and used by the Allies for propaganda purposes. This propaganda was enhanced by Belgian refugees, fleeing to the relative safety of Britain or France, who readily confirmed the atrocity stories. These stories made good newspaper copy at a time when the retreat from Mons landed the British Army knocking on the gates of Paris and the newspapers had little positive about which to write. Better to focus on the evils of the enemy than on military defeats. And this propaganda was repeated, repeated and embellished by the gullible and artless, culpable and mendacious.

How did the 'truth' become propaganda?

The sequence of 1914 newspaper reportage in Source S shows how a relatively insignificant event can be turned into propaganda material.

Source S

(i) From the *Kölnische Zeitung*
When the fall of Antwerp became known, the church bells were rung not only in Antwerp but throughout Germany.

(ii) From *Le Matin*
According to the *Kölnische Zeitung*, the clergy of Antwerp were compelled to ring the church bells when the fortress was taken.

(iii) From the *Corriere della Sera*
According to what *The Times* has heard from Cologne, via Paris, the unfortunate Belgian priests who refused to ring the church bells when Antwerp was taken, have been sentenced to hard labour.

Continued overleaf . . .

Source S continued . . .

(iv) From *Le Matin*

According to information that has reached the *Corriere della Sera* from Cologne via London, it is confirmed that the barbaric conquerors of Antwerp punished the unfortunate priests for their heroic refusal to ring the church bells by hanging them as living clappers to the bells with their heads down.

A sequence of extracts from German, French and Italian newspapers in October 1914 following the fall of Antwerp to German forces

SKILLS BUILDER

How do you account for the changes in reportage?

It does seem that some of the most valuable propaganda work was done, inadvertently, by the Germans themselves. Much of this can be attributed to the German concept of total war involving, as it did, the deaths of non-combatants – a concept not readily grasped by the British until 1939:

- The execution, by firing squad, of nurse Edith Cavell is a case in point. Working in occupied Belgium, she not only provided nursing care for all sick and wounded soldiers, but was also actively involved in helping the British to escape. This was, strictly speaking, espionage, and she was shot for her pains. This was excellent grist for the British propaganda mill; had the German authorities simply imprisoned her or deported her to England, no such opportunity would have been given.

- The striking of the *Lusitania* medal was intended to draw attention to British hypocrisy by pointing out that the ship had, in fact, been carrying arms and that warnings to such ships had been ignored. In reality, the medal was seized upon by the propaganda machine, claiming that it was congratulating the successful U-boat crew.

- The shelling of Scarborough and Hartlepool in December 1914 had no military significance whatsoever, and served not only to heighten British fears of invasion but also as a marvellous propaganda opportunity.

Source T

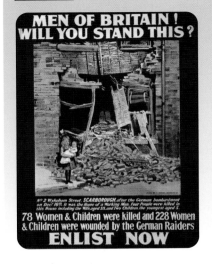

10.3 Poster issued in 1915 by the Parliamentary Recruiting Committee following the German bombardment of the seaside town of Scarborough, North Yorkshire

SKILLS BUILDER

1 Compare this recruitment poster to the ones on pages 142–3. How far is it similar in message and appeal?

Plain, straightforward lies

As the war dragged relentlessly into its third year, *The Times* newspaper provided the newly constituted War Aims Committee with what was to be the most famous propaganda achievement of the whole war.

Source U

Herr Karl Rosner, the correspondent of the Berlin 'Lokalanzeiger' on the Western Front, who lately gave such glowing accounts of the devastation of France, published last Tuesday the first definite German admission concerning the way in which the Germans use dead bodies. In a description of the battlefield north of Reims, he writes:

'We pass through Evernigcourt. There is a dull smell in the air, as if lime were being burnt. We are passing the great Corpse Exploitation Establishment (Kadaververwertungsansralt) of this Army Group. The fat that is won here is turned into lubricating oils, and everything else is ground down in the bones-mill into a powder which is used for mixing with pigs' food and as manure.'

Herr Rosner conveys this information with no comment but the remark that 'nothing can be permitted to go to waste.'

From *The Times* newspaper, 16 April 1917

Very shortly, a leaflet was produced by the Department of Information.

Source V

Out of their own mouths, the military masters of Germany stand convicted of an act of unspeakable savagery which has shocked the whole civilised world, including, probably, now that the truth has come out, many of the German people themselves. Attila's Huns were guilty of atrocious crimes, but they never desecrated the bodies of dead soldiers – their own flesh, as well as the fallen of the enemy – by improvising a factory for the conversion of human corpses into fat and oils, and fodder for pigs.

That is what the autocrats of Prussia have done – and admitted. 'Admitted' is too mild a word. They have boasted of it. It is an illustration of their much-vaunted efficiency! A sign of their pious Kultur! Proof of the zeal to waste nothing! Further evidence of the Kaiser's self-imposed deification! 'There is one law, mine!'

How was the discovery made? Quite simply. Herr Karl Rosner, the Special Correspondent of the Berlin 'Lokalanzeiger' on the Western Front, made the announcement in his published dispatch on 10 April.

From a 1917 Department of Information leaflet *A Corpse Conversion Factory* subtitled 'A Peep behind the German Lines'. Following this extract, the pamphlet gave a reproduction of a German language version of the supposed dispatch followed by an English translation.

SKILLS BUILDER

1 How has the Department of Information used the report in *The Times* to create propaganda?

2 How has the Department of Information tried to make its account believable?

3 Why do you think so many people believed it?

It was not until 1925 that it was admitted in the House of Commons that the whole story was a lie, put about for propaganda purposes.

What was the role of the cinema?

The cinema was in its infancy in the years 1914–18, but this did not stop its manipulation for propaganda purposes. It must be remembered, however, that films directly relating to the war amounted to around ten per cent of those produced and shown in British cinemas. The cinema was largely used for entertainment and escapism.

Cartoons

Some cartoons were basic in the extreme, and provided audiences with crude images and an unsophisticated, impossible to miss, message.

Source W

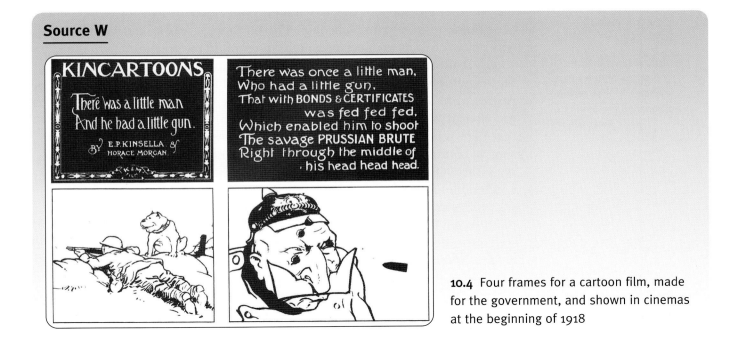

10.4 Four frames for a cartoon film, made for the government, and shown in cinemas at the beginning of 1918

Less crude, with a greater need for sensitivity and with an outcome that was difficult to predict, were images from the front.

Images of the front

Despite initial reluctance on the part of the War Office to allow photographers and film companies anywhere near the front, the formation of an official film unit was agreed sometime between March and July 1915. Newsreels began offering 'authentic' scenes from the front and going to the cinema became, for many, a patriotic duty and a way of contributing, albeit vicariously, to the war effort. Cinema audiences, hungry for information and to understand the experiences of their 'boys' overseas,

Source X

You must not leave the public with a bitter taste in their mouth at the end. The film takes you to the grave, but it must not leave you there; it shows you death in all its grim nakedness, but after that it is essential that you should be restored to a sense of cheerfulness and joy. That joy comes out of the knowledge that in all this whirlpool of horrors, our Lads continue to smile the smile of victory.

Geoffrey Malins, the official director of newsreels, explains in 1916 how he approached the filming of war scenes

were sitting targets for the purveyors of propaganda. However, to their credit, the government did not allow the use of film as a provider of information to be overridden by its value as a propaganda vehicle. By 1918 over 700 films of one kind or another had been made. Most were realistic portrayals of a nation at war; while distressing material may have been edited out, it does not seem that any fictitious scenes were edited in.

The Battle of the Somme

The Battle of the Somme was a film made almost by accident. Geoffrey Malins and J.B. McDowell were sent to the 4th British Army simply to do some background filming. Postponement of the battle enabled them to film scenes of preparation, and on 1 July, Malins filmed the famous sequence of the detonation of a large British mine under the German Hawthorn Redoubt. It seems likely, too, that although the preliminary bombardment and the march of the battalions to the front-line trenches were filmed on the Somme, the shots of the actual battle were taken miles away, probably at a trench mortar training school. Trench footage was staged, but there was no real intent to deceive, simply to recreate the truth in a situation where real trench conditions made filming impossible. Malins and McDowell left the Western Front on 10 July. Back in London, the first rushes were seen on 12 July and William Jury of Imperial Pictures, a member of Wellington House's Cinema Committee immediately realised that here was a documentary in the making, even though it had not been shot as continuous narrative and a lot of cutting and splicing would be necessary. On 24 August 1916, *The Battle of the Somme* opened in 34 London cinemas and in the provinces a week later. It was an instant success, with 2,000 bookings in the first two months of its release. Overall, the film made some £30,000 profit but that was not really the point. For the first time the general public could see what a significant battle on the Western Front was really like. Or so they thought.

Source Y

14 August 1916

We went to a private view of the Somme films, i.e. the pictures taken during recent fighting. To say that one enjoyed them would be untrue; but I am glad I went. I am glad I have seen the sort of things our men have to go through, even to the sortie from the trench and the falling in the barbed wire. There were pictures, too, of the battlefield after the fight and of our gallant men lying crumpled and helpless. There were pictures of men mortally wounded being carried out of the communication trenches with the look of agony on their faces. It reminded me of what Paul's last hours were [Paul was her brother] I have often tried to imagine to myself what he went through, and now I know: and I shall never forget. It was like going through a tragedy. I felt something of what the Greeks must have felt when they went in their crowds to witness those grand old plays – to be purged in their minds through pity and terror.

From the diary of Frances Stevenson. She was David Lloyd George's secretary, his mistress and, later, his second wife.

Source Z

A DUTY YOU OWE TO
THE IMPERIAL GOVERNMENT

SEE
The Battle of the Somme.

COME AND SEE
The Battle of the Somme.

The very punch of the Allies, Backed
by the hall-mark of
THE IMPERIAL GOVERNMENT.

10.5 A poster outside the Harehills Picture House in Leeds advertising *The Battle of the Somme* showing there in August 1916

SKILLS BUILDER

Study Sources W, X, Y and Z and use your own knowledge.

To what extent would you regard the film *Battle of the Somme* as government propaganda?

How successful was government propaganda?

Most British people had their attitudes towards Germans moulded by propaganda and by the personal experiences of those engaged in front-line activities. The only Germans the British on mainland UK met face-to-face were prisoners of war.

Source AA

10.6 Women workers at a clothing factory in London, 1918 with German prisoners of war who worked there too. The factory made uniforms for German prisoners of war in Britain and British prisoners of war in Germany.

Source BB

Rioting was going on quite near here. It is a mercy that they have interned the Germans at last. It ought to have been done long ago. It is a pity that our folk descended to lawlessness, but it was the only way our people could show their feelings in the matter. We have a great camp of German prisoners of war not far from here. Would you believe that some people were actually asking for cakes for them!

Part of a letter from Margaret Lilley of Stroud Green, London, written in May 1915

Source CC

Monday 4 March 1918

The German prisoners are hard at work on the aerodrome at Chelmsford. They have Quarters in the Workhouse and are marched back there from their work at 4.30 p.m. each day. They are said to be happy, laughing and joking with each other as they pass along the street. Several Chelmsford girls have been taken before the magistrates for giving them stamps and chocolate.

Thursday 29 August 1918

A girl was driving a baker's van in a lane at Leaden Roding. She was stopped by a group of German prisoners, who demanded bread, and threatened her if she refused to give it. They took six loaves, but paid for them. She was summoned before a magistrate at Dunmow for supplying bread to German prisoners. The magistrates dismissed the case, adding that it is a pity that prisoners are allowed on Essex lanes without a guard.

Mrs Matthews has four German prisoners doing work on her farm. They are brought in a lorry at 8.00 a.m. They have a meal at the Chelmsford Workhouse before they start in the morning, and bring another meal with them. She does not think this is enough, because they work until 7 or 8 p.m. She is annoyed because the authorities forbid her giving them more food, but quietly ignores the prohibition. The men are excellent workers.

Extracts from the diaries of the Rev Andrew Clark, vicar of Great Leighs, Essex

SKILLS BUILDER

Study sources AA, BB and CC.

1 How do you account for the differences in the attitudes of British people to the German prisoners of war?

2 List the positive attitudes towards Germans that you can find. Does this mean that the British propaganda machine failed?

Source DD

There is considerable debate as to the effect of wartime propaganda in general, and it is wise to get the propaganda effort into perspective. Famous recruiting posters such as Alfred Leete's 'Kitchener Wants You', an image first published in Britain on 5 September 1914, did not arrest the decline in military recruitment. While the Parliamentary Recruiting Committee eventually printed almost 6m posters and over 14m leaflets at a total cost of £24,000, this was less than Rowntrees of York had spent on advertising a single brand of cocoa in 1911–12. Similarly, for every PRC leaflet produced in 1914–15, at least ten had been produced by the three main political parties during the 1910 election campaigns. Clearly, bearing in mind the limits of technological and media development in this period, military victory and not propaganda was the most significant factor in Germany's defeat.

From Ian Beckett *Home Front 1914–18* published in 2006

Source EE

British propaganda during the war was characterised by terrible chaos and lack of direction. The early reliance upon voluntary bodies made it impossible for any cohesion to be developed. When the government began to intervene more actively, it did so on a piecemeal basis, such that contradictory policies were pursued by competing departments. The establishment of a Ministry of Information improved matters, but Beaverbrook still found that 'the sphere of the Ministry's work was not defined with sufficient clearness. No charter of rights and duties was drawn up'. Given these deficiencies, one doubts that propaganda made a significant contribution to maintaining home front morale. Even the best propagandist would have had difficulty in putting a gloss on such a static and costly war. For the first four years of the war the British people had little reason to feel cheerful, yet their morale held. They were not duped by their government; a propaganda effort so chaotic could not have contributed to mass mind control. The steadfast patriotism of the British people and their unquenchable faith in eventual victory instead arose from within themselves.

From Gerard J. DeGroot *Blighty: British Society in the Era of the First World War* published in 1996

Question

How far do sources DD and EE support each other in their views about the effectiveness of propaganda?

And finally . . .

Samuel Johnson, the English poet, critic and lexicographer, wrote in 1758 that:

> Among the calamities of war may be numbered the diminution of the love of truth.

He wasn't wrong, was he?

What have you learned in this unit?

You have learned about the role of the government in setting up various departments, as the war progressed, to deal with propaganda and you will have understood that the apparently chaotic and disorganised way in which this aspect of total war was addressed was probably partially the result of organised mass propaganda being a relatively new field in which the government was engaged. You have learned about the ways in which the war was reported and people were made aware of the 'enemy within' and have understood that this affected members of the public differently. You have considered the importance of the media in disseminating and developing propaganda, and in particular the role of the more extreme newspaper proprietors such as Horatio Bottomley and the role and impact of film. Finally, you have considered the impact of propaganda on people insofar as their reactions to individual Germans in their midst were concerned.

What skills have you used in this unit?

You have used your analytical skills to consider one definition of propaganda and have cross-referenced to specific sources in order to evaluate them against this definition in order to determine whether or not they 'qualify' as propaganda. You have worked with a number of different sorts of propaganda and assessed the effectiveness of their 'message' and the appropriateness of the media used. You have investigated rumours and atrocity stories in order to understand how they originated and spread and have understood the roles of both Germany and the British government in this. You have used your empathetic skills to understand how, no matter how illogical and unfair it was, some people turned against all things they associated with Germany and the German people while others remained supportive of the German prisoners of war with whom they worked and who lived in their communities.

SKILLS BUILDER

- What is the difference, in your view, between propaganda and bias?
- Is it ever justifiable to twist the truth of an event so that it serves a purpose other than providing information?
- To what extent would you regard First World War British propaganda as a waste of time?

Exam style question

This is the sort of question you will find appearing on the examination paper as a (b) question.

Study Sources D, BB and EE, and use your own knowledge.

Do you agree with the view, expressed in Source EE, that 'British propaganda during the war was characterised by terrible chaos and lack of direction'?

Exam tips

You have worked on (b) style questions at the end of Units 3, 5, 8 and 10.

You have experimented with different sorts of plans and considered different styles of question.

You should by now have a good idea of the way in which you prefer to plan your answer. So go ahead and plan an answer to this question.

Now test yourself! Look at your plan and check what you have drawn up.

Continued overleaf . . .

Exam tips continued . . .

Have you:

- **Analysed** Sources D and BB for points that support and points that challenge the view expressed in Source EE that 'British propaganda during the war was characterised by terrible chaos and lack of direction', and noted these points in your plan?
- Shown how you will **cross-reference** between the sources for points of agreement and disagreement?
- Shown where you will use your **wider knowledge** both to reinforce and challenge the points you have derived from the sources?
- Thought about how you will combine the points you have made into an **argument** for or against the view that women gained nothing from their war-time experience, and noted this on your plan?
- Shown how your **evaluation** of the points you have used in argument has considered the **quality of the evidence** used?
- Noted what your conclusion will be, and how you will ensure it is **balanced and supported**?

RESEARCH TOPIC

Some of the men who fought on the Western Front wrote poetry about their experiences.

Two of the most well-known of these were Siegfried Sassoon and Wilfred Owen, but there were many others. There are a number of others mentioned throughout the book.

Research the experience of war and the war poetry of one such man. How far would you regard his poetry as propaganda?

11 The Home Front 1914–18: how was the economy mobilised for total war?

What is this unit about?

The main focus of this unit is on the ways in which the British government geared up the economy for total war. It explores the implications of the Defence of the Realm Act and the Munitions of War Act, considers the impact on the economy of the enlistment of so many men of military age and of the necessary 'dilution' of the workforce by women. It considers how the munitions industry was turned round in order to respond to the shell shortage, and addresses the ways in which the mining, transport and agriculture industries attempted to meet the demands of total war. The problem of alcohol, the resultant impact this had on industrial production and government action to prevent absenteeism due to drunkenness is considered. The reactions of trade unions and sections of the workforce to the directing of the economy to meet the demands of total war are addressed as, finally, is the cost of the war in financial and human terms.

Key questions

- How did the government organise the country's economy for total war?
- How far was the workforce willing to accept the government's initiatives?

Timeline

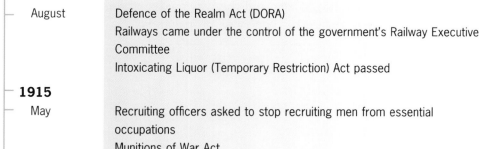

1914

August	Defence of the Realm Act (DORA)
	Railways came under the control of the government's Railway Executive Committee
	Intoxicating Liquor (Temporary Restriction) Act passed

1915

May	Recruiting officers asked to stop recruiting men from essential occupations
	Munitions of War Act
	Shell shortage scandal breaks
	Coalition government formed
	Ministry of Munitions formed with David Lloyd George as Minister of Munitions
	Tramway Workers' Union dubious about employment of women
June	Central Board of Control established to restrict the sale of alcohol in specific areas
July	Miners' strike

1916
- February — London General Omnibus Company begins employing women
- July — TUC passes resolution supporting Haig and setting aside all holidays for the duration of the war
- December — DORA extended to cover South Wales coalfield

1917
- Jan — Women's Land Army founded
- February — Coal controller appointed
  Shipping controller appointed
- March — Canal company takes over all canals not under the control of the railways
- May — Navy controller appointed
  Lord Rhondda appointed Minister of Food

1918
- November — Armistice; the war ends

An all powerful state?

It is important to remember that Britain had no written constitution that guaranteed the rights of individuals against an overbearing state. What Britain did have, however, was a long history of custom and practice, a judiciary separate from the executive and a free press. There were thus checks and balances upon what a government could, in practice, do. In a situation of total war, government had to be given (not take) specific and far-reaching powers to override these checks and balances.

The Defence of the Realm Act, 1914

Parliament surrendered some of its authority to the government on 8 August 1914 when it agreed to the Defence of the Realm Act (DORA). This Act gave the government wide powers '*for securing the public safety and defence of the realm.*' Its provisions were extended at various points throughout the war, as the need to do so arose. DORA meant that the government could react quickly to crises, without the long-drawn-out procedures and processes involved in setting up relevant acts of parliament.

Source A

An Act to confer on His Majesty in Council power to make regulations during the present War for the Defence of the Realm.

Be it enacted by the King's most Excellent Majesty by and with the advice and consent of the Lords Spiritual and Temporal, and Commons, in this present Parliament assembled, and by the authority of the same, as follows:

Continues overleaf . . .

Source A continued . . .

1 His Majesty in Council has power during the continuance of the present war to issue regulations as to the powers and duties of the Admiralty and Army Council, and of the members of His Majesty's forces, and other persons acting on His behalf, for securing the public safety and defence of the realm; and may by such regulations authorize the trial by courts martial and punishment of persons contravening any of the provisions of such regulations designed –

(a) to prevent persons communicating with the enemy or obtaining information for that purpose or any purpose calculated to jeopardize the success of the operations of any of His Majesty's forces or to assist the enemy; or
(b) to secure the safety of any means of communication, or of railways, docks or harbours;

in a like manner as if such persons were subject to military law and had on active service committed an offence under section five of the Army Act.

From *The Defence of the Realm Act*,
passed on 8 August 1914

SKILLS BUILDER

Acts of parliament are written in legal language that can be tricky to understand if you are not a lawyer.

Read the Act in Source A carefully.

Could it:

(i)   prevent spying?
(ii)   protect centres of communication?
(iii) enable the government to control industry?
(iv)   censor the press?
(v)   detain suspected people without trial?
(vi)   withdraw from the war?
(vii) decide where people were to work?

Explain how.

These powers were essential if an economy was to be developed that was capable of coping with total war – a 'war economy'.

What is a 'war economy'?

The First World War was probably the first time that the entire economy of a country was transformed to meet the needs of a military struggle.

Source B

The aim was to win, no matter what the cost. Therefore the main economic priority was to produce the necessary quantity of goods to defeat the enemy. Consequently the ultimate economic purpose was quite different from that of peacetime, and the kind of economy that was created has come to be known loosely by the term 'war economy'. The term is a loose one, for it is a matter of historical fact that most of the 'war economies' that have existed have neither had such simple priorities as, nor much resemblance to, the war economies which existed in Britain. It may even be questioned whether historians have not exaggerated the degree of unanimity of purpose which informed the economy of Britain during the two world wars. Nevertheless, it must be stated that it is a matter of almost universal agreement that the British nation twice bent its united energies to create an economy whose dominating purpose was to defeat the enemy, sweeping aside, gradually in the First World War, and almost from the beginning in the Second, most other claims on that economy.

From A.S. Milward *The Economic Effects of Two World Wars on Britain*
published in 1984

SKILLS BUILDER

1   Using the evidence in Source B, how would you define a 'war economy'?

2   How do you think a 'war economy' would differ from a 'peacetime economy'?

3   What evidence would you look for in order to determine whether or not Britain in 1914–18 was on a 'war economy' footing?

How was the workforce managed?

The most valuable resource any country can posses is its people. Without an effectively and appropriately organised workforce, little of worth can be achieved in a peace-time economy, let alone in a war-time one. The first problem to be faced by the government was one of manpower. '*In a war of machines*', wrote historian Arthur Marwick '*it was at least as necessary to look to the supply of machine-makers at home as to the machine-users on the field of battle.*'

Where had all the workers gone?

Ironically, the main hindrance to effective deployment of manpower was the patriotic rush of young men to enlist in the early months of the war.

Source C

A table showing the occupations of men who volunteered for the British Army, August 1914–February 1916.

Occupation	Men employed July 1914 (000s)	Men enlisting (000s)	% pre-war labour force volunteering
Industry	6,165	1,743	28.3
Of which mines and quarries	1,266	313	24.7
Agriculture	920	259	28.2
Transport	1,041	233	22.4
Finance and commerce	1,249	501	40.1
Professions	144	60	41.7
Entertainment	177	74	41.8
Central government	311	85	27.3
Local government	477	126	26.4
All occupations	10,484	3,081	29.4

Questions

1 How do you account for the differences in volunteering from the various occupational groups?
2 How would enlistment from these industries and occupations affect Britain's ability to create and run a war economy?

By May of 1915 the War Office was becoming aware of the situation, and issued circulars to recruiting officers, asking them to avoid recruiting men from certain occupations. At the same time, efforts were made to bring skilled men back from the trenches. Later in the war, when losses on the Western Front mounted, there were continual reviews of the 'reserved occupations', with thousands of men being 'combed out' and sent into the services. There was, thus, always this tension between the demands of the front-line commanders and the demands of those supplying them.

What was the Munitions of War Act?

In May 1915, a Munitions of War Act was passed. This put on to a legal footing the Treasury Agreement that had been made two months previously between the Trades Union Congress (TUC) and the Chancellor of the Exchequer, David Lloyd George. The Act applied to all industries engaged in war work:

- Strikes and lock-outs were prohibited.
- All workplace differences were to be 'solved' by compulsory arbitration.
- Wage rates were safeguarded and any wage rate increases had to be approved by the government.
- Trade unions were to abandon restrictive practices for the duration of the war, and permit unskilled and semi-skilled men and women to take the place of skilled men who were away in the armed services. This was commonly known as 'dilution'.

- Profits within these 'controlled' industries were to be limited.
- The government had the power to direct people to work in specific industries in specific parts of the country.
- No worker could leave his job without the consent of his employer obtained in a 'Certificate of Discharge'.
- No worker could refuse to take on a new job, regardless of the rates of pay on offer.
- No worker could refuse overtime even if it was unpaid.
- People committing offences under this Act were to be tried in special Munitions Tribunals.

SKILLS BUILDER

What were (a) employers and (b) workers reactions likely to be to the Munitions of War Act? Which clauses would they find the most troublesome?

How was the munitions industry managed?

The most important industrial sector during a time of total war was **munitions**. The equation was simple. Without an adequate supply of weaponry, the war would be lost:

- On 22 February 1915, David Lloyd George, Chancellor of the Exchequer, circulated his colleagues with a memorandum arguing that the whole economy had to be geared up for total war and that this meant reorganising factories and engineering works to focus on the production of munitions. This was in direct opposition to Kitchener, who wanted to continue with the existing War Office contracts. The battle between the two men continued through April and May.
- A shortage of shells on the Western Front quickly became a national scandal.
- Sir John French, Commander-in-Chief of the British forces (see page 102) had previously assured Kitchener that he had all the ammunition he needed (though this wasn't widely known at the time). Here was crisis indeed.
- On 19 May Prime Minister Herbert Asquith announced that he was restructuring his ministry.
- On 21 May the House of Commons debated the munitions crisis.
- In the new ministry formed at the end of May, the Conservatives joined the Liberals in a wartime coalition under Prime Minister Asquith and, importantly, David Lloyd George headed the newly formed **Ministry of Munitions**.

Question

How did the Munitions of War Act of 1915 help create a war economy?

Definition

Munitions

Military weapons, ammunition and stores.

Source D

We had not sufficient high explosives to lower the enemy's parapets to the ground, after the French practice. The infantry did splendidly, but the conditions were too hard. The lack of an unlimited supply of high explosives was a fatal bar to our success.

Part of an article from the military correspondent of *The Times* newspaper, Colonel Repington, and published in that newspaper on 14 May 1915. He is referring to the second Battle of Ypres.

Definition

Ministry of Munitions
The Ministry of Munitions was staffed at the top levels by businessmen, recruited by the minister, David Lloyd George, and loaned by their companies for the duration of the war. These men were able to coordinate the needs of big business with those of the state, and reach a compromise on price and profit that was acceptable to both sides. In addition, government agents bought essential supplies from abroad. Once bought, their distribution had to be controlled in order to prevent speculative price rises and to enable normal marketing to continue. The whole of the Indian jute crop, for example, was bought and distributed in this way. Steel, wool, leather and flax came under similar controls. By 1918, the Ministry of Munitions had a staff of 65,000 employing some 3 million workers in over 20,000 factories.

SKILLS BUILDER

1 How similar is the message of this poster to that of the recruitment posters on pages 136–7?

2 How different is the technique used to convey that message?

Source E

THESE WOMEN ARE DOING THEIR BIT

LEARN TO MAKE MUNITIONS

11.1 One of a series of posters issued by the Ministry of Munitions urging people to take up various posts in the armaments industry

How was the mining industry managed?

The coal strike 1915

Most industrial concerns were powered by coal, and thus a steady and reliable supply was essential to the maintenance of Britain's economy and so to the war effort:

- This supply was compromised in the early days of the war by the vast numbers of miners (see Source C) who volunteered for the armed services. Production fell and prices soared. The situation was additionally complicated by a bitter coal strike in July 1915.
- All mines were privately owned and the mine owners had separate, and sometimes very different, wage agreements with their employees.
- The South Wales Miners' Federation had a five-year agreement with their mine owners that was due to expire on 1 April 1915. Prior to this, however, miners throughout the country had successfully pressed the government for a war bonus, and a national agreement had been reached. However, the Welsh miners made it clear that they preferred their local agreements to the national one. They were anxious to secure a permanent pay increase, rather than a 'war bonus' that could be taken away when the war ended.

- All attempts at mediation failed and a strike was declared for 14 July. At this point, the government, aware of the catastrophic effects of a coal strike, moved in.

- On 13 July the government invoked the Munitions of War Act, declaring the South Wales coalfield a 'controlled establishment'.

- Nevertheless, 15 July saw some 200,000 Welsh miners out on strike. Horrified at the impact this would have on the war economy, the government promptly conceded to all the miners' demands, and work began again on 20 July.

- Further brief, spasmodic stoppages occurred throughout the war. South Wales set a pattern for the settlement of wage disputes in key industries during the war, with the government realising that confrontation was counter-productive.

State control?

Various proposals for direct state control of the coal mines were made by committees of enquiry, but all were stalled by the government, partly because the Liberal Party was heavily dependent on contributions from coal owners to its party funds. However, by the beginning of December 1916, DORA had been extended to cover the South Wales mines and a coal controller appointed in February 1917. Although mines remained in private ownership throughout the war, their profits were fixed at 1913 levels and national, rather than local, pay negotiation was permitted. This was possible because any surplus profits went to the Treasury, where they were used to make up any falling profits in individual mines to the 1913 level.

Source F

11.2 Cartoon from the *Daily Mirror* commenting on the miners' strike, published on 19 July 1915

SKILLS BUILDER

1 Is the cartoon attacking trade unions or the miners? (Hint: identify the man on the left and the man on the right.)

2 What is the message of the cartoon?

3 How far would you regard this cartoon as government propaganda?

Source G

Practically all the families were very poor, like us. We were all very proud, too, but it was very difficult to make ends meet. Dad used to work nights and weekends to get everything he could. We still had to go on the parish to get extra, though. Dad was a quiet, patriotic man and he would rather not have struck, especially with the war on. He supported the war, he volunteered for the army but they told him he would be more useful as a miner. He didn't go to all the meetings that the police tried to break up, but he decided to go along with the majority when they came out on strike. When they were out, I used to get up early to go up the slagheap with my dad and my brother to get coal for the fire. I can't remember how long the coal strike lasted, but they got what they wanted. I think they were awarded two shillings a week extra and then Dad had to admit that perhaps it was worth it after all. Everyone was jubilant and we even sang a song at school to celebrate the end of the strike.

Gwen Herford was one of nine children of a miner living in the village of Pontycymmer in the Garw valley, South Wales. Here she remembers a miners' strike in 1917.

SKILLS BUILDER

How far does Source G challenge the message in Source F?

How was the transport industry controlled?

It was clearly essential at a time of total war to be able to move troops and civilians, raw materials and manufactured goods, quickly and efficiently to where they were needed, both within Britain and overseas.

Railways

The necessity of government control of the railways had been recognised as early as 1871, when the Regulation of Forces Act stated that in time of war the railways were to be placed at the disposal of the government. So, in August 1914, the railways passed easily into the control of the government's Railway Executive Committee. In reality, however, they were run by the managers of the main railway companies, and were administered not by the government but for the government. This arrangement worked well: profits were kept at 1913 levels and the Treasury, in return for free transport of troops, made up any deficits.

Shipping

The merchant marine was as essential to survival in total war as the Royal Navy, yet by December 1916 fewer than half of Britain's merchant ships and none of its great passenger liners had been requisitioned by the government. This was all changed by the appointment of Sir John Maclay, a Scottish shipowner, as shipping controller working in conjunction with a committee of management comprising all significant British shipowners. In May 1917, Eric Geddes, as controller of the navy, headed up a separate department. By 1918 almost all merchant shipping had been requisitioned by the Ministry of Shipping.

A Canal Company, set up in March 1917, was responsible for all inland waterways not owned and run by railway companies.

How far were women involved?

Source H

(a) Railways

At the outbreak of war women fulfilled a number of functions on the railways such as booking clerks, telegraph and telephone operators, carriage cleaners and charwomen; they also worked on the clerical side and in domestic service in the railway companies' hotels and restaurants. There were 12,423 women thus employed. Four years later this figure had risen to over 65,000 and included those doing what might be termed 'new' jobs [like ticket collecting and signal operators]. The impact of women in the transport industries, particularly on the railways, was short-lived, and the high-profile nature of the work such as ticket collecting did not really reflect where the main increase in women's labour lay. It was in the clerical and telephone side of the industry that the rate of increase was most noticeable. That figure rose from 2,800 in 1914 to just short of 21,000 by 1918.

(b) Buses

Male opposition to the advent of women were considerable. The Amalgamated Association of Tramway and Vehicle Workers had opened their membership to women, but prejudice was implicit in the Tramway Workers' resolution of May 1915, which emphasised that the employment of women in such work was 'dangerous' and 'unwise'. In fact, it was not until February 1916 that the London General Omnibus Company started to employ women. Only 100 had started work by March, although the training schemes were designed to provide an increase of 500 a month.

From Diana Condell and Jean Liddiard *Working for Victory?* published in 1987

Source I

11.3 Women porters working in the goods department of the South East and Chatham Railway Company Depot, 1918

Question

Would the photograph of women porters (Source I) be more or less likely to remove prejudice against women working in the transport system?

How was the agricultural industry organised?

There was initially little government involvement in organising agriculture, largely because it was complacently assumed that the war would be over by Christmas and that food supplies would continue as normal. There was, too, a reluctance to interfere in the countryside, which was traditionally conservative, suspicious of change and dominated by large landowners who were doing nicely out of the increasing profits as the war extended beyond Christmas 1914, and food became scarcer and prices soared.

Source J

The food production on Britain's farms was actually falling. The calorific value of the food they produced fell from 21.4 billion calories in 1914 to 19.3 billion calories in 1916. There were a number of factors involved. Overseas supplies of artificial fertilisers were cut off and the supply of imported animal feeds disrupted. Large numbers of farm workers, who were traditionally amongst the lowest wage earners in the country, followed Kitchener's call to arms. They were lured by the promise of better money, regular meals and military glory. Around 15% of the rural labour force, self-selected from the young and fit, and many of them with vital skills in animal husbandry and ploughing, were lost from the countryside.

From Richard van Emden and Steve Humphries
All Quiet on the Home Front published in 2003

The situation was exacerbated by government requisitioning of horses for the front.

Source K

I think the one thing that affected me, apart from my brother George being killed, was when they took the horses. They used to come from the War Office and say, 'We're going to buy three or four of your horses.' You had no redress. You couldn't say, 'I don't want to sell them.' We only had four and two of them were beautiful shire horses. They took those and another bay mare which wasn't quite as big, and left us with just one horse. It upset me very much. It was a morning before I went to school, oh, I was so sad all day at school. I think I cried myself to sleep that night. They weren't pets, but I knew them by their names and they meant an awful lot to us. Boxer, Duke and Violet were their names. Never saw them again, of course.

The men said, 'We'll send you some more horses.' We waited a day or two and a very large mule arrived, that was their replacement. He was a wonderful mule, really. Lots of army mules were vicious things but he was as quiet as a mouse. He turned out to be a good asset, but it was strange to see my father ploughing with one horse and one mule, that was the only power on the farm. Poor old things, they had to work so hard. But it was all part of the war, I suppose. Animals suffered the same as human beings.

Len Whitehead, a farmer's son, remembers what happened on his father's farm in 1915

SKILLS BUILDER

1 Was horse-power or man-power more necessary on Britain's farms?

2 How sensible would it have been for the government to have designated some farm work as 'reserved occupations'?

The government finally got a grip on the situation:

- In May 1917 Lord Rhondda replaced the ineffective Lord Devonport as Minister of Food and the food supply was brought under control.

- He set up a system of rationing for essential foodstuffs by establishing statutory food control committees throughout the country, each area with a food office that issued registration cards. Local initiatives were encouraged. For example, Birmingham went ahead with its own scheme.

- Bacon, butter, margarine, meat, sugar and tea were among the essential foodstuffs to be rationed.

- Bread was never rationed, but people's biggest grievance was its expense. In the spring of 1917, bread cost 1s for a 4lb loaf, twice its 1914 price. Lord Rhondda persuaded the government to subsidise the cost of bread (the staple of the working classes) at 9d for a 4lb loaf. From November 1917, the government subsidised the cost of potatoes (another working-class staple).

- Widespread administrative machinery was set up, reaching into every hamlet and farmstead, with the aim of encouraging the growth of essential foodstuffs and all-round greater efficiency.

- The basic aim was to boost the production of wheat, barley and potatoes and many livestock farmers were persuaded to turn to crop production by government assurances that the price of corn would not only be doubled from its pre-war level but would be held for five years.

- The Board of Agriculture undertook to ensure that the land was properly cultivated and in 1917 some 2.1 million acres of pasture were ploughed up for food crops.

- Sixty-one War Agricultural Executive Committees were set up throughout the country to supervise farmers and ensure they managed their lands effectively.

- A Wages Board was established to ensure that farmers paid their male workers a minimum wage of £1 5s 0d a week.

- In January 1917 the Women's Land Army was founded, with the aim of replacing the men lost to agriculture and providing a permanent skilled and mobile female labour force for work on farms and in forestry. Most of the women recruited into the WLA were middle- and upper-class town girls, viewed with suspicion by many farmers. In Hampshire as late as 1918 it was reported that farmers would *'take on anything that comes along, boys, old men, cripples, mentally deficients, criminals or anything else'* rather than women.

- WLA members were paid eighteen shillings a week – seven shillings less than unskilled male farm workers.

- Despite widespread government propaganda, only 16,000 WLA members helped bring in the 1918 harvest. Most of the women workers on the land were not the uniformed members of the WLA. They were the women who were the wives, sisters, mothers, aunts and cousins of farm labourers and village craftsmen.

Source L

I had a good job in a factory. I'd taken the foreman's place, and had a lot of girls under me. But I wanted to help on the land. I was so proud to do my bit for the war effort, and I was so proud of my uniform. I had no idea how hard it was going to be. That winter it was bitterly cold, it was very bad and it seemed to rain all day, every day. The farmer was hard and he had me cutting cabbages in the fields and driving a horse wagon around. I got soaked through, there was no shelter, no escape from the rain, I just had to keep on working. Well, as a child I had been a delicate, petite girl and the wet and the cold started to make me very ill. I got a severe chest problem, bronchitis it was, I couldn't do anything. It stayed with me for years. So after a few months I ended up coming back to Sheffield. That was the end of the Land Army for me.

Edith Storey from Sheffield recounts her time in the Women's Land Army in 1917

Source M

We do have fun, though the most part is really heavy, dirty work. I was knocked over by a calf this morning, and my hand is pretty badly hurt, but the experience did not equal that of being chased by an old sow, as I was the other day; she took a dislike to me as I was carrying a huge sack of potatoes up the field. Of course I ran as fast as I could, but she kept up with me until I backed through a hedge, tearing my dress on a piece of barbed wire. My revenge was complete, though. Yesterday we went (the farmer and his wife and I) to the market and sold the offensive animal for £9 and ten shillings. My farmer is also the village blacksmith and I am learning to shoe a horse and blow the bellows: the sparks fly from the anvil and make holes in your clothes – not to mention yourself. Some people tell me I will not be able to go on with my farm work in the winter because it will make my hands so bad. But I intend to stick to it. Our men don't stop fighting in the cold weather and neither shall I. My only brother is in the trenches, so you know how I feel.

Dorothy Chalmers writes about her time on a farm near Nantwich, Cheshire in 1917

SKILLS BUILDER

How do you account for the different attitudes to farm work shown by the members of the Women's Land Army in Sources L and M?

Source N

11.4 A recruitment poster for the Women's Land Army, 1917.

Question

How far is the propaganda poster (Source N) supported by the experience of women in the Women's Land Army (Sources L and M)?

The demon drink

In the years before 1914, all establishments selling alcohol had to be licensed and had a set closing time. There were some regional variations but, in general, pubs were open for most of the day. Opening hours of 5.00 a.m. until midnight were usual. Men and women could drink as much as they liked, whenever they liked. Drunkenness was common, but wasn't limited to the working classes. Working men spilled out of the public houses and were highly visible – unlike the drunken 'gentlemen' in their clubs. Many thousands of men right across the social spectrum were drinking far too much. In 1914 alone, there were over 3,300 convictions a week in England and Wales for drunkenness.

What was the impact of drunkenness on the war effort?

On the outbreak of war, both the War Office and the Admiralty reported servicemen appearing either drunk on duty or with heavy hangovers. In April 1915 a report on timekeeping in the shipping, transport and munition industries was published, reporting poor timekeeping and absenteeism because of drunkenness and associated conditions.

Source O

We are fighting Germany, Austria and drink, and, as far as I can see, the greatest of these deadly foes is drink.

From a speech by David Lloyd George when he was Chancellor of the Exchequer in the spring of 1915

SKILLS BUILDER

Read Source O. Do you think that David Lloyd George was exaggerating?

What did the government do about the problem of drunkenness?

- The Intoxicating Liquor (Temporary Restriction) Act passed on 31 August 1914 gave licensing authorities the power to restrict public house opening hours.

- 10 June 1915, in response to the April 1915 report, the government used DORA to set up a Central Board of Control to restrict the sale of alcohol in areas considered important to the war effort. Fourteen areas were initially named within which alcohol could only be sold for 4.5 hours a day. In Plymouth (a naval town) for example, women could not buy drinks after 6.00 p.m. although men could buy them until 9.00 p.m. In London, women, unlike men, could not buy alcoholic drinks before 11.30 a.m.

- By 1917, the Central Board of Control was regulating the drinking habits of 93 per cent of the population.

- The government encouraged the setting up of 'model' pubs, cheap restaurants and canteens.

- DORA was used to ban the sale of spirits in bottles of less than quarts, restrict the purchase of beer with a 'chaser', and the buying of alcoholic drink for another individual.

- The alcohol content of beers was steadily lowered on governmental instructions and the alcohol content of spirits was pegged at 70 per cent.

- Duties were increasingly imposed on alcoholic drinks; in 1914 the price of a pint was 3d. This had risen to 10d by the end of the war, mainly due to excise duty. The price of spirits had risen by 500 per cent.

Source P

PUNCH, OR THE LONDON CHARIVARI.—April 14. 1915.

THE ENEMY'S ALLY.

11.5 A cartoon from the magazine *Punch* published in 1915

SKILLS BUILDER

1 How similar are the messages of Sources O and P?

2 Which Source, O or P, do you consider would have been the more effective in persuading people to consume less alcohol?

Were the government measures successful?

Convictions for drunkenness and assault in England and Wales stood at 62,882 in 1908; by 1918 these had been reduced to 1,670; the weekly conviction rate for drunkenness in England and Wales had fallen from 3,388 in 1914 to 449 in 1918. In Scotland the figures were 1,485 and 355. Public drunkenness had declined as a feature of the British social scene and the war effort was enhanced as a result. Ships crossing the Atlantic did not have to carry so much grain for brewing but could carry other goods. But it wasn't all good news. As drinking and drunkenness became unacceptable, the middle classes turned to their other drug of choice – cocaine – to the extent that the government had to forbid its importation except under licence.

Cooperation or conflict?

It is clear that industrial relations deteriorated as the war dragged on, but this should not be taken as an indication that workers' patriotism and their devotion to the war effort diminished. It must be remembered that, in 1914, it was generally thought that this would be a quick war. But as 1915 led to 1916 and 1917 with no end in sight, traditional issues that troubled working people came to the fore. Many strikes were the result of wage claims arising from steadily escalating prices, understandable in the context of a 27 per cent rise in the cost of living and with increasing numbers of workers finding their wages subject to income tax.

Source Q

> *RESOLUTION*
> *passed at Trade Union Conference*
> *at Caxton Hall, July 18th, 1916*
>
> # WORKERS' REPLY
> ## TO GEN. SIR DOUGLAS HAIG.
>
> This meeting of representatives of organised trades, including both men and women engaged in munition work and in other occupations, assure you, and through you the British Army, that we will not relax our efforts to maintain and increase the supply of ammunition, guns, and other war material which is necessary to enable you and the Army to bring to a victorious conclusion the great task which you have so gallantly and successfully begun.
>
> For this purpose we have resolved to recommend the POSTPONEMENT OF ALL HOLIDAYS, general and local, which involve interruption of production UNTIL SUCH TIME AS WE ARE ASSURED BY YOU THAT MILITARY EXIGENCIES PERMIT of the postponed holidays being taken.
> *(signed)* ARTHUR HENDERSON
> *(Chairman)*

11.6 A government poster reporting on a resolution passed by the Trade Union Conference on 8 July 1916

The cooperation of the Trades Unions, implied by this government poster, was essential if the workforce left behind in Britain was to work effectively within the war economy that was being developed. The strikes and working days lost shown in Source R, though appearing dramatic, were in fact, usually about pay and working conditions and were settled relatively easily. Indeed, during the war some 8,000 awards made by arbitration tribunals were accepted without further protest.

Source R

A table showing the number of strikes, the working days lost and union membership in the years 1913–20.

Year	Strikes	Working days lost	Union membership
1913	1,459	9,804,000	4,135,000
1914	972	9,878,000	4,145,000
1915	672	2,953,000	4,359,000
1916	532	2,446,000	4,644,000
1917	730	5,647,000	5,499,000
1918	1,116	5,875,000	6,533,000
1919	1,352	34,969,000	7,927,000
1920	1,607	26,568,000	8,348,000

Definitions

Skills differential

Skills differential is the established difference in the level of skill of work between men and women.

Dilution

The employment of an unskilled or semi-skilled worker to do a skilled person's work, involving the breakdown of the job into its constituent parts, with the dilutee(s) taking on a specific part(s). This sometimes involved as many as five dilutees taking on the process previously undertaken by one skilled worker.

Substitution

The employment of an unskilled or semi-skilled worker as a direct substitute for a skilled worker, slotting completely into the job.

The problem of dilution

Dilution remained a contentious issue throughout the war. Agreements signed between employers and unions allowed for the employment of unskilled or semi-skilled workers in jobs hitherto reserved for skilled workers. Thus, at a stroke, the unions had agreed to the undermining of the **skills differential** upon which workers' security was based, and abandoned what had been won after years of struggle. The dilutees were often women, as has been seen. These were dangerous, because they were working for a lower wage and were generally not unionised, but were usually accepted as a necessary wartime aberration. Male dilutees, however, were seen by many unionised workers as constituting a real threat because they appeared to challenge craft privilege.

Source S

It is perhaps understandable that the workers' loyalty was doubted in some quarters. The period since 1910 had witnessed considerable industrial turmoil. But incessant strikes tended to obscure the fact that the trade union movement, despite containing left-wing elements, was predominantly reformist and pragmatic. Those characteristics explain its willingness to cooperate with the war effort – first demonstrated by the Trades Union Congress's declaration of an industrial truce shortly after the outbreak of war. Thus, the trade unions immediately surrendered their most effective weapon – the strike – without extracting anything significant in return. The only conceivable explanation for this cooperation is simple patriotism, strengthened by a conviction that a thankful government would reward the workers when peace returned.

From Gerard J. DeGroot *Blighty* published in 1996

Question

How far do the statistics shown in Source R support the views of the historian Gerard J. DeGroot expressed in Source S?

What did it all cost?

Paying for the war: in cash terms

It cost the government roughly £3.85m a day to keep the war going. Where did the money come from?

- Increasing the **national debt** from £625m in 1914 to £7,980m in 1918 met about 70 per cent of the total expenditure.
- The remaining 30 per cent was made up from taxation, and successive chancellors of the exchequer steadily raised revenue in this way:
  - Lloyd George (1914–15) increased the standard rate of income tax from 9d in the pound to 1s 6d in the pound.
  - McKenna (1915–16) raised income tax to 3s 6d in the pound and introduced a tax on large (excess) profits.
  - Bonar Law (1916–18) raised income tax to 6s in the pound and excess profits tax to 80 per cent.

  In 1914, 1.5 million people paid income tax; by 1918, the number had risen to 7.75 million.
- The government persuaded people to buy war bonds. These were, in effect, loans from individuals and institutions to the government that were to be paid back at the end of the war, plus interest. This formed part of the national debt but, for the individuals concerned, it was a form of saving.
- The banks stopped issuing gold in exchange for bank notes. The gold was kept in reserve for a government emergency – and, overall, more bank notes were printed than there was gold to back them.

Definition

National debt

This is the total money owed by the government as a result of borrowing from its own people, from foreign governments and from international institutions. At the end of the war, the government owed so much that about 25 per cent of the revenue raised by the government was spent just on paying the interest charges.

Paying for the war: in human terms

The mobilisation of a volunteer and then conscript army, together with spasmodic raids by the Germans on coastal towns and London, meant that there was scarcely a family in the land that was untouched by tragedy. Herbert Asquith lost one son and Andrew Bonar Law, two. Neither politician completely recovered from his loss. Nearly 750,000 British servicemen were killed. Thousands more were injured: of these over 240,000 had leg or arm amputations. Most of those who died, or were hurt mentally and physically, were young men aged between 18 and 25. These were the 'lost generation' and losing them meant that tens of thousands of children grew up fatherless; widows grew old alone; young women never married and remained childless all their lives. A huge range of potential talent was lost. The cost in human terms was incalculable.

Unit summary

What have you learned in this unit?

You have learned about the ways in which the economy was geared up for total war, about the ways in which a war economy was created, and in particular about the importance of the Defence of the Realm Act and the Munitions of War Act. You have understood why the government needed to control and manage the workforce and the measures it took to do this. You have considered vital areas of the economy: munitions and mines, transport and agriculture and the ways in which these attempted to meet the demands of total war. You have addressed the extent to which the workforce cooperated with the government in its efforts to create a war economy. Finally, you have considered the cost of the war in monetary and human terms.

What skills have you used in this unit?

You have analysed the Defence of the Realm Act and the Munitions of War Act in order to assess their impact on the economy and the people who ran it, and you have used your skills of empathy to understand the reactions of employers and employees to the ways in which the government attempted to create a war economy. You have worked with data in order to calculate the damage done to the war economy by strikes and days lost, and by the voluntary enlistment of men from a variety of industries and occupations. You have considered the role of cartoons and posters as government propaganda and in doing this you have prepared yourself for the next unit. Finally, you have assessed controversial evidence regarding the reactions of various sections of the population to the establishment of a war economy.

SKILLS BUILDER

1 How successfully had the government created a war economy?
2 To what extent was the work of women indispensable to the success of a war economy?
3 How far did the workforce accept the government's policies that were aimed at creating a war economy?
4 Is it ever acceptable for workers to strike during a time of national emergency?

Exam style question

This is the sort of question you will find appearing on the examination paper as a (b) question.

Study Sources Q, R and S and use your own knowledge.

Do you agree with the view that people in the workplace demonstrated 'simple patriotism' throughout the war?

Exam tips

You have worked on (b) style questions at the end of Units 3, 5, 8 and 10.

You have experimented with different sorts of plans and considered different styles of question.

You should by now have a good idea of the way in which you prefer to plan your answer. So go ahead and plan an answer to this question.

Now test yourself! Look at your plan and check what you have drawn up. Have you:

- **Analysed** sources Q, R and S for points that support and points that challenge the view that people in the workplace demonstrated 'simple patriotism' throughout the war, and noted these points in your plan?
- Shown how you will **cross-reference** between the sources for points of agreement and disagreement?
- Shown where you will use your **wider knowledge** both to reinforce and challenge the points you have derived from the sources?
- Thought about how you will combine the points you have made into an **argument** for or against the view that women gained nothing from their wartime experience, and noted this on your plan?
- Shown how your **evaluation** of the points you have used in argument has considered the **quality of the evidence** used?
- Noted what your conclusion will be, and how you will ensure it is **balanced** and **supported**?

RESEARCH TOPIC

Agitation in the Clydeside shipyards came to result in the area being nicknamed 'Red Clydeside'.

Research these disturbances in order to discover why they happened, how they were resolved and what their impact was on the war economy.

12 What was the Impact of the First World War 1919–29?

What is this unit about?

This is an attempt to examine what effect the war had on Britain in the decade after the Armistice. There were economic, social and political changes, all of which could be traced in part to the war. Some changes were wholly bad: the number of wounded and damaged young men, for instance. But there were other results which can be viewed in a much more positive light: the creation of a vast aircraft industry and improvements in surgery techniques. Some changes were only partially a product of the war, such as the enfranchisement of women, and here the war was more a determinant of timing rather than a prime cause.

Key questions

- Did the war damage the British economy?
- Did the war produce social and political change?

Timeline

1918		
	June	Representation of the People Act: vote given to women over 30 and men over 21
	December	General Election: two Liberal parties stand
1919		Versailles Peace Conference
		Sex Disqualification Removal Act: all professions opened to women except the Church
1920		Trade union membership reaches over 8 million, nearly double pre-war numbers
1921–22		Major post-war slump: massive rise in unemployment
1922		Geddes 'Axe': drastic cuts in government spending
1924		First Labour Government formed
1925		Return to the Gold Standard
1926		General Strike
1928		Death of Field Marshall Haig: vast crowds pay tribute
		Equal Franchise Act: votes for women over 21
1929		*All Quiet on the Western Front* by E.M. Remarque: international bestseller
		Goodbye to All That by Robert Graves
		Journey's End: a popular play by R.C. Sherriff
		Wall Street Crash

Demographic Effects

The most devastating result of the war must have been the deaths of mainly young men. Out of 6,146,574 serving soldiers, sailors and airmen, 722,785 were killed (11.8%). There was in consequence much talk of a lost generation. In reality 11.8% does not add up to a lost generation but, as Source B points out below, a vast amount of human suffering. Every Prime Minister between 1940 and 1963 had served in the trenches, emphasising that survival was the norm. In fact, amongst the ruling elite of Britain there was a higher risk of death than amongst other ranks (i.e. officers stood a greater chance of death or injury than ordinary soldiers). A curious analysis of the ducal peerage, a peculiarly narrow sample it must be admitted, reveals that 48% of male members born between 1880 and 1939 died violent deaths.

Despite the death rate there is little evidence that the war altered the demographic pattern of Britain. The fall in infant mortality during the war, the period of fastest fall in the first thirty years of the twentieth century, probably outweighed the impact of violent deaths. Life expectancy at birth rose between 1911 and 1921, from 49 for men to 56 and from 53 for women to 60. There is ample evidence to suggest that the whole civilian population was markedly healthier at the end of the war than at the beginning. The war appears to have accelerated developments already underway, such as better maternity care. More work and better pay for the bulk of the population seems to have been the case. Industrial canteens and subsidized meals for workers became more common and the provision of school meals for children was extended. In Scotland the sums spent on feeding children rose from £7 million in 1912–13 to £29 million in 1917–18. Health insurance, established in 1911, was given automatically to all the armed services and their wives now received maternity benefits.

The trend towards smaller families began before the war continued, possibly encouraged by the encounter of many men with contraception offered in the numerous brothels officially provided in France for the troops. Changes in emigration patterns, which declined markedly after the war, also had an impact as it became more difficult to move to the USA. All this indicates that it is too simplistic to argue that the war had a devastating effect on the population of Britain.

A.E. Housman's poem 'Here Dead We Lie' must rank as amongst the shortest but most poignant reflections on the war.

Source A

Here dead we lie,
Because we did not choose to shame the land from which we sprung.
Life to be sure is but a little thing to lose,
But young men think it is, and we were young.

Source B

The balance of females over the age of fourteen, therefore (discounting any other minor factors involved), rose from 595 per thousand in 1911 to 638 per thousand in 1921, and the proportion of widows per thousand of the population rose from 38 to 43. There is no exact measure of the quantity of personal agony concealed behind these figures, but society, in later years, exhibited all the signs of having suffered a deep mental wound.

From Arthur Marwick *The Deluge: British Society and the First World War*
published in 1965

The Effects on the Economy

The effects on the economy are equally difficult to assess. It might be thought that the sinking of millions of tons of shipping, the deaths of hundreds of thousands of energetic young men and the vast production of destructive armaments and explosives at the expense of other goods would all have damaged the British economy. Some British markets were lost overseas forever. Japan began to make serious inroads into the important British markets in China and even British India. The USA captured British markets in South America, particularly Argentina. It was the export of traditional products like cottons and coal that were to be particularly hard hit and these never recovered. Even in the best of the boom years in 1927–28 exports reached only 84% of those in 1913. Some of Britain's vast overseas investments had been sold off to maintain the value of the pound and cover borrowing from the USA during the war. Some contemporary estimates put these losses at £1 billion, a colossal amount at the time.

Careful research into the impact on the economy has tended to modify the impression of negativity. If many young men died, many more babies survived. The shipping losses were rapidly made good by rebuilding and the problem of the 1920s was an excess capacity of shipping. British national income per head actually grew between 1915 and 1918. New industries such as aircraft manufacture had received a vast boost and new steel plants were established in various places. In fact, as with ships, there was too much steel by the 1920s and the industry entered a slump from which it did not escape until the approach of the next war. If exports declined, Britain gained from cheaper imports as the price of food, boosted during the war, rapidly declined in the 1920s as the world had a surplus. To pay for its imports Britain had to sell less abroad, meaning that the decline of exports was not too damaging, and Britain gained by the falling price of the goods imported. The loss of investments has been reinterpreted and recent research indicates that the losses were about a quarter of the figure believed to be the case in 1918, and by 1928 the British investment portfolio abroad had been more than rebuilt. In fact, investment abroad had continued during the war.

Social Effects

Some social effects have been partly addressed under the section on population, but there were many more – from the quaint and possibly trivial, to serious long-term consequences – for British society. Rationing encouraged the habit of queuing. British Summer Time was introduced and is still with us. Alcohol consumption fell as taxation rapidly increased. The excise duty on beer went up by more than a factor of ten and the price of a pint nearly doubled. Cigarettes became much more popular, replacing the pipe amongst many of the working class. They were much more convenient in the cramped conditions of the trenches and often freely available. Cigars attracted a heavier tax and thus even the middle and upper classes often switched to cigarettes. This changing leisure habit touches upon a more serious development: greater social equality. Class divisions continued to exist but hierarchies were crumbling and the divisions were becoming more fuzzy, as Sources C and D make clear.

Source C

Levelling was inevitable in a period when a Duke's son served under his gardener's boy; or a duke's daughter hoed turnips while 'her social inferiors' were buying themselves fur coats out of their earnings in the munition factories. It is significant that you seldom hear nowadays the phrase which was once so common: 'I know my station.' In the same way the line which formerly demarcated so clearly the province of women from that of men has now become so blurred as to be often scarcely visible. During the war, women undertook men's jobs and showed unexpected capability. Since then they have managed, not without a good deal of ill-feeling, to retain their footing in business and most of the professions, not to mention the now all important world of sport.

From F.W. Hirst *The Consequences of the War to Great Britain* published in 1934

Source D

Not only was the population healthier, there is much to suggest that the war prompted greater social equality. Wage rates improved and the average working week was reduced from 55 to 48 hours. It was the poorest group in society who came out best and the gap in wage rates between skilled and unskilled narrowed. The very rich lost out due to much heavier taxation and their share of national income decreased. The number of servants fell dramatically as women found more profitable work elsewhere. The rigid class divisions, particularly between middle- and working-class families began to erode. The possession of a servant and the paying of income tax had been the hallmark of middle-class respectability before 1914. By 1918 fewer had servants and many more paid income tax. Britain had become a more socially equal society as a result of her struggle with Germany.

From Malcolm Pearce and Geoffrey Stewart *British Political History 1867–1995* published in 1996

Political Effects

As in many areas, the First World War accelerated trends rather than simply starting them, and this is particularly true in terms of the political effects: the damage to the Liberal Party, the boost to the Labour Party and trade unions, the enfranchisement of women and the growth in the power and role of the state. In the case of the latter, the acceleration was enormous. Taxation massively increased and never again in the twentieth century returned to its pre-war levels. In the Boer War income tax had risen to 5p in the £. The Liberals before the war had raised it to 6p but by 1919 it was 30p. Death duties rose from 15% to 40%. An Englishman's home was no longer his castle. In fact, if it was a castle, it was likely to pass to the state upon his death. The number of civil servants employed by central government tripled and regulations covering drinking hours, the consumption of drugs and the strength of alcoholic beverages all increased. If Britons were healthier in 1919 they were also more controlled by the state.

The Liberal Party was damaged by the wartime split between its two leaders, Asquith and Lloyd George. The Labour Party entered government for the first time as part of the coalition and gained from both the rapid growth in trade union membership and the enfranchisement of all males in 1918. It was clearly impossible to ask a man to fight for his country and then deny him the vote, at least when he reached 21. The enfranchisement of all men made it impossible to delay any longer the enfranchisement of women, which already enjoyed widespread support before the war. It is often said that women were rewarded for their part in the war. This can only be regarded as partially true at best, as only women over 30 were given the vote in 1918 and it was women under 30 who had made the biggest contribution to war work. Despite this, the Representation of the People Act of 1918 really made Britain a democracy, tripling the electorate. Ironically, such a development made money all the more important in elections to manipulate the increased numbers of voters. Party organisation and propaganda became more important. The Liberals were the poorest of the three parties and suffered accordingly. The Conservatives achieved the most votes in every one of the next seven elections although this did not always result in them retaining power, as in 1929 when Labour narrowly won more MPs.

Source E

There was no sudden post-war emancipation of women and their gains were deceptive. In 1919 parliament admitted them to all professions and simultaneously deprived them of access to industrial jobs through the Restoration of Pre-War Practices Act passed in the same year. This legislation and the subsequent behaviour of employers and unions were reminders that the mass recruitment of women during the war had been a temporary measure. Men took back their old jobs and the number of women workers fell dramatically; where they kept their jobs their wages were lower than men's. Admitted to full citizenship, however, women were now able to exert political pressure, particularly on issues that directly involved them such as family and welfare.

From Lawrence James *Warrior Race: A History of the British at War*
published in 2001

Remembering and Interpreting the War

Initially, the war was presented in the early twenties in bloody but patriotic terms. *Peter Jackson, Cigar Merchant* by Gilbert Frankau, published in 1919, was a popular novel of these years based on first-hand experience. It sold over 100,000 copies and did not seek to challenge the validity of the war as a justified patriotic triumph. The poetry of Wilfred Owen, later to be the force-fed diet of British schoolchildren from the 1960s onwards, was not widely known. By 1929 less than a thousand copies of his verse had sold. By comparison 300,000 copies of the collected works of the more patriotic Rupert Brooke had been bought. All over the land memorials and cenotaphs were erected to the 'fallen'. Remembrance Day became a national institution, blending sorrow and national pride. Churchill's best-selling history of the war was as fair and objective about events and the leading players as was possible so soon after the ending of the conflict, but he clearly sought to play up his role and the importance of developments with which he was associated, such as the tank. In the words of Baldwin, the then Tory leader, 'I hear Winston has written a large book about himself and called it *The World Crisis*.' When Haig, who had devoted his last years to helping former soldiers through the British Legion, died in 1928, there was an outpouring of genuine sorrow and widespread appreciation of his positive role in the winning of the war.

1929 is perhaps the significant year in the onset of bitter criticism and the development of the counter myth that the war was futile and conducted with idiocy. Pointless suffering rather than patriotic endurance increasingly became the trade description of the conflict. The publication of the German best-selling novel *All Quiet on the Western Front* by E.M. Remarque caught the mood of the age and triggered a spate of memoirs and creative writing based on the war. R.C. Sherriff's play *Journey's End* was a hit and remained popular through the 1930s. Two of the main characters die in the play, as do most of those in Remarque's novel. Robert Graves' fictionalised memoir *Goodbye to All That* was justifiably popular. It was brilliantly written and hailed as masterpiece of anti-war literature. This is not what Graves intended. He was clearly proud of his war service but passages could be quoted to emphasise the horror that was now the dominant theme.

Source F

After the first day or two the corpses swelled and stank. I vomited more than once while superintending the carrying. Those we could not get in from the German wire continued to swell until the wall of the stomach collapsed, either naturally or when punctured by a bullet; a disgusting smell would float across. The colour of the dead changed from white to yellow-grey, to red, to purple, to green, to black, to slimy.

From Robert Graves *Goodbye to All That* published in 1929

Source G

Every sector becomes a bad one, every working party is shot to pieces; if a man is killed or wounded his brains or entrails always protrude from his body; no one ever seems to have a rest. The soldier is represented as a depressed and mournful spectre helplessly wandering about until death brought his miseries to an end.

From Cyril Falls *War Books: A Critical Guide* published in 1930

Siegfried Sassoon added his influential *Memoirs of an Infantry Officer* the following year and he, unlike Graves, clearly aimed to produce an anti-war tract. The flood of anti-war literature produced an inevitable reaction but at this time a somewhat muted one. Nevertheless, the great divide in historical interpretation can be discerned as dating from this period. Charles Carrington, much favoured by the revisionist school, brought out his *A Subaltern's War* in 1929. In 1930 the historian Cyril Falls, who had served through the war and was outraged by the new fashionable tendency to see the war purely in terms of mud, blood and futility, sarcastically commented:

The battle of alternative viewpoints has continued to rage ever since, but then 'History is argument without end'. The last word is given to Siegfried Sassoon, and in particular the last verse of the poem 'Aftermath' that he wrote in March 1919.

> Do you remember that hour of din before the attack –
> And the anger, the blind compassion that seized and shook you then
> As you peered at the doomed and haggard faces of your men?
> Do you remember the stretcher cases lurching back
> With dying eyes and lolling heads – those ashen-grey
> Masks of the lads who once were keen and kind and gay?
>
> Have you forgotten yet? . . .
> Look up and swear by the green of the spring that you'll never forget.

Thematic review: source-based debate and evaluation

It is important, especially when dealing with a topic that addresses change over time, to stand back and review the period you have been studying. You need to ask yourself not only what happened, but why it happened and why it happened then and not, say, twenty years later. What had driven change? Which factors were significant and which were not? Were there any events that were critical turning points? Thematic review questions, spanning the whole time period, will help to focus your thinking. These are the thematic review questions that relate to' The Experience of War 1854-1929'. You can probably think of more, but for the moment these are the ones with which you will be working.

- What explains the growing scale of the three conflicts ?

- How far did British Army adapt successfully to rapid technological changes in the period 1854–1918?

- To what extent had the reporting of war changed in the period 1854-1918?

- How far did the three wars encourage political reform and change in the years 1854–1929?

- To what extent was war an agent of social and economic change during this period 1854–1929?

- How far did attitudes to war and patriotism change in the period 1854–1929?

Choose one of these thematic review questions that you plan to answer. Working through this section will make much more sense if you have an actual question in mind.

Answering a thematic review question

There are two keys to answering a thematic review question: **select** and **deploy.**

Select	You need to select appropriate source material You need to select appropriate knowledge
Deploy	You need to deploy what you have selected so that you answer the question in as direct a way as possible.

Unpacking 'Select'

You will see that all the thematic review questions are asking for an evaluation. They ask 'How far . . .' To what extent . . .' How significant . . .' which means that you will have to weigh up the evidence given by the sources you have selected. You will, therefore, have to select sources that will give you a range of evidence. Six diary entries, for example, will not give you the range you want. You will also need to select sources that seem to provide evidence that pulls in different directions. Eight sources saying more or less the same thing but in different ways will not help you weigh up the significance of different sorts of evidence and reach a reasoned, supported conclusion.

So now go ahead.

(i) Look back through this book and select the sources, primary and secondary, that you think will give you the appropriate range, balance and evidence.

(ii) Make notes of the knowledge you will need to use to contextualise the sources and create an argument.

You can't, of course, simply put some sources into an answer and hope that whoever is reading what you have written can sort things out for themselves. You need to evaluate the sources you have selected and use that evaluation to create the argument you will be making when you answer the question. You have already had practice of doing this in the Exam Café section of this book, but here is a reminder of some of the questions you will need to ask of a source before you can turn it into evidence:

- Is the **content** appropriate for the question I am answering?
- Can I supply the appropriate **context** for the source?
- How **reliable** is the source as evidence? Was the author or artist **in a position to know** what he or she was talking / painting about?
- What was the intended **audience** of the source? What was the **purpose** of the source?
- If the source is a photograph, did the photographer **pose** the people in the picture? Was the photographer **selective** in what he or she chose to photograph?
- How **useful** is this source in developing an answer to the question? Remember that a source that is unreliable can still be useful.

Now you have your selection of source material, you need to think about it as a package. Does it do the job you want it to do? Does it supply you with enough evidence to argue your case, while at the same time providing you with enough evidence of different points of view so that you can show you have considered what weight the evidence will bear in reaching a reasoned, supported conclusion? In other words, can you effectively **cross-reference** between the sources, showing where they support and where they challenge each other?

Unpacking 'deploy'

The key to successful deployment of evidence and knowledge in answering a question like the one you have selected is always to keep the question in the forefront of your mind, Keep focused! Don't be tempted to go off into interesting by-ways. Make every paragraph count as you build your argument.

You have already had a lot of practice in essay planning and writing as you have worked through the Exam Café, so this is just a reminder of the main things you need to bear in mind.

Plan carefully how you are going to construct your answer and make out your case.

Structure your answer, and you could use this framework as a guide.

Introduction Here you 'set out your stall' briefly outlining your argument and approach

Paragraphs These should develop your argument, using the evidence you have created by questioning the sources. As you create the case you are making, remember to cross-reference between the sources you are using so as to weigh the evidence, showing on which you place the greater weight.

Conclusion Here you should pull your case together, giving a supported summary of the arguments you have made and coming to a reasoned, supported judgement.

In other words, say what you are going to do, do it, and show that you have done it.

You do not, of course, have to respond to these thematic review questions by writing an essay all by yourself. You could work collaboratively in a small group, or you could use one or more of the questions to prepare for a class debate. In whatever way you are going to use these thematic review questions, the approach will be the same: select, deploy and keep to the point.

Good luck!

Exam zone

1. Relax and Prepare

Hot Tips

From GCSE to AS level

- I really enjoyed studying modern world History at GCSE but I am glad that I had the chance to look at some nineteenth and twentieth century English history at AS level. It has been challenging but enjoyable to study a different period.

- Many of the skills that I learned at GCSE were built upon at AS level, especially in Unit 2 where the skills of source evaluation and analysis are very important.

- AS level History seems like a big step up at first with more demands made on independent reading and more complex source passages to cope with. However by the end of the first term I felt as if my written work had improved considerably.

- The more practice source based questions I attempted, the more confident I became and quite quickly I picked up the necessary style and technique required for success.

- I found it really helpful to look at the mark schemes in the textbook. It was reassuring to see what the examiners were looking for and how I could gain top marks.

What I wish I had known at the start of the year

- I used the textbook a lot during the revision period to learn the key facts and practice key skills. I really wished that I had used it from the beginning of the course in order to consolidate my class notes.

- I wished that I had taken more time reading and noting other material such as the photocopied handouts issued by my teacher. Reading around the subject and undertaking independent research would have made my understanding more complete and made the whole topic more interesting.

- AS History is not just about learning the relevant material but also developing the skills to use it effectively. I wish that I had spent more time throughout the year practising source questions to improve my style and technique.

- I wish I had paid more attention to the advice and comments made by my teacher on the written work I had done. This would have helped me to improve my scores throughout the year.

How to Revise

- I started my revision by buying a new folder and some dividers. I put all my revision work into this folder and used the dividers to separate the different topics. I really took pride in my revision notes and made them as thorough and effective as I could manage.
- Before I started the revision process, I found it helpful to plan out my history revision. I used the Edexcel specification given to me by my teacher as a guideline of which topics to revise and I ticked off each one as I covered it.
- I found it useful to revise in short, sharp bursts. I would set myself a target of revising one particular topic in an hour and a half. I would spend one hour taking revision notes and then half an hour testing myself with a short practice question or a facts test.
- I found it useful to always include some practice work in my revision. If I could get that work to my teacher to mark all the better, but just attempting questions to time helped me improve my technique.
- Sometimes I found it helpful to revise with a friend. We might spend 45 minutes revising by ourselves and then half an hour testing each other. Often we were able to sort out any problems between us and it was re assuring to see that someone else had the same worries and pressures at that time.

2. Refresh

Revision Checklist

1. The Crimean War 1854-56: 'Theirs not to reason why'

- Causes of the war
- Conditions under which the men fought
- Significance of the charge of the Light Brigade
- The war reportage of Roger Fenton and William Russell

2. The Crimean War 1854-56: 'Someone had blundered'

- Problems of supplying the troops and reactions to this in Britain
- Medical services and supplies available in the Crimea
- Significance, in the Crimea and in Britain, of the work of Florence Nightingale
- Significance, in the Crimea and in Britain, of the work of Mary Seacole

3. The Crimean War 1854-56: What were the outcomes?

- Reaction in Britain to the Peace of Paris.
- Development of nursing as a profession
- Changes to British institutions: the army and the civil service
- Attitudes to coloured people evidenced by the treatment of Mary Seacole

4. **How and why was the 2nd Boer War fought?**
   - Attitudes of the British public and politicians to the British Empire in general and South Africa in particular
   - Structure of the British Army in 1899
   - Attitudes to the British Army of soldiers and the public
   - Strengths and weaknesses of the British Army in South Africa

5. **What was the impact of the Boer War in Britain 1899-1902?**
   - Development of the press
   - Importance of Churchill's work as a war correspondent
   - Changing public support for the war
   - Effect on party politics

6. **What was the wider significance of the Boer War?**
   - Army reforms
   - Impact on attitudes to Empire and Imperialism
   - National efficiency and Liberal reforms.
   - Historians' interpretations of the war

7. **Why and how was the First World War fought?**
   - Reasons for going to war
   - Nature of trench warfare
   - The significance of the Battle of the Somme (1916) to the conduct of the war and on attitudes to war in Britain
   - The reasons for the Allies' victory

8. **What was the nature of Army life in France during the First World War?**
   - The organisation, weaponry and deployment of the British Army in France.
   - Maintaining morale and discipline.
   - Life behind the lines
   - Health and medical services

9. **The Home Front 1914-18: mobilising a fighting force**
   - Persuading men to volunteer: propaganda, recruitment and Pals' battalions
   - Conscription: nature and need
   - The treatment of conscientious objectors
   - The role of women in the armed forces

10. **The Home Front 1914-18: how were people's minds mobilised for total war?**
   - Official management of propaganda
   - Unofficial management of propaganda: the role of the press
   - The role of the cinema
   - The success of propaganda in shaping attitudes to war and the enemy

11. The Home Front 1914-18: how was the economy mobilised for total war?

- The importance of DORA
- Organising the workforce, women and industrial relations
- Managing industry, agriculture and transport
- The cost of the war in cash and human terms.

This revision check-list looks very knowledge based. The examination, however, will test your source-based skills as well. So remember that when dealing with sources you must be able to:

- Comprehend a source and break it down into key points

- Interpret a source, drawing inferences and deductions from it rather than treating it as a source of information. This may involve considering the language and tone used as well.

- Cross-reference points of evidence between sources to reinforce and challenge.

- Evaluate the evidence by assessing its quality and its reliability in terms of how much weight it will bear and how secure are the conclusions that can be drawn from it. This will include considering the provenance of the source.

- Deal with the sources as a set to build up a body of evidence

3. Result

You have spent a lot of time working on plans and constructing answers to the (a) and (b) questions. So you now have a pretty good idea about how to plan an answer and write a response to the questions on the examination paper. But what are the examiners looking for? And what marks will you get?

What will the exam paper look like?

There will be three questions on the paper.

(a)	Compulsory: everyone has to do this.
(b) (i) and (b) (ii)	You will have a choice here and will only have to answer one (b) question.
Sources	There will be nine sources on the examination paper. But don't worry: you won't have to deal with them all! You'll only need to deal with six sources – three for each of the questions you will be answering. And here is the good news. So far, you have worked with very long sources, some of which were complicated. In the examination, because you will only have one hour and twenty minutes to answer the two questions, the sources will be much shorter. You'll probably be dealing with no more than around 550 words altogether.

Question (a)
What will you have to do, and what marks will you get for doing it?

(a)   You will have to focus on reaching a judgement by analysis, cross-referencing and evaluation of source material. The maximum number of marks you can get is 20. You will be working at any one of four levels. Try to get as high up in the levels as you can. Remember that the only knowledge, outside of that which you can find in the sources, is what examiners call 'contextual' knowledge. This means you can write enough to enable you to interpret the source, but no more. For example, if one of the three sources is by Mary Seacole, you should show the examiners that you know she was self-funded in the Crimea, but you should not describe the work she did in Jamaica unless this information helps the understanding of a particular source.

Level 1   Have you shown that you understand the surface features of the sources, and have you shown that you have selected material relevant to the question? Does your response consist mainly of direct quotations from the sources?

1–5 marks   This is what you will score.

Level 2   Have you identified points of similarity and difference in the sources in relation to the question asked? Have you made a least one developed comparison or a range of undeveloped ones? Have you summarised the information you have found in the sources? Have you noted the provenance of at least one of the sources?

6–10 marks   This is what you will score

Level 3   Have you cross-referenced between the sources, making detailed comparisons supported by evidence from the sources? Have you shown that you understand you have to weigh the evidence by looking at the nature, origins, purpose and audience of the sources? Have you shown you have thought about considering 'How far' by trying to use the sources as a set?

11–15 marks   This is what you will score

Level 4   Have you reached a judgement in relation to the issue posed by the question? Is this judgement supported by careful examination of the evidence of the sources? Have you cross-referenced between the sources and analysed the points of similarity and disagreement? Have you taken account of the different qualities of the sources in order to establish what weight the evidence will bear? Have you used the sources as a set when addressing 'How far' in the question?

16–20 marks   This is what you will score.

Now try this (a) question

(a) Study sources A, B and C. How far does Sources C challenge the views expressed in Sources A and B about attitudes in Britain towards Germans during the First World War?

Source A

The loss of the great Cunard liner, the *Lusitania*, was a shock to the world. There was a fierce clamour for reprisals. The meanest elements among the jingoes worked up the first of the anti-German riots. These were deliberately organised, in no sense a spontaneous popular outburst; but the prospect of looting without fear of punishment made its appeal to certain sections of the poor and ignorant. Many a home was wrecked; many a peaceable working family lost all. Stones were flung, children injured.

(From Sylvia Pankhurst *The Home Front* published in 1932. She lived and worked through the times she describes here)

Source B

Rioting was going on quite near here. It is a mercy that they have interned the Germans at last. It ought to have been done long ago. It is a pity that our folk descended to lawlessness, but it was the only way our people could show their feelings in the matter. We have a great camp of German prisoners of war not far from here. Would you believe that some people were actually asking for cakes for them!

(Part of a letter from Margaret Lilley, of Stroud Green, London, written in May 1915.)

Source C

Thursday 29 August 1918

Mrs Matthew has four German prisoners doing work on her farm. They're brought in a lorry at 8.00am. They have a meal at the Chelmsford Workhouse before they start in the morning, and bring another meal with them. She does not think this is enough, because they work until 7.00pm or 8.00pm. She is annoyed because the authorities forbid her to give then more food, but quietly ignores the prohibition. The men are excellent workers.

(From the diary of the Rev Andrew Clark, vicar of Great Leighs, Essex)

Now use the marking criteria to assess your response.

How did you do?

What could you have done to have achieved a better mark?

Question (b)
What will you have to do and what marks will you get for doing it?

(b)   You will have to analyse and evaluate a historical view or claim using two or three sources and your own knowledge. There are 40 marks for this question. You will get 24 marks for your own knowledge and 16 marks for your source evaluation. You can be working at any one of four levels. Try to get as high up in the levels as you can. The examiners will be marking your answer twice: once for knowledge and a second time for source evaluation.

This is what the examiners will be looking for as they mark the ways in which you have selected and used your knowledge to answer the question:

Level 1   Have you written in simple sentences without making any links between them? Have you provided only limited support for the points you are making? Have you written what you know separately from the sources? Is what you have written mostly generalised and not really directed at the focus of the question? Have you made a lot of spelling mistakes and is your answer disorganised?

1–6 marks   This is what you will score

Level 2   Have you produced a series of statements that are supported by mostly accurate and relevant factual material? Have you make some limited links between the statements you have written? Is your answer mainly 'telling the story' and not really analysing what happened? Have you kept your own knowledge and the sources separate? Have you made a judgement that isn't supported by facts? Is your answer a bit disorganised with some spelling and grammatical mistakes?

7–12 marks   This is what you will score

Level 3   Is your answer focused on the question? Have you shown that you understand the key issues involved? Have you included a lot of descriptive material along with your analysis of the issues? Is your material factually accurate but a bit lacking in depth and/or relevance? Have you begun to integrate your own knowledge with the source material? Have you made a few spelling and grammatical mistakes? Is your work mostly well organised?

13–18 marks   This is what you will score.

Level 4   Does your answer relate well to the question focus? Have you shown that you understand the issues involved? Have you analysed the key issues? Is the material you have used relevant to the question and factually accurate? Have you begun to integrate what you know with the evidence you have gleaned from the source material? Is the material you have selected balanced? Is the way you have expressed your answer clear and coherent? Is your spelling and grammar mostly accurate?

19–24 marks   This is what you will score.

This is what the examiners are looking for as they mark your source evaluation skills.

Level 1   Have you shown that you understand the sources? Is the material you have selected from them relevant to the question? Is your answer mostly direct quotations from the sources or re-writes of them in your own words?

1–4 marks   This is what you will score.

Level 2   Have you shown that you understand the sources? Have you selected from them in order to support or challenge from the view given in the question? Have you used the sources mainly as sources of information?

5–8 marks   This is what you will score

Level 3   Have you analysed the sources, drawing from them points of challenge and/or support for the view contained in the question? Have you developed these points, using the source material? Have you shown that you realise you are dealing with just one viewpoint and that the sources point to other, perhaps equally valid ones? Have you reached a judgement? Have you supported that judgement with evidence from the sources?

9–12 marks   This is what you will score

Level 4   Have you analysed the sources, raising issues from them? Have you discussed the viewpoint in the question by relating it to the issues raised by your analysis of the source material?

Have you weighed the evidence in order to reach a judgement? Is your judgement fully explained and supported by carefully selected evidence?

13–16 marks This is what you will score.

Now try this (b) question.

Read sources D, E and F and use your own knowledge.

Do you agree with the view, expressed in Source F, that 'the élite were simply unable to meet the challenges of modern warfare and society'?

Source D

We have failed in everything because in almost all our recent appointments, civil and military, we have promoted men without reference to merit, and refused to remove them without regard to failure. Our commander-in-chief missed the opportunity of taking Sebastopol when almost undefended, neglected his commissariat, disregarded his communications, and sat quietly at home while his army was perishing. But he was appointed by the Whigs and politically connected with the Tories, so he remains our commander-in-chief still.

(From *The Times* 5 May 1855)

Now use the marking criteria to assess your response.

How did you do?

What could you have done to have achieved higher marks?

The examiners will not be nit-picking their way through your answer, ticking things off as they go. Rather, they will be looking to see which levels best fit the response you have written to the question, and you should do the same when assessing your own responses.

How will I time my responses?

You have 1 hour 20 minutes to answer two questions. Remember that the (a) question is compulsory and that you will have a choice of one from two (b) questions. Take time, say, five minutes, to read through the paper and think about your choice of (b) question. The (a) question is worth half the marks of the (b) question, so you should aim to spend twice the time on the (b) question. This means that, including planning time, you should spend about 25 minutes on the (a) question and about 50 minutes (again, including planning) on the (b) question.

You have now had a lot of practice in planning, writing and assessing your responses to the sort of questions you can expect to find on the examination paper. You are well prepared and you should be able to tackle the examination with confidence.

Good luck!

Source E

If ever a generous or kind-hearted man – yes, a soldier's friend – then that man's name is Raglan. He is not only a brave soldier but his moral character stands second to none. I speak not only from my heart but from my long service under that glorious soldier and man.

(From a letter written by an officer serving in the Crimea to his wife, dated 15 January 1855)

Source F

The wave of criticism of Britain's institutions in early 1855 stemmed from the sufferings of the army in the Crimea and the perceived inability of the army leadership, dominated as it was by the aristocracy, to remedy the situation. Critics argued that the role of the aristocracy – especially the wave of promotions in 1854 when more experienced officers, who were less well connected socially, were passed over – called into question aristocratic predominance in all fields. It was argued that the elite were simply unable to meet the challenges of modern warfare and society.

(From Clive Ponting *The Crimean War* published 2004)

References

Amery, L.S. (1900–09) *The Times History of the War in South Africa, 1899–1902*, 7 vols, Sampson Low & Co.

Barnett, C. (1970) *Britain and Her Army, 1509–1970: A Military, Political and Social Survey*, Allen Lane

Beaverbrooke, M.A. (1956) *Men and Power*, Hutchinson

Beckett, I. (2006) *The Home Front 1914–18: How Britain Survived the Great War*, National Archives

Begbie, H. (1915) *On the Side of the Angels*, 2nd edn, Hodder and Stoughton

Benson, A.C. (1902) *Land of Hope and Glory*, song lyrics, Boosey & Co.

Blake, R.L.V. ffrench (1971) *The Crimean War*, Cooper

Bloem, W. (1930) *The Advance from Mons 1914*, trans. By G.C. Wynne, Peter Davies Ltd

Brittain, V. (1933) *A Testament of Youth: An Autobiographical Study of the Years 1900–1925*, Gollancz

Brooke, R. (1914) *Peace*, poem

Burdett-Coutts, W. (1900) *The Times*, 28 April

Carrington, C. (1965) *Soldier from the Wars Returning*, Hutchinson

Carver, Field Marshall Lord (1998) *Britain's Army in the Twentieth Century*, Macmillan with the Imperial War Museum

Chamberlain, J. (1899) Cabinet Memorandum, 6 September

Chenery, T. (1854) *The Times*, September

Churchill, W.S. (1898) *The River War: An historical account of the reconquest of the Soudan*, edited by F. W. Rhodes, Longman, Green and Co.

Churchill, W.S. (1900) *Morning Post*, January

Condell, D. and Liddiard, J. (1987) *Working for Victory?: Images of women in the First World War, 1914–18*, Routledge & Kegan Paul

Coppard, G. (1969) *With a Machine Gun to Cambrai: The tale of a young Tommy in Kitchener's army 1914–1918*, H.M.S.O.

Corrigan, G. (2003) *Mud, Blood and Poppycock: Britain and the First World War*, Cassell

Cronin, J.E. (1983) *Labour and Society in Britain 1913–1979*, Batsford Academic and Educational

DeGroot, G.J. (1996) *Blighty: British Society in the Era of the Great War*, Longman

Department of Information (1917) *A Corpse Conversion Factory*, Department of Information

Dickens, C. (1854) *Hard Times*, Bernhard Tauchnitz

Dixon, N. (1976) *On the Psychology of Military Incompetence*, Cape

Duffy, C. (2006) *Through German Eyes: The British & The Somme 1916*, Weidenfeld & Nicolson

Farrar, M.J. (1998) *News From the Front: War correspondents on the Western Front 1914–18*, Sutton

Farrar-Hockley, A.H. (1967) *Ypres 1914: Death of an army*, Pan Books

Fryer, P. (1984) *Staying Power: The history of Black people in Britain*, Pluto

German General Staff (1919) *Die Schlacht bei Mons*, Stalling

Grant, S. (2008) 'A terrible beauty', available online at www.tate.org.uk/tateetc/issue5/aterriblebeauty.htm

Haig, Field Marshall Sir D. (1917) 'Official Dispatch', 25 December

Haig, Field Marshall Sir D. (1918) 'Special Order of the Day', 11 April

Harrison, J.F.C. (1990) *Late Victoria Britain, 1870–1901*, Fontana

Hobsbawm, E.J. (1987) *The Age of Empire 1875–1914*, Weidenfeld and Nicolso

Jack, J.L. (1964) *General Jack's Trench Diary 1914–1918*, Eyre & Spottiswoode

Judd, D. (1975) *The Crimean War*, Hart-Davis

Keegan, J. (1998) *The First World War*, Hutchinson

Kipling, R. (1890) *The Queen's Uniform*, poem first published on 1 March 1890

Kipling, R. (1899) *The Absent Minded Beggar*, song

Kipling, R. (1902) *The Lesson*, poem

Lasswell, H.D. (1927) *Propaganda Technique in the World War*, Kegan Paul & Co.

Leviseur, S. (1982) *A Boer Women in Bloemfontein*, publisher unknown

von Ludendorff, General (1919) *War Mermoirs*, Hutchinson

Longfellow, H.W. (1857) *Santa Filomena*, poem first published in November 1857

Machen, A. (1915) *The Bowmen and Other Legends of the War*, Simpkin

Marwick, A. (1965) *The Deluge: British Society and the First World War*, Bodley Head

MacRae, J. (1915) *In Flanders Fields*, poem

Milward, A.S. (1984) *The Economic Effects of Two World Wars*, Macmillan Education

Nettleton, J. (1979) *The Anger of the Guns: An infantry officer on the western front*, Kimber

Newbolt, Sir H. (1897) *Vitai Lampada*, poem

Noakes, F. (1952) *The Distant Drums: the personal history of a guardsman in the Great War*, published privately

Osburn, A. (1932) *Unwilling Passenger*, Faber and Faber

The Oxford History of the British Empire (1999) Vol. III, Oxford University Press

The Oxford History of the British Empire (1999) Vol. IV, Oxford University Press

Packenham, T. (1979) *The Boer War*, Weidenfeld & Nicolson

Pegler, M. (2006) *Attack on the Somme: Haig's offensive 1916*, Pen & Sword Books

Phillips, P. (1917) *Daily Express*, 2 August

Ponting, C. (2004) *The Crimean War*, Chatto & Windus

Ramdin, R. (2005) *Mary Seacole*, Haus

Rees, R. (1993) *Britain and the Great War*, Heinemann Educational

Rees, R. (2003) *Britain 1890–1939*, Heinemann

Repington, Colonel (1915) *The Times*, 14 May

Reynolds, F. (1988) *War in Britain*, publisher unknown

Roberts, A. (1999) *Salisbury, Victorian Titan*,

Robinson, J. (2005) *Mary Seacole*,

Rowland, P. (1975) *Lloyd George*, December

Russell, B. (1914) *The Nation*, 15 August

Russell, W. (1854) *The Times*, September

Russell, W. (1854) *The Times*, 8 November

Russell, W. (1854) *The Times*, 14 November

Russell, W. (1854) *The Times*, 25 November

Russell, W. (1855) *The Times*, January

Sassoon, S. (1930) *Memoirs of an Infantry Officer*, Faber & Faber

Seacole, M. (1857) *Wonderful Adventures of Mary Seacole in Many Lands*, Blackwood's London Library

Seely, Captain J.E.B. (1901) *The Times*, July

Seely, Captain J.E.B. (1930) *Adventure*, William Heinemann

Shaw, G.B. (1900) *Fabianism and the Empire: A manifesto by the Fabian society*, G. Richards

Sheffield, G. (2001) *Forgotten Victory: The First World War – myths and realities*, Headline

Small, H. (1998) *Florence Nightingale: Avenging Angel*, Constable

Smurthwaite, D. (2002) *The Boer War 1899–1902*, Hamlyn

Snow, P. and Snow, D. (2007) *The World's Greatest Twentieth Century Battlefields*, BBC

Sterling, Lt. Col. A. (1895) *The Story of the Highland Brigade in the Crimea*, Remington & Co.

Swinton, E.D. (1932) *Eyewitness*, Hodder and Stoughton

Taylor, A.J.P. (1965) *English History 1914–45*, Clarendon Press

Tennyson, Alfred Lord (1854) *The Charge of the Light Brigade*, publisher unknown

Turner, W.J. (1939) *Death's Men*, poem

van Emden, R. and Humphries, S. (2003) *All Quiet on the Home Front*, Headline

Vieth, F.H.D. (1907) *Recollections of the Crimean Campaign and the Expedition to Kinburn in 1855*, John Lovell & Son

Viljoen, B.J. (1902) *My Reminiscences of the Anglo-Boer War*, Hood, Douglas & Howard

Wilson, A.N. (2002) *The Victorians*, Hutchinson

Winter, D. (1978) *Death's Men*, Allen Lane

Winter, J.M. (1988) *The Experience of World War I*, Macmillan

Glossary

Araba An ox- or horse-drawn carriage used in Turkey

Batman A soldier from the ranks who acted as a servant to an officer

Brass hats A derogatory term for very senior officers, so-called because of their extensive gold braid

Calvinism The Boers were predominately Calvinist in their beliefs. This means that they followed the strict teachings of seventeenth-century Protestant reformer John Calvin

Census A survey of the population undertaken once very ten years. The first census was in 1801

Chinese slavery A major issue of the general election in 1906. Chinese indentured labourers were imported in South Africa to repair damage done by the Boer War. They were not slaves but bound by the terms of the contract to work off the cost of their passage

Church of the Holy Sepulchre This church in Bethlehem is said to have been built on the site of Jesus' crucifixion and burial. It was and is an important shrine for Christian pilgrims to visit

Conscientious objectors These were people whose consciences would not let them fight

Dilution The employment of a skilled or semi-skilled worker to do skilled work, broken down into constituent parts, with the dilutee(s) taking on specific parts

Independent Labour Party Established at a conference in Bradford in 1893, it included a number of socialist organisations

Khaki A Hindi word for dusty. It originated as a colour for uniforms in the British Indian Army and was generally adopted as service uniform for service overseas in the British Army from the 1880s

Lee Enfield Magazine rifle weighing just over 9 lbs. It was a very effective precision weapon with a magazine of 10 bullets

Litter A stretcher for carrying the sick or wounded

Meritocratic When position and power are based on talent and merit, not birth

Ministry of Munitions The Ministry of Munitions was staffed at top levels by businessmen, recruited by David Lloyd George and loaned by their companies for the duration of the war

Munitions Military weapons, ammunition and stores

Music Hall One of the most popular venues for entertainment in the late Victorian period.

National debt Total money owed by the government from borrowing from its own people, foreign governments and international institutions

Non-Combatant Corps Set up in March 1916 as part of the army and run by regular officers. Conscientious objectors had the rank of army privates, but did not carry weapons or take part in battle. They provided physical labour to support the military

Pacifist A person who rejects war and violent action as a means of solving disputes, especially disputes between nations

Poilu Means 'hairy one', affectionate slang to describe a French infantryman

Propaganda Control of opinions and attitudes by direct manipulation of social suggestion, rather than by altering the conditions of the environment

Quaker A member of the Society of Friends, a Christian movement founded by George Fox c.1620

Reserved occupations These were occupations that the government thought so important to the war effort that the workers could not be released for military service

Salient A military term for part of a line which juts into enemy held territory so that it is semi-surrounded and vulnerable to attack

'Separate spheres philosophy' A philosophy that maintained that men and women occupied 'separate spheres' in society. The woman's sphere was home and all things domestic; the man's was the world of work, finance and government

Skills differential Established difference in the level of skill of work between man and women

Substitution The employment of an unskilled or semi-skilled worker as a direct substitute for a skilled worker, slotting completely into the job

Tariff Reform This was the key issue in the general election of January 1906, being the imposition of duties on imported goods from outside the Empire

Unrestricted submarine warfare is a term applied to the German naval strategy of abandoning the accepted rules of trade war. These had evolved to relate to commerce raiding by surface ships and involved stopping a merchant ship and searching it before either sinking it or taking it as a prize. It was almost impossible for submarines to do this. The Germans, after much internal debate, decided to sink merchant ships on sight in a zone around the British Isles. The danger was that it would bring the USA into the war, which it helped to do

Voluntaryism This is relying on people to volunteer rather than forcing them to contribute

Index

Page references in *italics* indicate illustrations.